Panayotis G. Michaelides

21 Equations that Shaped the World Economy

Understanding the Theory Behind the Equations

palgrave
macmillan

Panayotis G. Michaelides
National Technical University of Athens
Athens, Greece

ISBN 978-3-031-76139-3 ISBN 978-3-031-76140-9 (eBook)
https://doi.org/10.1007/978-3-031-76140-9

This Palgrave Macmillan imprint is published by the registered company Springer Nature Switzerland AG.
The registered company address is: Gewerbestrasse 11, 6330 Cham, Switzerland

21 Equations that Shaped the World Economy

"This important book presents and examines the meaning and limitations of the elementary mathematical expressions used in Economics and Finance for better understanding the world of human economic action."

—Professor Dr Vernon L. Smith, *Chapman University, USA, Nobel Laureate in Economics*

"With clarity and precision, the author demystifies key economic equations, making them accessible to readers of all backgrounds. An invaluable addition to the literature on economic theory!"

—Professor Dr Dieter Bögenhold, *University of Klagenfurt, Austria*

"Engaging and informative, this book sheds light on the key equations that have shaped our understanding of the global economy."

—Professor Dr Stéphane Goutte, *UMI SOURCE, University Paris-Saclay, France*

"A must-read for anyone! Brilliantly written and well researched, the author magisterially illustrates the power of equations to critically influence our understanding of economic science, while thoughtfully addressing their extensive limitations and alternative critiques."

—Professor Dr John Milios, *National Technical University of Athens, Greece*

"This book offers a comprehensible and insightful exploration of how certain equations have impacted the world economy."

—Professor Dr Antonis Papapantoleon, *Delft University of Technology (TU Delft), The Netherlands, National Technical University of Athens, and Foundation for Research and Technology-Hellas (FORTH)*

"A fascinating journey through economic science, illustrating how simple equations shape our understanding of the field."

—Professor Dr Panos Xidonas, *ESSCA Grande École, France*

"The author, one of the leading scholars of his generation, elucidates how simple equation-based models explain our economic reality in this landmark book. A must-read to learn from one of the best!"

—Professor Dr Stavroula Yfanti, *Queen Mary University of London, United Kingdom*

If you want to go fast, go alone
If you want to go far, go together
African Proverb

Dedicated to those minds and hearts who do things differently…

Preface

There have been few phenomena worldwide that have exerted a stronger influence on societies than the workings of the global economy throughout history. For centuries, civilizations have risen and fallen, fortunes have been made and lost, and destinies have been shaped by economic forces. Yet, amid this complex interplay lie the equations that underpin the mosaic of our economic system. This intellectual journey stands at the intersection of real-world Economics and Finance, daring to unravel the web of equations that have shaped our reality.

As we journey through the pages of this book, we shall encounter an ensemble of equations, some elegant and quite well known, others still veiled in obscurity. All these equations have left an indelible mark on Economic Science. From the theory of General Equilibrium to Chaos Theory, from the equations governing International Trade to those shaping the Profit Rate, each equation we will encounter holds a key to unlocking the enigmatic secrets of our economic past and future.

However, this book is by no means an esoteric exercise in mathematical conjecture. On the contrary, it seeks to connect these equations to the realities of Economic Science, stressing the connection between economic theory and social dynamics. By unraveling the threads that tie equations to a realistic view of the economy, we aim to foster a deeper understanding of the mechanisms driving the economic and financial systems.

Of course, we recognize that the academic field of Economic Science can sometimes appear inaccessible, with its jargon, complex mathematical models, and abstract concepts. However, our aim is to demystify this subject, breaking it down into more digestible terms. We have deliberately chosen a language that avoids most unnecessary academic technicalities, ensuring that readers from all backgrounds can engage with the content and grasp the profound ideas presented.

This deliberate choice of language serves a crucial purpose in making complex concepts accessible to a diverse readership. By opting for a very simple, clear, and straightforward communication style, we bridge the gap between experts and individuals from various backgrounds, enabling a broader audience to engage with and comprehend the ideas that are being conveyed. When complex ideas are translated into simpler language, it not only enhances understanding, but also fosters inclusivity and diversity in the conversation. Readers who may not have formal training in Economics or Mathematics are less likely to feel discouraged from studying these topics. This inclusivity is especially important in a scientific world where interdisciplinary collaboration is becoming increasingly necessary.

Moreover, using accessible language does not dilute the significance or depth of the concepts being discussed. On the contrary, it reflects an effort to distill ideas into digestible forms without sacrificing accuracy or depth. This expresses an effort to bridge the gap between specialized knowledge of Economics and Mathematics and general understanding, thereby creating a platform for dialogue.

In advocating for this approach, we promote an equitable dissemination of knowledge. When knowledge is presented in a manner that resonates with a wide range of readers, it empowers individuals from various walks of life to participate in discussions, form opinions, and contribute meaningfully to societal debates. This, in turn, nurtures a more informed and engaged citizenry, capable of critically analyzing economic policies, making informed decisions, and advocating for positive change. By embracing this approach, we open the doors to a more diverse and informed discourse, where ideas are not confined to academic circles.

Whether you are a first-year student studying Economics for the first time, a postgraduate seeking to broaden your knowledge, or an inquisitive reader, this book will serve as a friendly companion. Regardless of your level of familiarity with Economics and Mathematics, this book aims to provide an introductory foundation. In this context, the mathematical concepts utilized in this book assume an understanding of pre-university Mathematics, along with foundational principles of university-level Mathematics, such as matrix algebra and advanced calculus, which are briefly covered in Chap. 23, "Mathematical Appendix."

In closing, this book represents the culmination of several years of research and a deep passion for sharing valuable insights with a broader audience. While the core ideas are firmly grounded in my own work, I have embraced the power of artificial intelligence (AI) throughout this journey. In this context, the text leverages the innovative capabilities of AI, as these tools have been instrumental in ensuring both analytical consistency and originality, as well as in detecting errors and suggesting phrasings. Of course, any remaining errors or omissions are my responsibility alone. I hope that the final result meets your expectations!

Athens, Greece Panayotis G. Michaelides

Acknowledgments

In embarking on this scholarly journey, I stand on the shoulders of giants, indebted to those who have paved the path of economic inquiry throughout the ages. It is through the collective efforts and tireless contributions of the entire research community that I made an effort at expanding our understanding of the extremely complex world of Economics and Finance.

I extend my deepest gratitude to the mentors, colleagues, and institutions whose support and guidance have been instrumental in the realization of this intellectual journey. More precisely, I wish to thank the National Technical University of Athens, the London School of Economics, the Delft University of Technology, the University of Groningen, the University of Klagenfurt, the Athens University of Economics and Business, the National and Kapodistrian University of Athens, the University of Piraeus, and the Hellenic Open University. Their wisdom and collaboration have been invaluable.

I would also like to thank my current team members, Panagiotis Cheilas, Theodoros Daglis, Georgios Evangelidis, Konstantinos N. Konstantakis, Giorgos Kotsompolis, Pavlos Koulmas, Ioannis Melissaropoulos, Theocharis Marinos, Despoina Paraskeuopoulou, Arsenios-Georgios Prelorentzos, Dimitrios Stamos, Efthymios Stamos, Olga Theodoratou, Eleftherios-Theodoulos Papadakis, Theofanis Papageorgiou, and Maria Vlachou, for helpful feedback. Additionally, I am grateful to the following colleagues, for the useful discussions we have had over all these years: Marios Angelopoulos, Aristidis Arageorgis, Christos Bagavos, Simone Baglioni, Loukas Balafoutas, Athena Belegri-Roboli, Seraina Anagnostopoulou, Dieter Bögenhold, Apostolos Christopoulos, Tryfonas

Christou, Gonul Colak, Aggeliki Demertzi, Constantine Dimoulas, Ioannis Dokas, Byron Kaldis, Kyriakos Drivas, Claire Economidou, George Economakis, Alexandros Eskenazis, Paraskevas Georgiou, Drossos Gintides, Dimitris Gounopoulos, Stephane Goutte, Iason Karafyllis, Aikaterini Karadimitropoulou, Dimitris Karamanis, Vassilis Karasmanis, Sotiris Karkalakos, Ioannis Katselidis, Konstantinos Kirytopoulos, Dimitris Konstantios, Stelios Kotsios, Christos Kountzakis, Aris Koutougos, Sofia Labropoulou, Spyros Lapatsioras, Spyridon Lazarakis, Petros Livas, Michalis Loulakis, Magdalini Maniou, Theodore Mariolis, Mania Markaki, Stavros Mavroudeas, Maria Mexi, John Milios, Dimitrios Milonakis, Sevastianos Moirasgentis, Antonis Papapantoleon, Marita Papada, Lefteris Papagiannakis, Marios Papaspyrou, Panagiotis Patrinos, Ioannis Polyrakis, Nikos Progoulis, Giouli Rapti, Leonidas Rompolis, Aristeidis Samitas, George Soklis, Robert Solow, Dimitris Sotiropoulos, Ioannis Stamatoudis, Nikolaos Stavrakakis, Spyridon Stelios, Nicholas Theocarakis, Kostas Theologou, Dimitrios Thomakos, Kien Tran, Evgenia Tzannini, Panos Tsakloglou, Persefoni Tsaliki, John Tsinias, Efthymios G. Tsionas, Ioannis Tsolas, Lefteris Tsoulfidis, Petros Varthalitis, Vanghelis Vassilatos, Angelos Vouldis, Panos Xidonas, Stavroula Yfanti, and Michel Zouboulakis.

Of course, special thanks go to Professor Vernon L. Smith, Nobel Laureate in Economics, for his encouragement!

Furthermore, I must express my sincere gratitude to friends and loved ones for their continuous support throughout this journey. Their patience and understanding have sustained me, always reminding me of the importance of balance and deep human connection in the pursuit of scholarly excellence. Additionally, a special thank you is due to the two anonymous referees who provided constructive feedback. Finally, I am deeply grateful for Palgrave Macmillan's highly efficient processes, particularly for the dedication and efforts of Wyndham Hacket Pain and Leonie Sittner. Their support has been truly invaluable.

Contents

About the Author

Panayotis G. Michaelides is Full Professor at the School of Applied Mathematical and Physical Sciences, National Technical University of Athens (NTUA), and a former Research Associate at the London School of Economics (LSE). Recognized among the top 1% of economists worldwide (ScholarGPS, 2025), his research ranks among the most downloaded globally (IDEAS-RePEc, 2025). A prolific scholar, Michaelides has authored over 250 papers (ResearchGate, 2025), including more than 100 articles in refereed Journals. He was honored with the Highly Commended Paper Award for Excellence from Emerald. His recent book, *History of Economic Ideas: From Adam Smith to Paul Krugman*, published by Palgrave Macmillan in 2023, has attracted thousands of downloads. He has mentored over 150 students in their PhD theses or MSc/MEng dissertations in Applied Mathematics, Economics, or Finance, and has designed innovative curricula for 20 different courses, with 25 years of teaching experience at all levels by now.

Michaelides's research lies at the intersection of *Economics*, *Finance*, *Data Science*, and *Political Economy*. His work integrates insights from various schools of economic thought, leveraging historical, mathematical, statistical, quantitative, and computational methods. He explores topics such as instability, global production, sustainable development, technological change, and the effects of natural phenomena on economic and financial systems.

Michaelides has been selected twice as a referee for works by Nobel Prize laureates and has led large interdisciplinary teams in numerous EU-funded and nationally funded projects. He has served as an expert consultant, scientific director, principal investigator, and senior researcher for international corporations and the banking sector. His advanced degrees in Mathematics, Economics, and Business complement his academic foundation, which began with a robust five-year degree (MEng) in Mechanical Engineering from NTUA, providing a very strong foundation in *Physics*, *Mathematics*, *Operational Research*, and *Computer Science*.

His articles have been published in top-tier Journals across various fields, including:

Quantitative Methods and Statistics: *Journal of the Royal Statistical Society; European Journal of Operational Research; Annals of Operations Research.*

Economics: *Cambridge Journal of Economics; Journal of Economic Dynamics and Control; Energy Economics.*

Financial Economics: *Journal of Financial Stability*; *Journal of International Financial Markets, Institutions and Money*; *International Journal of Finance and Economics.*

Finance and Accounting: *Review of Quantitative Finance and Accounting; International Review of Financial Analysis.*

Infrastructure Economics: *Annals of Tourism Research; Journal of Technology Transfer; Transportation Research-Part E.*

List of Tables

Introduction

Equations constitute the backbone of science, technology, and the economy, and interact with the modern world we inhabit. From cryptography to satellite navigation, from music to broadcasting, from invention to innovation, equations have propelled humanity forward. They underpin our understanding of the economic world. However, equations hold too much significance to remain concealed. They offer insight and beauty, akin to poetry, accessible to a wider audience than presumed.

In Economic Science, equations assume an essential role. They try to uncover hidden facets of economic phenomena. Although overshadowed by historical accounts of rulers, wars, and disasters, equations possess transformational power. While words offer another means of comprehension, their inherent subjectivity and imprecision sometimes fall short in capturing the deeper expressions of complex phenomena. Equations usually provide a universal language for unraveling profound truths.

Over the course of history, their influence has pervaded economic processes, from macroeconomic models to microeconomic decision-making. Just as equations have reshaped the physical world, they have subtly and partly shaped economic and financial systems. Their role may be unassuming, yet it is undeniable. Equations illuminate the complexities of economic and financial dynamics, casting light on both visible and often concealed forces driving economic progress.

In what follows, we will focus on the equations that have been the silent 'architects' of our economic and financial systems, societal progress, and even human behaviors. Equations, those seemingly abstract symbols on the page, possess an ability to breathe life into economic theories and try to shed new light on the complex mechanisms underlying economic and financial dynamics. Much like the notes that compose a symphony, each equation carries a distinct melody, a melody that has resonated through the corridors of economic discourse and, to some extent, transformed the course of nations. They often stand as the backbone of economic and financial models, serving as the bridges between theory and practice, allowing economists to quantify the impact of policies, and to decipher the enigma of human decision-making.

As we embark on this intellectual journey, we will uncover the ways in which equations have lent their insight to the economic world. From the foundations of the General Equilibrium Theory to the fascinating mosaics of modern Game Theory, these equations have often been both the guiding stars that illuminate our path and the source of intense debates that have shaped Economic Science. What follows is an analysis of how these mathematical constructs have been both instruments of enlightenment and triggers for skepticism. As we examine each equation, we shall briefly unearth its historical context, trace its evolution, and examine its implications, all the while gaining a deeper appreciation for the dynamic forces that drive economies and societies. In the world of Economics, equations are not mere symbols; they are the keys that unlock the vault of understanding. In most instances, they have served as the compasses that guide policy decisions, and the mirrors that reflect human behavior, but not without failure.

Yet, the allure of equations extends far beyond their quantitative elegance. Beneath their formal exterior lies a world of ideas, criticisms, controversies, debates, and *paradigm shifts*. Our book will not be a simple mathematical investigation; it will also be a brief analysis of the theory and applications behind the equations. We will witness how equations have been both intellectual milestones and sparks for further inquiry. In our quest to understand the role of equations, we shall not be confined to a traditional perspective. We shall cast our gaze wider, embracing alternative voices that challenge the popular approaches and advocate for a broader, more inclusive understanding of economic and financial systems, shedding light on the limitations and biases that can arise from their usage.

Equations, while a valuable tool, often rest on assumptions and simplifications that may not accurately capture the multifaceted reality of economic and financial interactions. These assumptions can sometimes lead to a narrow and incomplete understanding of economic phenomena, omitting crucial factors such as power or class dynamics, historical context, and cultural influences. Moreover, the equation-centric approach tends to characterize individuals as rational, self-interested actors, disregarding the interplay of psychology, emotions, and social norms that shape economic behavior.

In addition, the emerging complexity inherent in economic and financial systems poses a challenge to the equation-based models. Such perspectives emphasize that equations may struggle to account for the complex and often unpredictable outcomes that arise from interactions among numerous agents in dynamic systems. This limitation prevents equations from fully capturing the emergent patterns that are often crucial in understanding economic dynamics.

Another central concern raised is the potential 'homogenization' of economic analysis due to an overemphasis on equations. Numerous economists advocate for a more open-minded approach that accommodates diverse viewpoints and methodologies, recognizing that alternative ways of understanding economic phenomena may offer valuable insights. Distributional concerns, too, come to the forefront as equations in modern Economics may prioritize efficiency and aggregate measures while overlooking the critical impact of income and wealth distribution on societal well-being.

Moreover, while equations provide a structured and quantitative means of understanding economic systems, they often perpetuate power asymmetries and exclude marginalized voices. The equation-centric paradigm can reinforce existing economic paradigms, limiting the investigation of alternative economic theories and solutions that diverge from the established framework.

In response to these limitations, we advocate for an alternative, more inclusive, interdisciplinary, and context-sensitive approach to Economic Science. In this framework, we propose that equations should be regarded as just one tool among many in the economist's toolkit, allowing for a broader and more holistic understanding of economic realities. By embracing a more diverse range of theories, methodologies, and perspectives, we can move beyond the confines of equations to uncover a richer and more comprehensive understanding of complex economic and financial systems.

CHAPTER 1

Compound Interest Rate

Learning Objectives

- Understand the Development of Interest Rates
- Explore the Interconnection Between Interest Rates and the Economy
- Analyze the Role of Interest Rates in Decision-Making
- Critically Evaluate the Limitations of Interest Rates
- Formulate a Balanced Approach to Financial Management

1.1 Introduction

The concept of compound interest emerges as a dynamic force that defies the linear nature of time, exerting its influence on the growth and accumulation of wealth with exponential precision. While simple interest merely adds a fixed percentage of the principal amount to the total over regular intervals, compound interest introduces an innovative twist. It includes the compounding effect, which capitalizes on the interest earned in previous periods, essentially allowing interest to earn interest. This compounding effect transforms the financial landscape, paving the way for the potential multiplication of wealth over time.

P. G. Michaelides, *21 Equations that Shaped the World Economy*,
https://doi.org/10.1007/978-3-031-76140-9_1

The roots of simple and compound interest can be traced back through human history, appearing in various forms and practices across cultures and civilizations. From the ancient merchants who engaged in lending and borrowing at interest to the medieval bankers who pioneered innovative financial instruments, the concept has long captivated human imagination. Its impact was said to be documented in, among others, the *Code of Hammurabi*, a legal text from ancient Mesopotamia that addressed the terms of loans and interest rates. Over time, the concept spread its influence, shaping medieval European banking practices and influencing the trajectory of Renaissance-era commerce.

Yet, it was only with the refinement of mathematical principles and the emergence of modern Finance that compound interest found its systematic footing. It revolutionized the way we understand the dynamics of financial growth. With this formula, individuals and institutions gained a tool to calculate the potential outcomes of different compounding scenarios, enabling informed decisions about investments, loans, and savings strategies.

The implications of compound interest extend far beyond the individual level, infiltrating the core of economic systems and influencing macroeconomic trajectories. Central banks and policymakers factor in compound interest when crafting monetary policies and determining interest rates, recognizing its ability to influence consumption patterns, investment behaviors, and overall economic stability. The ripple effects of these decisions impact everything from inflation rates to currency values, creating a complex interplay of forces that shape the economic landscape.

Furthermore, compound interest highlights the interplay between risk and reward in the financial system. While it has the power to amplify returns on investments, it also introduces the potential for losses to compound, magnifying the impact of poor decisions or economic downturns. This duality underscores the importance of prudent financial management, as individuals and businesses operate in pursuit of their respective goals.

In conclusion, the concept of compound interest is a captivating force that bridges Economics and Finance, transcending time and space to shape the growth and accumulation of wealth. Its historical journey reflects humanity's evolving understanding of financial dynamics, while its mathematical foundations provide a tangible tool for decision-making in an ever-changing world.

1.2 Interest Rate in Economics

As we have seen, the concept of simple interest can be traced back to ancient civilizations where lending and borrowing practices were commonplace. In these early societies, interest was often charged as a straightforward percentage of the initial principal, with no consideration for the compounding of interest over time. This concept laid the groundwork for future discussions on the value of money and the potential for it to earn more money. The emergence of simple and compound interest rates in economic history is also linked to the development of modern banking practices, with notable roots extending to the flourishing city-states of medieval Italy. These financial pioneers laid the groundwork for understanding the dynamics of lending and borrowing, setting the stage for the evolution of interest rate concepts that continue to shape our financial world today.

It was against this backdrop that the foundations of simple interest began to crystallize. Merchants engaged in lending ventures and sought compensation for the temporary relinquishing of their capital. Interest rates were applied to loans in a straightforward manner, typically calculated as a percentage of the principal amount. While simple in concept, this practice introduced a pivotal shift in how individuals perceived the value of money over time. As financial activities burgeoned, so too did the need for more sophisticated mechanisms to account for the compounding effect of interest.

The emergence of simple and compound interest rates marked a watershed moment in the history of Finance. The practices and innovations that originated in some bustling city-states laid the groundwork for modern banking systems, investment strategies, and economic theories. These early financial pioneers illuminated the potential of money to grow over time, creating a dynamic interplay between present decisions and future outcomes.

However, it was the emergence of compound interest that truly revolutionized financial thinking in this context. The recognition that money could not only generate returns based on its initial value, but also accumulate interest upon interest introduced a shift in how individuals and institutions approached savings, investments, and loans. Compound interest found its place in the world of Finance, offering a mechanism that could potentially lead to exponential growth or, conversely, exponential debt.

The conceptualization of compound interest took time to solidify, with its mathematical formulation evolving over centuries. The seeds of compound interest could be seen in the works of early mathematicians and scholars, including ancient Greek philosophers. The emergence of both simple and compound interest rates marked a turning point in the field of Finance, offering individuals and institutions the tools to make educated financial decisions. Simple interest, with its linear approach to interest accrual, remains relevant in certain contexts where compounding is minimal. Compound interest, on the other hand, has proven to be a foundational concept, underpinning investment strategies, loan structures, and economic modeling. While the principles behind simple and compound interest rates have been refined and expanded upon, their emergence in historical contexts expresses the evolution of human thought regarding the value of money and its potential to grow over time.

In conclusion, as we journey through economic history, it becomes evident that the roots of simple and compound interest are deeply intertwined with the rise of banking institutions, the study of innovative financial instruments, and the pursuit of understanding the dynamics of wealth accumulation. The lessons learned continue to resonate in the modern financial world, underscoring the enduring relevance of these interest rate concepts in shaping the economic landscapes of today and tomorrow.

1.3 The Equation

Let's take a look at the notions of simple and compound interest rates in Economics and Finance, examining their mathematical insights, and broader implications for financial decision-making and economic growth. Simple interest, as previously mentioned, is a linear method of calculating interest based solely on the initial principal amount. While it may seem straightforward, its application is crucial in various financial contexts. Simple interest is often employed in scenarios where compounding is infrequent or when the growth of money over time is not a significant factor. Consider a case where one invests \$10,000 in a bank account with a simple annual interest rate of 5%. At the end of each year, the account earns an additional 5% of \$10,000, i.e., \$500, and this amount remains constant throughout the investment period.

In general, simple interest is a linear method of interest calculation. As we have seen, it is usually expressed as a percentage of the initial principal amount and remains constant throughout the duration of the loan or investment. The equation for calculating simple interest is as follows:

$$I = P \cdot r \cdot t \tag{1.1}$$

where:

- I represents the interest earned or paid
- P is the principal amount
- r denotes the annual interest rate, and
- t signifies the time period, usually in years

Hence, the aforementioned formula calculates the interest I earned on the principal amount P over a period of time t at an annual interest rate r. Consequently, the total amount A after time t can be expressed as:

$$A = P + I \tag{1.2}$$

By plugging Eq. (1.1) in Eq. (1.2), we get:

$$A = P + P \cdot r \cdot t$$

and

$$A = P \cdot (1 + r \cdot t) \tag{1.3}$$

Simple interest is commonly used in scenarios where the compounding effect is negligible, making calculations relatively straightforward. However, it fails to account for the exponential growth potential that compound interest offers. In contrast, compound interest introduces a dynamic element that reflects the exponential growth potential of money over time. It accounts for the accumulation of interest on both the principal amount and any interest previously earned. This compounding effect accelerates the growth of an investment or the escalation of a debt, often leading to substantial differences compared to simple interest calculations.

To derive the compound interest formula from this understanding, we'll assume that interest is compounded n times per year. First, if the interest is compounded annually, the amount A after one year plugging $t = 1$ in Eq. (1.3) would be:

$$A = P \cdot (1 + r) \tag{1.4}$$

However, if the interest is compounded n times a year, the annual interest rate r is divided by n, and the interest is applied n times. Therefore, plugging the new interest rate $\frac{r}{n}$ in Eq. (1.4), the amount after the first compounding period (e.g., first month if compounded monthly) would be:

$$A_1 = P \cdot \left(1 + \frac{r}{n}\right) \tag{1.5}$$

After the second compounding period in one (1) year, the amount becomes:

$$A_2 = A_1 \cdot \left(1 + \frac{r}{n}\right)$$

Or, plugging in the expression of A_1 based on Eq. (1.5), we get:

$$A_2 = P \cdot \left(1 + \frac{r}{n}\right) \cdot \left(1 + \frac{r}{n}\right)$$

or

$$A_2 = P \cdot \left(1 + \frac{r}{n}\right)^2$$

After n compounding periods in one (1) year, the amount is:

$$A_n = P \cdot \left(1 + \frac{r}{n}\right)^n \tag{1.6}$$

Finally, if the interest is compounded for t years, the number of compounding periods is $n \cdot t$, and Eq. (1.6) becomes:

$$A = P \cdot \left(1 + \frac{r}{n}\right)^{n \cdot t} \tag{1.7}$$

where:

- A expresses the final amount, including interest
- P represents the principal amount
- r is the annual interest rate in decimal
- n expresses the number of compounding periods *per year*
- t signifies the time period in years

Compound interest takes into account the frequency of compounding (annually, semi-annually, quarterly, monthly, etc.), which can impact the final amount. As the compounding periods increase, the interest is applied more frequently, leading to a higher overall return on investment.

Here is a very simple numerical example illustrating the concepts of interest and compound interest. Let's say you invest \$1000 at an annual simple interest rate of 5% for three (3) years. By plugging the numbers in Eq. (1.1) we get:

$$I = 1000 \cdot 0.05 \cdot 3 = 150$$

So, the total interest earned over three (3) years is \$150. The total amount A after three (3) years by plugging numbers in Eq. (1.2) is:

$$A = 1000 + 150 = 1150$$

Now, let's use the same principal amount of \$1000, an annual compound interest rate of 5%, and a period of three (3) years. We'll assume the interest is compounded annually. We plug the numbers in Eq. (1.7), and calculate the amount A, which is the amount of money accumulated after n years, including interest.

$$A = 1000 \cdot \left(1 + \frac{0.05}{1}\right)^{1 \cdot 3} = 1000 \cdot 1.157625 = 1157.63$$

So, the total amount after three (3) years with compound interest is \$1157.63.

By plugging these numbers in Eq. (1.2), we get:

$$1157.63 = 1000 + I$$

Or, solving for *I*:

$$I = 1157.63 - 1000$$

and

$$I = 157,63$$

Consequently, with simple interest, the total amount after three (3) years is \$1150, and the interest earned is \$150. With compound interest, the total amount after three (3) years is \$1157.63, and the interest earned is \$157.63.

This simple example illustrates how compound interest can result in a higher return compared to simple interest over the same period, even with the same principal and interest rate. The effect of earning interest on the interest accrued in previous periods makes compound interest more beneficial in the long run.

As demonstrated by Eq. (1.7), the more frequent the compounding, the higher the final amount. This illustrates the exponential nature of compound interest and underscores its relevance in long-term investments and savings strategies. These two distinct approaches to calculating the cost of borrowing and the returns on investments provide an understanding of how the value of money evolves over time, influencing both individual financial choices and broader economic trends. From an economic perspective, simple and compound interest rates influence a plethora of financial decisions.

1.4 Insights and Consequences

The complex web of economic implications woven by interest rates, whether manifesting as simple or compound interest, underscores their multifaceted role in driving the gears of economies and shaping financial landscapes. These rates are not mere numbers; they hold the power to orchestrate the symphony of economic activity, influencing behavior from the microcosm of individual financial decisions to the macrocosm of national and global economic trajectories. Central banks around the world utilize interest rates as a primary tool to implement monetary policy. By adjusting interest rates, central banks aim to control borrowing and spending behavior in the economy. For instance, lowering interest rates stimulates economic activity during periods of stagnation or recession, while raising rates helps control inflation and prevent an overheated economy. These policy decisions have a cascading impact on lending rates, consumer spending, business investment, and ultimately the overall economic outlook.

At the micro- level, interest rates act as lighthouses guiding the financial choices of individuals and businesses. A decrease in interest rates can spark a wave of optimism, encouraging households to take on mortgages for their dream homes, entrepreneurs to invest in new ventures, and students to pursue education with more manageable loan terms. These actions, in turn, ripple through the economy, generating demand for housing, fostering innovation, and nurturing human capital. Conversely, elevated interest rates can tighten the reins, altering spending and saving patterns. The allure of low borrowing costs diminishes, prompting a reevaluation of investment decisions. Savers may feel incentivized to allocate more funds to interest-bearing accounts, seeking higher returns on their money. This recalibration of financial strategies can have a dampening effect on short-term economic growth but might aid in curbing inflationary pressures.

Interest rates also cast their influence across the global stage, choreographing the dance of capital flows and exchange rates. When an economy's interest rates rise, international investors may find the prospect of higher yields attractive, leading to an influx of capital and potentially strengthening the domestic currency. Conversely, when a country's interest rates dip, capital outflows might weaken the local currency. These currency fluctuations carry implications for trade balances, export competitiveness, and even geopolitical dynamics.

Within the corridors of the financial world, interest rates are the architects of financial products and instruments. Banks design loan products with meticulously calculated interest rates, shaping the landscape of consumer and corporate borrowing. Investors assess bond yields and equity valuations through the lens of prevailing interest rates, making decisions that reverberate through stock markets and pension funds. The real estate market also dances to the tune of interest rates. As interest rates drop, the cost of borrowing for home purchases diminishes, fostering demand. This phenomenon can also raise concerns about housing affordability and speculative bubbles.

In sum, the implications of interest rates—whether simple or compounded—resonate far beyond numerical values on financial statements. They are the not-so-'invisible hands' shaping the trajectory of economies, molding the decisions of individuals and institutions alike, and influencing the balance between growth, stability, and inflation. An understanding of these implications is essential for understanding economic life, allowing stakeholders to chart courses through the complex currents of finance and ensuring that economic vessels sail toward prosperous horizons.

1.5 Conclusion, Limitations, and Critiques

In Economic Science, the concepts of simple and compound interest rates are woven into the mosaic of financial decision-making, investment strategies, and macroeconomic policy. These concepts have historical roots that reach back through the ages, reflecting humanity's evolving understanding of wealth accumulation and the time value of money. They serve as tools for individuals, businesses, and governments to cope with the dynamic currents of Finance, influencing a wide spectrum of economic behaviors and outcomes.

The implications of interest rates, whether in the form of simple or compound interest, are far-reaching and profound in the fields of Economics and Finance. When borrowing or investing, individuals and firms evaluate the potential returns and costs in relation to prevailing interest rates. As we have seen, lower interest rates can incentivize borrowing for investments in homes, businesses, and other assets, spurring economic growth. On the contrary, higher interest rates can discourage borrowing and encourage saving, potentially slowing down spending and economic expansion.

However, like any powerful tool, the concepts of simple and compound interest rates are not without their limitations and critiques. One of the primary limitations lies in their assumptions, which often simplify the complexities of real-world financial transactions. For instance, both simple and compound interest rate calculations assume a static interest rate over time, whereas real-world rates can fluctuate due to economic, political, and market dynamics. Additionally, these calculations sometimes overlook external factors such as taxes, fees, and inflation, which can significantly impact the actual returns or costs experienced by individuals and institutions. Moreover, the implications of interest rates can have unintended consequences that challenge conventional economic wisdom. Critiques often question the reliance on interest rates as the primary tool for monetary policy. They argue that the focus on interest rates can lead to financial speculation, bubbles, and income inequalities.

Furthermore, the effects of interest rates on financial markets and economies can sometimes be nonlinear and unpredictable. As interest rates reach extremely low levels, the conventional understanding of their impact may break down, leading to unexpected outcomes and potentially distorting market behaviors. In light of these limitations and critiques, it is crucial to recognize that interest rates are not a *panacea* for all economic challenges. A holistic approach to economic policy must consider a range of strategies to promote stability, and equitable distribution of resources. This might involve examining alternative policy frameworks, which challenge traditional notions of government borrowing and debt.

In conclusion, the concepts of simple and compound interest rates have played a pivotal role in shaping economic thought and practice throughout history. They offer useful insights into the dynamics of investment, guiding decisions at individual, corporate, and governmental levels. However, these concepts are not without their limitations and critiques, reminding us that the economic landscape is multifaceted and subject to diverse forces.

Key Takeaways

- The roots of interest rates can be traced back to ancient civilizations and innovative financial instruments of medieval Europe.
- Simple interest is linear and straightforward, while compound interest accounts for interest accumulation over time.
- Compound interest introduces a compounding effect that allows interest to earn interest, revolutionizing financial growth and wealth accumulation.
- Compound interest's exponential growth potential impacts investments, loans, and savings, necessitating prudent financial management.
- Interest rates guide individual and business financial decisions, impacting real estate, investments, and debt management.
- Central banks use interest rates to regulate economic activity, influencing borrowing, spending, and inflation.
- Unconventional low or negative interest rates can lead to unpredictable market behaviors and require alternative policy approaches.
- Critiques highlight limitations of interest rates, including assumptions, external factors overlooked, such as taxes, fees and inflation.
- Interest rates are essential but not exclusive tools in economic policy; holistic strategies are needed for sustainable growth.
- The economic landscape is multifaceted, and understanding interest rates requires considering diverse forces and dynamic interactions.

Revision Questions

1. How have interest rates evolved throughout history?
2. Explain the formula for calculating simple interest. What variables are involved?
3. What is the compounding effect, and how does it differentiate compound interest from simple interest?
4. How does interest impact financial decisions?
5. How do interest rates influence individual financial choices and behaviors in the market?
6. How do central banks leverage interest rates to influence borrowing, spending, and growth?
7. Describe the potential implications of extremely high/low interest rates for financial markets.
8. What are some critiques of relying solely on interest rates as a tool for economic management?
9. What key factors contribute to the multifaceted nature of the economic landscape, and how do they interact with interest rates?
10. Why is it important to consider a holistic approach to economic policy beyond just interest rates?

CHAPTER 2

The Normal Distribution

Learning Objectives

- Analyze the Characteristics of the Normal Distribution
- Understand the Central Limit Theorem in Economics
- Use the Normal Distribution for Economic Modeling
- Discuss the Impact of Extreme Events
- Evaluate the Limitations of the Normal Distribution

2.1 Introduction

In the dynamic world of Economic Science, where countless variables shape markets, behaviors, and outcomes, the concept of the normal distribution emerges as a powerful tool. Rooted in Mathematics and Statistics, the normal distribution, often referred to as the 'Gaussian distribution,' embodies a symmetrical 'bell-shaped' curve that has become a cornerstone in economic analysis. Its prevalence in various economic contexts underscores its significance as a fundamental pillar in understanding the distribution of data points and the inherent patterns they unveil.

From the distribution of household incomes within an economy to the dispersion of stock returns in financial markets, the normal distribution

P. G. Michaelides, *21 Equations that Shaped the World Economy*,
https://doi.org/10.1007/978-3-031-76140-9_2

serves as a versatile lens through which economists can observe and interpret the behavior of economic variables. By mapping data onto this curve, researchers gain insights into the central tendencies, dispersions, and probabilities that shape economic events. Moreover, the normal distribution's elegance extends beyond mere representation; it also facilitates the application of various formal and rigorous statistical methods and hypothesis testing. The concept of 'z-scores' and the empirical rule, which states that a large portion of data falls within a specific range around the mean, exemplify the distribution's practical utility. Economists employ these tools to assess risk, make predictions, and inform policy decisions in a range of domains.

This statistical distribution is particularly well known for its symmetrical, 'bell-shaped' curve, which signifies a remarkable alignment with the natural rhythms of randomness and variability that permeate economic systems. At its core, the normal distribution is a manifestation of the so-called central limit theorem (CLT). In very simple words, this theorem asserts that the average (or sum) of a sufficiently large number of independent and identically distributed (i.i.d.) random variables follows a normal distribution, regardless of what the original distribution of those variables was, which sounds surprising. This property lends the normal distribution its pervasive presence in economic contexts, as it arises organically from the aggregation of myriad individual factors.

The normal distribution's prevalence in Economics is far from coincidental. Its shape reflects a balance between positive and negative deviations from the mean, encapsulating the concept of 'typical' or 'average' behavior. This balance is a reflection of the symmetry and fragile equilibrium that often characterizes economic systems, where forces of supply and demand, consumption and production, and risk and return interact to shape outcomes.

One of the most compelling features of the normal distribution lies in its parameterization through the mean and standard deviation where the mean represents the value around which data points congregate, and the standard deviation, in turn, quantifies the dispersion of data points, providing insights into the extent of variability within the distribution. These parameters offer economists a powerful framework for quantifying and comparing economic phenomena, enabling them to measure the magnitude of deviations from the norm. As we focus on the normal distribution in Economics, we will discuss its basic mathematical properties, and its role in shaping economic models. By mastering this foundational concept, economists acquire a better understanding of the role played by randomness and variability in shaping economic landscapes.

2.2 The Normal Distribution in Economics

The emergence of the normal distribution as a cornerstone traces back to a confluence of intellectual curiosity, statistical advancements, and a growing need to comprehend and model economic phenomena. Its journey from a mathematical concept to an indispensable analytical tool reflects the evolution of economic thought and the pursuit of understanding the regularities of economic systems.

The seeds of the normal distribution were sown during the Enlightenment, a period characterized by an explosion of scientific inquiry and a burgeoning interest in quantifying natural and societal phenomena. Visionaries like Carl Friedrich Gauss, known as the 'Prince of Mathematicians,' played a pivotal role in formulating the normal distribution. Gauss, in his pursuit of describing the distribution of errors in astronomical observations, is said to have formulated the mathematical foundation for what would later be recognized as the Gaussian distribution.

However, the formal integration of the normal distribution into Economics gained traction in the late nineteenth and early twentieth centuries, paralleling the rise of quantitative methods in the social sciences. The field of Economics was undergoing a transformation, transitioning from qualitative analyses to quantitative approaches that demanded rigorous mathematical frameworks. The normal distribution, with its properties and applicability to a wide range of economic phenomena, offered economists a versatile toolkit to make sense of increasingly complex datasets. Certainly, one of the watershed moments in the integration of the normal distribution into Economics was the emergence of Econometrics. Pioneers like Jan Tinbergen paved the way for the application of statistical methods in economic analysis, contributing to the establishment of econometric models and hypothesis testing. The normal distribution found a 'natural home' in these methodologies, providing a solid footing for parameter estimation, significance testing, and model validation.

As the twentieth century progressed, the normal distribution became more deeply ingrained in economic theory and practice. From macroeconomic models that describe the behavior of aggregate variables to microeconomic analyses of individual consumer behavior, the normal distribution's versatility allowed economists to bridge the gap between theoretical constructs and empirical realities. Moreover, the rise of financial economics and risk assessment further solidified the normal distribution's role as useful toolkit for understanding market movements and investment behavior. In the modern era, the normal distribution continually evolves alongside advancements in statistical methodologies and computational capabilities. Its emergence and integration reflect the dynamic interplay between mathematical innovation and the quest for insights into economic behavior.

2.3 The Equation

As we have discussed, the normal distribution plays a key role in Economic Science by offering a helpful context for understanding the distribution of data and analyzing various economic phenomena. This symmetrical, 'bell-shaped' curve is defined by its probability density function (PDF) and is characterized by specific mathematical properties that make it an indispensable tool in economic analysis.

The equation of the normal distribution's probability density function (PDF) is:

$$\Phi(x) = \frac{1}{\sqrt{2\pi\sigma^2}} \cdot e^{-\frac{1}{2}\left(\frac{x-\mu}{\sigma}\right)^2} \tag{2.1}$$

where:

- x represents the variable of interest, such as income, price, quantity, etc.
- μ is the distribution's mean, indicating the average value around which the data tends to cluster.
- σ^2 is the variance of the distribution, which quantifies the spread or dispersion of the data points around the mean. The square root of the variance (σ) is known as the standard deviation (s.d).
- e is the base of the so-called natural logarithm, a mathematical constant equal to 2.71828, approximately.
- π is a mathematical constant equal to 3.14159, approximately.

The normal distribution possesses certain key properties that make it an ideal fit for various economic scenarios. Firstly, the curve is symmetric around its mean, with half of the data points falling on either side. This symmetry reflects the distribution often observed in economic and social systems. Secondly, as previously mentioned, the normal distribution can be seen as a direct consequence of the central limit theorem (CLT). When the sample size is sufficiently large, the distribution of the sample mean (or sum) follows a normal distribution regardless of the original distribution of the data. Thirdly, the concept of 'z-scores' is a critical feature, which expresses the number of standard deviations a data point is from the mean. It is calculated using the formula:

$$Z = \frac{X - \mu}{\sigma} \tag{2.2}$$

Consequently, the standard normal variable, Z, is related to any normal variable X through the z-score formula in Eq. (2.2) above. The standard normal distribution is a special case of the normal distribution with a mean of 0 and a standard deviation of 1. Any normal distribution can be transformed into the standard normal distribution using the 'z-score.' The standard normal distribution table (or z-table) provides the cumulative probability associated with each z-score.

This standardization allows economists to compare and analyze data from different contexts on a common scale. Fourthly, the so-called 68-95-99.7 rule states that within one standard deviation of the mean, about 68% of the data falls; within two standard deviations, about 95% falls; and within three standard deviations, about 99.7% falls. This rule expresses the concentration of data around the mean.

We can now use the fundamental properties of the normal distribution and the standard normal distribution to accurately determine probabilities for normally distributed data. Therefore, for a given value X in a normal distribution with mean μ and standard deviation σ, first, we calculate the z-score based on Eq. (2.2):

$$Z = \frac{X - \mu}{\sigma}$$

This transformation converts the value x from the original normal distribution to the standard normal distribution, and practically standardizes any normal variable to a common scale.

Next, we find the probability:

$$P(X \leq x)$$

This is the probability that the random variable X is less than or equal to x. This can be found using the standard normal distribution:

$$P(X \leq x) = P\left(\frac{X-\mu}{\sigma} \leq \frac{x-\mu}{\sigma}\right) \tag{2.3}$$

Now, plugging Eq. (2.2) in Eq. (2.3), we get:

$$P(X \leq x) = P\left(Z \leq \frac{x-\mu}{\sigma}\right) \tag{2.4}$$

Next, to find the probability that X is greater than x, we use the complement rule. This rule is based on the idea that the total probability of all possible outcomes must equal 1. Since the event $X > x$ and its complement $X \leq x$ together cover all possible outcomes, this implies mathematically:

$$P(X > x) + P(X \leq x) = 1$$

which leads us to the equation below:

$$P(X > x) = 1 - P(X \leq x) \tag{2.5}$$

Now, plugging Eq. (2.4) in Eq. (2.5), we get:

$$P(X > x) = 1 - P\left(Z \leq \frac{x-\mu}{\sigma}\right) \tag{2.6}$$

Therefore, given a specific value x in the original distribution, the probability that X is greater than x can be expressed by Eq. (2.6).

Or, if we let $z = \frac{x - \mu}{\sigma}$, then:

$$P(X > x) = 1 - P(Z \leq z) \tag{2.7}$$

The normal distribution's equation and its associated equations offer a structured and standardized framework for quantifying and analyzing economic variables. By plugging specific values into the equations, economists can compute the probability of observing a particular outcome or range of outcomes. This mathematical precision empowers economists to make informed predictions, assess risk, and devise strategies in various economic contexts. Hence, the equation of the normal distribution serves as a fundamental tool that enables economists to translate real-world observations into a mathematical language, facilitating rigorous analysis and enhancing our understanding of the dynamics that govern economic systems.

Let's see a very simple numerical example. Suppose the monthly incomes in a small town are normally distributed with a mean (μ) of €3000 and a standard deviation (σ) of €500. In our example, $\mu = 3000$ and $\sigma = 500$.

Now, let's calculate some probabilities for different income ranges using the properties of the normal distribution, presented earlier.

- *Within one ($1 \cdot \sigma$) Standard Deviation (68% Rule):*

According to the empirical rule, about 68% of the data falls within one (1) standard deviation of the mean. Hence, the range is: €3000 ± €500, i.e., from €2500 to €3500.

- *Within two ($2 \cdot \sigma$) Standard Deviations (95% Rule):*

According to the empirical rule, about 95% of the data falls within two (2) standard deviations of the mean. Hence, the range is: €3000 ± €1000, i.e., from €2000 to €4000.

- *Within three ($3 \cdot \sigma$) Standard Deviations (99.7% Rule):*

According to the empirical rule, about 99.7% of the data falls within three (3) standard deviations of the mean. Hence, the range is: €3000 ± €1500, i.e., from €1500 to €4500.

Furthermore, let's calculate the *z*-score for an income of €3800, by plugging the numbers in Eq. (2.2):

$$z = \frac{3800 - 3000}{500} = 1.6$$

A z-score of 1.6 means that an income of €3800 is 1.6 standard deviations away from the mean. Now, we can use the *z*-score to find the probability of an individual earning more than €3800. Using the standard normal distribution table, we can find the probability corresponding to a z-score of 1.6. The table gives us the probability that a value is less than or equal to $z = 1.6$. The value of $z = 1.6$ corresponds to the probability that an individual earns less than or equal to €3800, and, from the standard normal distribution tables, is equal to approximately 0.9452. Hence:

$$P(Z \leq 1.6) \approx 0.9452$$

This means that there is a 94.52% probability that an individual earns less than or equal to €3800, and reflects the cumulative probability provided by the standard normal distribution table.

To find the probability that an individual earns more than €3800, we plug the numbers in Eq. (2.7) to get:

$$P(X > 3800) = 1 - P(Z \leq 1.6)$$

$$P(X > 3800) \approx 1 - 0.9452$$

and

$$P(X > 3800) \approx 0.0548$$

Therefore, the probability that an individual earns more than €3800 is approximately 5.48%. This calculation demonstrates the application of the normal distribution and *z*-scores in determining the probability of a specific income range within a normally distributed dataset. This very simple example illustrates how the normal distribution can be applied to calculate probabilities for economic data.

2.4 Insights and Consequences

The implications of the normal distribution serve as a powerful lens through which economists can comprehend, model, and analyze economic data. Its applications extend across diverse areas, shaping our understanding of variability, risk, and decision-making. The normal distribution's influence extends across a wide spectrum of domains, enriching our understanding and enabling data-driven decision-making.

On the one hand, in financial markets, the normal distribution transcends risk assessment, underpinning concepts like the capital asset pricing model (CAPM) and the Efficient Market Hypothesis (EMH). These tools guide investors in portfolio construction, asset allocation, and risk evaluation. Moreover, it plays a pivotal role in the well-known Black-Scholes model, facilitating the valuation of derivatives by modeling future price distributions. On the other hand, econometric modeling heavily relies on the normal distribution. This distribution serves as a fundamental building block for estimating relationships between economic variables, thus enhancing our grasp of connections, policy implications, and the dynamics within economic systems.

In related fields, the normal distribution continues to yield insights. Health economics and public health benefit from its application in understanding the distribution of health-related data. This informs healthcare policies, guides resource allocation, and contributes to epidemiological studies aimed at improving public health outcomes. Environmental economics employs the normal distribution to model variables like pollution levels and natural resource availability. This offers a quantitative framework to assess the impacts of environmental policies and sustainability initiatives, guiding efforts toward a greener and more balanced future.

Additionally, analyzing exchange rates, and trade policies, the normal distribution provides economists with information on the likelihood of various trade scenarios and exchange rate movements. Similarly, in real estate and housing markets, it aids in comprehending property prices, rental yields, and market dynamics. This knowledge informs decisions about real estate investments, urban planning, and housing policy formulation. Central banks also utilize the normal distribution to guide monetary policy decisions. By assessing inflation trends and setting targets, central banks control interest rates, money supply, and economic stability, ultimately shaping the trajectory of economic growth.

Furthermore, labor economics also benefits from the normal distribution's application in modeling wage distributions and labor market outcomes. This enhances our understanding of income mobility and wage disparities, guiding policymakers in shaping equitable labor market conditions. Also, in the context of development economics, the normal distribution aids in analyzing poverty levels, income growth, and disparities in developing economies. It serves as a tool for designing effective poverty alleviation programs and development strategies, thereby contributing to sustainable and inclusive growth.

Furthermore, the intersection of the normal distribution with behavioral Economics yields insights into the deviations from rational decision-making. Understanding these deviations helps economists study biases, heuristics, and non-rational behavior, offering a richer understanding of economic decision processes. Lastly, the distribution plays a pivotal role in social welfare analysis. By modeling distributional outcomes, economists evaluate the impacts of social welfare programs, taxation policies, and redistribution efforts on diverse segments of the population, aiding the pursuit of more equitable and just societies. In each of these contexts, the normal distribution provides a quantitative framework that aids economists in making sense of complex data, conducting robust analyses, and developing informed strategies.

2.5 Conclusion, Limitations, and Critiques

As we have seen, the normal distribution stands as a crucial concept in the field of Economic Science. Its symmetrical, 'bell-shaped' curve provides a useful framework for understanding the distribution of economic data and analyzing a wide range of phenomena. From income distribution and market analysis to consumer behavior and macroeconomic modeling, the normal distribution offers valuable insights into central tendencies, dispersions, and probabilities that shape economic events.

The normal distribution's mathematical properties, such as symmetry and the central limit theorem (CLT), enhance its applicability in various economic contexts. The equation of the distribution's probability density function, anchored by parameters like the mean and standard deviation, enables economists to quantify and analyze economic variables with precision. This mathematical elegance empowers economists to assess risk, make predictions, and inform policy decisions across diverse domains.

Interestingly, one of the primary limitations is the assumption of normality itself. The Gaussian distribution by definition assumes that data follows a symmetric, 'bell-shaped' pattern, which is sometime unrealistic. Economic and financial variables frequently exhibit characteristics like skewness, heavy tails, or multimodal distributions that deviate from the idealized shape. These deviations challenge the applicability of the normal distribution to accurately represent all economic phenomena. Moreover, the Gaussian distribution tends to seriously underestimate the likelihood of extreme events, commonly referred to as 'fat tails.' In Economics, extreme events like financial crises or market crashes occur much more frequently than predicted by the distribution, leading to potential underestimation of risk. This discrepancy can have profound implications.

The normal distribution's sensitivity to outliers is another limitation. Outliers can exert a disproportionate influence on the parameters of the normal distribution. Even a single outlier could impact the estimated mean and standard deviation, potentially distorting the overall interpretation of the data and leading to inaccurate conclusions. Furthermore, the utility of the normal distribution relies on the assumption of a sufficiently large sample size, as justified by the central limit theorem (CLT). In this context, in cases of small sample sizes, the normal distribution may not always be appropriate. This challenges its widespread application, particularly when dealing with limited or non-representative data.

Theoretical criticisms of the normal distribution stem from a perspective that emphasizes the need for realism, particularly in representing the complexities and heterogeneity of economic systems. Economists argue for alternative distributional assumptions that better capture the diverse and dynamic nature of economic data. They contend that economic relationships often exhibit nonlinear patterns and non-constant variance, rendering the assumptions of the normal distribution inadequate for modeling. Behavioral deviations from rationality also factor into criticisms, as economists emphasize that behavioral insights reveal deviations from the idealized assumptions of the normal distribution. These behavioral deviations can lead to distributions that differ significantly from the normal, highlighting the need to incorporate human behavior and decision-making processes into economic models.

In response to these limitations and criticisms, economists can leverage alternative statistical distributions. These alternatives may offer better fits for specific economic data, addressing the shortcomings associated with the normal distribution's assumptions. In conclusion, criticisms raise valid concerns about the normal distribution's applicability to real-world economic phenomena, particularly in cases of extreme events, nonlinearity, and behavioral deviations. As Economic Science evolves, caution is indeed needed about when and how the normal distribution should be employed, and whether alternative distributions or methods may provide more accurate insights into economic behavior and outcomes. Such discussions enrich the field by encouraging a deeper understanding of the strengths and weaknesses of and potential alternatives to the normal distribution in economic analysis.

Key Takeaways

- The normal or Gaussian distribution is a foundational concept in Economic Science.
- Its symmetrical, 'bell-shaped' curve is characterized by the mean and standard deviation, offering insights into central tendencies and variability.
- The normal distribution aids economists in understanding economic data.
- It plays a pivotal role in risk assessment, financial modeling, and econometric analysis, guiding decision-making.
- The normal distribution's applications extend to various domains, including finance, health economics, and trade analysis.
- A deeper approach to using the normal distribution in economic analysis acknowledges its strengths while considering its limitations.
- The distribution's assumptions of normality and sensitivity to outliers raise limitations in representing economic complexities.
- Behavioral economics challenges the idealized assumptions of the normal distribution, emphasizing human decision-making deviations.
- Criticisms prompt economists to leverage alternative methods to better fit real-world economic data.
- Alternative distributions could provide options for capturing nonlinearity and extreme events.

Revision Questions

1. What is the normal distribution, and how does it relate to Economic Science?
2. In which areas of Economics and Finance is the normal distribution applied, and how does it enhance analysis?
3. How does the central limit theorem (CLT) contribute to the emergence of the Gaussian distribution in Economics?
4. Explain briefly the significance of the mean and standard deviation in the context of the normal distribution.
5. How does the normal distribution impact risk assessment and decision-making in financial markets?
6. What are some limitations of the normal distribution in representing economic data?
7. How does behavioral economics challenge the assumptions of the normal distribution?
8. What factors should economists consider when deciding whether to use the normal distribution or an alternative distribution?
9. Could alternative distributions address the shortcomings of the normal distribution?
10. How does a deeper approach to using the normal distribution enhance the understanding of economic complexities and behaviors?

CHAPTER 3

Ordinary Least Squares

Learning Objectives

- Understand the Mathematical Foundation of OLS
- Apply OLS in Various Contexts in Economics
- Analyze the Implications of OLS in Decision-Making
- Identify the Limitations and Critiques of OLS
- Evaluate the Role of OLS in Economic Research

3.1 Introduction

Economics, as a discipline, seeks to understand and analyze complex interactions. Researchers and economists often grapple with the challenge of unraveling the relationships between different variables and explaining economic phenomena. In the pursuit of this understanding, quantitative methods play a crucial role in modeling these relationships. One such powerful tool employed in Economics is Ordinary Least Squares (OLS) regression.

OLS is a fundamental technique leveraged in order to estimate the parameters of a linear model. At its core, OLS seeks to find the line (in one dimension) that minimizes the sum of the squared differences, between

P. G. Michaelides, *21 Equations that Shaped the World Economy*, https://doi.org/10.1007/978-3-031-76140-9_3

the observed and predicted values of the dependent variable. This approach serves as a fundamental tool for modeling and estimating parameters in various contexts. The method is widely employed for its simplicity, interpretability, and robustness in capturing the essence of relationships between variables. Whether examining the impact of policy changes, studying market dynamics, or forecasting economic trends, OLS provides economists with a reliable framework to analyze data and draw meaningful conclusions.

This chapter presents OLS, offering a concise examination of its principles, assumptions, and applications in the field of Economics. In this context, we will examine the foundations of OLS, discussing its mathematical underpinnings and the key assumptions that underlie its validity. We will illustrate how OLS serves as a powerful tool in empirical economic analysis, allowing economists to make informed decisions. For instance, OLS plays a crucial role in econometric analysis, enabling economists to make sense of the relationships between variables in economic models.

3.2 OLS IN *ECONOMICS*

The emergence of Ordinary Least Squares (OLS) in *Economics* can be traced back to the early developments in statistical methods and the growing need for systematic tools to analyze economic data. It was the early twentieth century when economists and statisticians began to explicitly formulate regression techniques for economic analysis. Notable contributions came from luminaries who developed methods for fitting a line to a scatterplot of data. These early efforts were foundational steps toward what would later evolve into the OLS method.

However, the breakthrough for OLS in Economics probably came with the works of economists who recognized its potential to estimate relationships between variables systematically. The widespread adoption of OLS gained momentum in the mid-twentieth century, notably with the seminal work of various economists such as Jan Tinbergen who emphasized the importance of rigorous statistical methods, including OLS, in testing economic theories against data. Since then, OLS has become a cornerstone of econometric analysis, finding applications in various branches of Economics and Finance. Its emergence and acceptance in the discipline can be attributed to its simplicity, interpretability, and the ability to provide meaningful insights into the relationships between economic variables. Today, OLS continues to be a fundamental tool in the economist's toolkit, with advancements in computing technology enhancing its applicability to large datasets and complex models.

3.3 The Equation

As we have seen, the OLS equation is a foundational method used for estimating the parameters of a regression model. In other words, it is a quantitative tool essential for analyzing relationships between variables. The linear regression model expresses the connection between a dependent variable Y and one or more independent variables $X_1, X_2, \ldots, X_k$, with corresponding coefficients $\beta_1, \beta_2, \ldots, \beta_k$.

A simple linear regression model takes the form:

$$Y = \beta_0 + \beta_1 \cdot X_1 + \varepsilon \tag{3.1}$$

Here, Y signifies the dependent variable, X_1 is the independent variable of interest, β_0 is the constant term, β_1 is the slope coefficient, indicating the change in Y for a one-unit change in X_1, and ε is the error term accounting for unobserved influences on Y.

For multiple linear regression with k independent variables, the equation extends to:

$$Y = \beta_0 + \beta_1 \cdot X_1 + \beta_2 \cdot X_2 + \ldots + \beta_k \cdot X_k + \varepsilon \tag{3.2}$$

The OLS method seeks to find the values of $\beta_0, \beta_1, \ldots, \beta_k$ that minimize the sum of squared differences between the observed Y_i values and those predicted by the model $\widehat{Y_i}$, where $i = 1, 2, \ldots n$ is the number of observations in the dataset.

Mathematically, this minimization problem is represented as:

$$min_{\beta_0, \beta_1, \ldots, \beta_k} \sum_{i=1}^{n} \left(Y_i - \left(\beta_0 + \beta_1 \cdot X_{1i} + \beta_2 \cdot X_{2i} + \ldots + \beta_k \cdot X_{ki}\right)\right)^2 \tag{3.3}$$

The solution to this minimization problem provides the OLS estimates, denoted as $\widehat{\beta_0}, \widehat{\beta_1}, \ldots, \widehat{\beta_k}$, which are used to construct the estimated equation:

$$\hat{Y} = \widehat{\beta_0} + \widehat{\beta_1} \cdot X_1 + \widehat{\beta_2} \cdot X_2 + \ldots + \widehat{\beta_k} \cdot X_k \tag{3.4}$$

Furthermore, the so-called R-squared (R^2) is a statistical measure that indicates the proportion of the variance in the dependent variable that is explainable from the independent variable(s), where the bar in its formula denotes the mean value of a variable. The formula for R^2 is as follows:

$$R^2 = 1 - \frac{\sum_{i=1}^{n} \left(Y_i - \widehat{Y_i}\right)^2}{\sum_{i=1}^{n} \left(Y_i - \overline{Y}\right)^2} \tag{3.5}$$

A high R^2 value close to 1 indicates that a large proportion of the variance in the dependent variable is explained by the independent variable(s) in the regression model. This suggests that the model fits the data very well and that the independent variables are good predictors of the dependent variable. Conversely, a low R^2 value close to 0 suggests that the independent variables in the model do not explain much of the variance in the dependent variable. This could indicate that the model is not a good fit for the data or that important predictors are missing from the model. There are no very strict ranges for good and bad fit.

For the case of simple linear regression, with one (1) independent variable, the estimated equation becomes:

$$\hat{Y} = \widehat{\beta_0} + \widehat{\beta_1} \cdot X \tag{3.6}$$

To derive the equation for the slope $\widehat{\beta_1}$ in the OLS method for simple linear regression, we proceed as follows. The OLS method minimizes the sum of the squared residuals, i.e., the differences between observed and predicted values. Mathematically:

$$S = \sum_{i=1}^{n} \left(Y_i - \widehat{Y_i}\right)^2 \tag{3.6a}$$

where Y_i are the observed values, and $\widehat{Y_i}$ are the predicted values on the OLS model:

$$\widehat{Y_i} = \widehat{\beta_0} + \widehat{\beta_1} \cdot X_i \tag{3.6b}$$

We expand the sum of squares, by plugging Eq. (3.6b) in Eq. (3.6a):

$$S = \sum_{i=1}^{n} \left(Y_i - \widehat{\beta_0} - \widehat{\beta_1} \cdot X_i\right)^2 \tag{3.6c}$$

We take the partial derivative of Eq. (3.6c) with respect to $\widehat{\beta_0}$ and set it to zero to obtain the first-order conditions (FOC) that are necessary to find the minimum (Sect. 23.1, Appendix A).

$$\frac{\partial S}{\partial \widehat{\beta_0}} = \sum_{i=1}^{n} 2 \cdot \left(Y_i - \widehat{\beta_0} - \widehat{\beta_1} \cdot X_i\right) \cdot (-1) = 0$$

$$\sum_{i=1}^{n} \left(Y_i - \widehat{\beta_0} - \widehat{\beta_1} \cdot X_i\right) = 0$$

$$\sum_{i=1}^{n} Y_i - \sum_{i=1}^{n} \widehat{\beta_0} - \widehat{\beta_1} \cdot \sum_{i=1}^{n} X_i = 0$$

$$\sum_{i=1}^{n} Y_i - n \cdot \widehat{\beta_0} - \widehat{\beta_1} \cdot \sum_{i=1}^{n} X_i = 0$$

$$\sum_{i=1}^{n} Y_i - \widehat{\beta_1} \cdot \sum_{i=1}^{n} X_i = n \cdot \widehat{\beta_0}$$

Now, we divide by *n*:

$$\frac{1}{n} \cdot \left(\sum_{i=1}^{n} Y_i\right) - \widehat{\beta_1} \cdot \frac{1}{n} \cdot \left(\sum_{i=1}^{n} X_i\right) = \widehat{\beta_0}$$

Therefore:

$$\overline{Y} - \widehat{\beta_1} \cdot \overline{X} = \widehat{\beta_0}$$

or the intercept $\widehat{\beta_0}$ is equal to:

$$\widehat{\beta_0} = \overline{Y} - \widehat{\beta_1} \cdot \overline{X} \tag{3.6d}$$

since:

$$\frac{1}{n} \cdot \left(\sum_{i=1}^{n} Y_i \right) = \overline{Y}$$

and

$$\frac{1}{n} \cdot \left(\sum_{i=1}^{n} X_i \right) = \overline{X}$$

Next, we take the partial derivative of Eq. (3.6c) with respect to $\widehat{\beta_1}$ and set it to zero to obtain the first-order conditions (FOC) that are necessary to find the minimum (Sect. 23.1, Appendix A):

$$\frac{\partial S}{\partial \widehat{\beta_1}} = \sum_{i=1}^{n} 2 \cdot \left(Y_i - \widehat{\beta_0} - \widehat{\beta_1} \cdot X_i \right) \cdot \left(-X_i \right) = 0$$

$$\sum_{i=1}^{n} (-X_i) \cdot \left(Y_i - \widehat{\beta_0} - \widehat{\beta_1} \cdot X_i \right) = 0$$

$$\sum_{i=1}^{n} (X_i) \cdot \left(Y_i - \widehat{\beta_0} - \widehat{\beta_1} \cdot X_i \right) = 0$$

$$\sum_{i=1}^{n} X_i \cdot Y_i - \widehat{\beta_0} \cdot \sum_{i=1}^{n} X_i - \widehat{\beta_1} \cdot \sum_{i=1}^{n} X_i^2 = 0 \tag{3.6e}$$

Now, we substitute Eq. (3.6d) in Eq. (3.6e):

$$\sum_{i=1}^{n} X_i \cdot Y_i - (\overline{Y} - \widehat{\beta_1} \cdot \overline{X}) \cdot \sum_{i=1}^{n} X_i - \widehat{\beta_1} \cdot \sum_{i=1}^{n} X_i^2 = 0$$

$$\sum_{i=1}^{n} X_i \cdot Y_i - \overline{Y} \cdot \sum_{i=1}^{n} X_i + \widehat{\beta_1} \cdot \overline{X} \cdot \sum_{i=1}^{n} X_i - \widehat{\beta_1} \cdot \sum_{i=1}^{n} X_i^2 = 0$$

$$\sum_{i=1}^{n} X_i \cdot Y_i - \overline{Y} \cdot \sum_{i=1}^{n} X_i = -\widehat{\beta_1} \cdot \overline{X} \cdot \sum_{i=1}^{n} X_i + \widehat{\beta_1} \cdot \sum_{i=1}^{n} X_i^2$$

$$\sum_{i=1}^{n} X_i \cdot Y_i - \overline{Y} \cdot \sum_{i=1}^{n} X_i = \widehat{\beta_1} \cdot \left(\sum_{i=1}^{n} X_i^2 - \overline{X} \cdot \sum_{i=1}^{n} X_i \right)$$

But, since:

$$\sum_{i=1}^{n} X_i = n \cdot \overline{X}$$

we get:

$$\sum_{i=1}^{n} X_i \cdot Y_i - n \cdot \overline{Y} \cdot \overline{X} = \widehat{\beta_1} \cdot \left(\sum_{i=1}^{n} X_i^2 - n \cdot \overline{X}^2 \right)$$

And solving for $\widehat{\beta_1}$ we obtain:

$$\widehat{\beta_1} = \frac{\sum_{i=1}^{n} X_i \cdot Y_i - n \cdot \overline{Y} \cdot \overline{X}}{\sum_{i=1}^{n} X_i^2 - n \cdot \overline{X}^2} \tag{3.6f}$$

This completes the derivation for the slope $\widehat{\beta_1}$ in simple linear regression, using the OLS method.

However, it can be shown that the slope $\widehat{\beta_1}$ is equal to:

$$\widehat{\beta_1} = \frac{\sum_{i=1}^{n} \left(X_i - \overline{X} \right) \cdot \left(Y_i - \overline{Y} \right)}{\sum_{i=1}^{n} \left(X_i - \overline{X} \right)^2} \tag{3.7}$$

Let's see why these two expressions are identical. We start by expanding the numerator of Eq. (3.7):

$$\sum_{i=1}^{n} \left(X_i - \overline{X} \right) \cdot \left(Y_i - \overline{Y} \right) = \sum_{i=1}^{n} \left(X_i \cdot Y_i - X_i \cdot \overline{Y} - \overline{X} \cdot Y_i + \overline{X} \cdot \overline{Y} \right)$$

Next, we break down each term:

First term: $\sum_{i=1}^{n} X_i \cdot Y$

Second term: $\sum_{i=1}^{n} X_i \cdot \overline{Y} = \overline{Y} \cdot \sum_{i=1}^{n} \cdot X_i = n \cdot \overline{X} \cdot \overline{Y}$

Third term: $\sum_{i=1}^{n} \overline{X} \cdot Y_i = \overline{X} \cdot \sum_{i=1}^{n} Y_i = n \cdot \overline{X} \cdot \overline{Y}$

Fourth term: $\sum_{i=1}^{n} \overline{X} \cdot \overline{Y} = n \cdot \overline{X} \cdot \overline{Y}$

So, putting these together, we get:

$$\sum_{i=1}^{n} \left(X_i - \overline{X}\right) \cdot \left(Y_i - \overline{Y}\right) = \sum_{i=1}^{n} X_i \cdot Y_i - n \cdot \overline{X} \cdot \overline{Y} - n \cdot \overline{X} \cdot \overline{Y} + n \cdot \overline{X} \cdot \overline{Y}$$

$$\sum_{i=1}^{n} \left(X_i - \overline{X}\right) \cdot \left(Y_i - \overline{Y}\right) = \sum_{i=1}^{n} X_i \cdot Y_i - n \cdot \overline{X} \cdot \overline{Y}$$

We proceed by expanding the denominator of Eq. (3.7):

$$\sum_{i=1}^{n} \left(X_i - \overline{X}\right)^2 = \sum_{i=1}^{n} \left(X_i^2 - 2 \cdot X_i \cdot \overline{X} + \overline{X}^2\right)$$

By breaking this down term by term:

First term: $\sum_{i=1}^{n} X_i^2$

Second term: $\sum_{i=1}^{n} 2 \cdot X_i \cdot \overline{X} = 2 \cdot \overline{X} \cdot \sum_{i=1}^{n} X_i = 2 \cdot \overline{X} \cdot n \cdot \overline{X} = 2 \cdot n \cdot \overline{X}^2$

Third term: $\sum_{i=1}^{n} \overline{X}^2 = n \cdot \overline{X}^2$

So, putting these together, we get:

$$\sum_{i=1}^{n} \left(X_i - \overline{X}\right)^2 = \sum_{i=1}^{n} X_i^2 - 2 \cdot n \cdot \overline{X}^2 + n \cdot \overline{X}^2$$

$$\sum_{i=1}^{n}\left(X_i - \overline{X}\right)^2 = \sum_{i=1}^{n} X_i^2 - n \cdot \overline{X}^2$$

Thus, we have shown that:

$$\sum_{i=1}^{n} X_i \cdot Y_i - n \cdot \overline{X} \cdot \overline{Y} = \sum_{i=1}^{n}\left(X_i - \overline{X}\right)\cdot\left(Y_i - \overline{Y}\right) \tag{3.7a}$$

And:

$$\sum_{i=1}^{n} X_i^2 - n \cdot \overline{X}^2 = \sum_{i=1}^{n}\left(X_i - \overline{X}\right)^2 \tag{3.7b}$$

By substituting Eqs. (3.7a) and (3.7b) in Eq. (3.6f), we get:

$$\widehat{\beta_1} = \frac{\sum_{i=1}^{n}\left(X_i - \overline{X}\right)\cdot\left(Y_i - \overline{Y}\right)}{\sum_{i=1}^{n}\left(X_i - \overline{X}\right)^2} \tag{3.7}$$

and the intercept $\widehat{\beta_0}$, based on Eq. (3.6d), is equal to:

$$\widehat{\beta_0} = \overline{Y} - \widehat{\beta_1} \cdot \overline{X} \tag{3.8}$$

where:

- i ranges from 1 to n, and n is the total number of observations or data points in the dataset.
- X_i and Y_i represent the values of the independent and dependent variables, respectively, for the i-th observation.
- $\overline{X}$ and $\overline{Y}$ are the means of the independent and dependent variables, respectively.

It should be noted that on the derivation of the OLS estimators for simple linear regression, we generally do not explicitly check the second-order conditions (SOC). The reason for this is that the OLS minimization

Table 3.1 Example data

Worker I	*Hours worked* (X)	*Units produced* (Y)
1	1	2
2	2	3
3	3	6
4	4	8
5	5	10

problem is known to be inherently quadratic and convex, ensuring that the solution derived from the first-order conditions is indeed a global minimum. More precisely, the minimization problem is inherently quadratic because the objective function, i.e., the sum of squared differences, is a quadratic function of the parameters. Therefore, it has a parabolic shape in terms of the parameter space. Since the problem refers to minimization, this implies that it is 'U-shaped' and, hence, there is a single global minimum.

Practically, statistical software is commonly utilized for OLS estimation. The OLS estimates exhibit some desirable mathematical properties, making them reliable for drawing inferences about the relationships between economic variables. Furthermore, hypothesis testing and confidence intervals can be conducted based on the OLS estimates, allowing for the assessment of the significance of the estimated coefficients in the context of econometric analysis.

Let's see a very simple linear regression example. Suppose we have data on the number of hours worked and the items produced by five (5) workers in a factory. We will use OLS to find the relationship between hours worked (independent variable, X) and units produced (dependent variable, Y). Table 3.1 shows the data:

Now, we need to plug the relevant numbers in Eqs. (3.7) and (3.8). First, we calculate the mean values of X and Y, respectively:

$$\bar{X} = \frac{1+2+3+4+5}{5} = 3 \text{ and } \bar{Y} = \frac{2+3+6+8+10}{5} = 5.8.$$

Then, we calculate the sum:

$$\sum_{i=1}^{n} \left(X_i - \bar{X}\right) \cdot \left(Y_i - \bar{Y}\right) =$$

$(1-3)\cdot(2-5.8)+(2-3)\cdot(3-5.8)+(3-3)\cdot(6-5.8)+(4-3)\cdot(8-5.8)+(5-3)\cdot(10-5.8)=(-2)\cdot(-3.8)+(-1)\cdot(-2.8)+(0)\cdot(0.2)+(1)\cdot(2.2)+(2)\cdot(4.2)=7.6+2.8+0+2.2+8.4=21$

Next, we calculate the sum:

$$\sum_{i=1}^{n}\left(X_i-\overline{X}\right)^2$$

$=(1-3)^2+(2-3)^2+(3-3)^2+(4-3)^2+(5-3)^2=10$

By plugging these numbers in Eq. (3.7) for the slope, we get:

$$\widehat{\beta_1}=\frac{21}{10}=2.1$$

Next, we plug the numbers in Eq. (3.8) for the intercept:

$$\widehat{\beta_0}=5.8-(2.1)\cdot 3=-0.5$$

Therefore, the estimated regression equation is: $\hat{Y}=-0.5+2.1\cdot X$

The value of the slope implies that for each additional hour worked, the produced output increases by 2.1 units, on average.

Next, we will calculate the R^2 based on Eq. (3.5). Given the original data and our regression model $\hat{Y}=-0.5+2.1\cdot X$, we first need to calculate the predicted values $\widehat{Y_i}$, and then the required sums, as shown in Table 3.2:

First, we calculate: $\sum_{i=1}^{n}\left(Y_i-\overline{Y}\right)^2=(2-5.8)^2+(3-5.8)^2+(6-5.8)^2+(8-5.8)^2+(10-5.8)^2=14.44+7.84+0.04+4.84+17.64=44.8$

Table 3.2 Example calculation

Worker j	*Hours worked* (X)	*Units produced* (Y)	*Predicted units produced* $(\widehat{Y})$
1	1	2	$-0.5+2.1\cdot 1=1.6$
2	2	3	$-0.5+2.1\cdot 2=3.7$
3	3	6	$-0.5+2.1\cdot 3=5.8$
4	4	8	$-0.5+2.1\cdot 4=7.9$
5	5	10	$-0.5+2.1\cdot 5=10.0$

Next, we calculate: $\sum_{i=1}^{n}\left(Y_i-\widehat{Y}_i\right)^2$ = (2 – 1.6)^2+ (3 – 3.7)^2 + (6 – 5.8)^2 + (8 – 7.9)^2 + (10 – 10)^2 = 0.16 + 0.49 + 0.04 + 0.01+ 0 = 0.7
We plug these numbers in Eq. (3.5):

$$R^2 = 1 - \frac{0.7}{44.8} = 1 - 0.016 = 0.984$$

The R^2 value for this regression model is 0.984, or 98.4%. This means that 98.4% of the variance in the units produced can be explained by the number of hours worked. This indicates that the regression model fits the data very well.

3.4 Insights and Consequences

The widespread application of OLS in Economics bears significant implications, fundamentally shaping the empirical analysis of economic relationships. One of the primary ramifications lies in its pivotal role in policy evaluation. OLS allows economists to discern relationships between variables, providing a foundational basis for assessing the effectiveness of policies. For instance, a substantial implication of OLS lies in its capacity for forecasting and prediction within the economic landscape. By modeling historical data, economists leverage OLS to forecast future economic trends. Consider an economist utilizing OLS to model the dynamic relationship between consumer spending and income across multiple years. This application enables the modeling of future consumer behavior, providing valuable foresight for businesses and policymakers engaged in strategic planning and decision-making. The versatility of OLS extends to market analysis and pricing strategies, where it offers invaluable insights into the dynamics of economic markets. OLS assists in optimizing pricing strategies by estimating how changes in variables, such as price, influence quantities demanded. For instance, businesses can utilize OLS to gain a better understanding of how alterations in pricing structures might impact consumer behavior.

In labor market studies, OLS plays a pivotal role in unraveling the complex relationship between variables like education levels and earnings. For instance, this application of OLS provides a comprehensive understanding of the returns on education and human capital investment, offering essential insights for policymakers and educational institutions alike. In the context of resource allocation in business, OLS empowers optimal decision-making by identifying key drivers of business outcomes. For instance, a firm might employ OLS to analyze the relationship between advertising expenditure and sales, allowing for data-driven decisions about resource allocation to maximize the impact of marketing efforts. The field of Finance also benefits significantly from OLS, particularly in understanding asset pricing and risk–return relationships. Investors and financial analysts routinely employ OLS to estimate parameters in models like the capital asset pricing model (CAPM). This not only aids in risk assessment but also contributes to informed investment decision-making by providing a quantitative framework for evaluating expected returns in relation to risk.

3.5 Conclusion, Limitations, and Critiques

It becomes evident that the impact of Ordinary Least Squares (OLS) extends across diverse domains, contributing substantially to the empirical understanding and interpretation of economic phenomena. By offering a systematic approach to discerning relationships between variables, OLS provides a crucial foundation for policymakers to assess the effectiveness of interventions and policy measures. Its application in modeling the deeper connections between variables serves as a powerful tool for policymakers seeking evidence-based insights. Whether predicting consumer behavior based on income trends or anticipating market dynamics, OLS contributes to strategic planning and risk management, offering valuable insights for businesses and policymakers. Moreover, OLS's role in econometric testing and model diagnostics ensures the reliability of empirical analyses. Rigorous diagnostic tests enhance the credibility of research findings, allowing economists to draw robust conclusions from their models. This commitment to methodological rigor contributes to the advancement of economic knowledge and the development of more accurate and reliable economic models.

Despite its widespread application in Economics, OLS is not without its limitations. The traditional method assumes linearity between dependent and independent variables, which may not align with real-world scenarios where relationships can be nonlinear. Moreover, OLS is sensitive to outliers, and the presence of influential data points can distort parameter estimates and compromise the robustness of the model. Another assumption of OLS is the independence of error terms. Violations, such as autocorrelation in time-series data, can lead to biased standard errors. Additionally, OLS assumes homoscedasticity, implying constant error variance across all levels of independent variables. Any departure from this assumption, known as heteroscedasticity, can affect OLS estimates. Multicollinearity, resulting from linear relations among independent variables, is another limitation, which makes it difficult to isolate the separate effects of each variable.

Critiques of OLS center on its distributional assumptions, particularly the normality assumption. They argue that in cases where normality may not be justified, alternative estimation techniques may be more appropriate. Economists also express concerns suggesting that the assumed relationships may be bi-directional or influenced by unobserved factors. To address this, other methods are proposed as alternatives. In this context, critics advocate for alternative estimation techniques beyond OLS, including Maximum Likelihood estimation, or Bayesian methods, which provide flexibility in modeling complex relationships.

Furthermore, critics argue that OLS oversimplifies economic relationships and may not adequately express the complexity of socio-economic systems. They propose embracing complexity and employing qualitative methods, such as case studies, for a more comprehensive understanding. Additionally, they emphasize the importance of considering the broader socio-economic context when applying OLS. They argue that a focus solely on statistical relationships may overlook structural factors, power or class dynamics, and historical context that shape economic phenomena.

In conclusion, the extended elaboration on the implications of OLS stresses its transformative influence across a spectrum of economic applications. Its adaptability, reliability, and versatility make it an extremely helpful tool for economists, policymakers, and businesses in the complexities of economic systems. Consequently, while OLS is a powerful tool in *Economics*, its limitations and critiques highlight the need for a cautious and context-aware approach to empirical modeling.

Chapter Takeaways

- OLS is a fundamental tool in *Economics* for estimating parameters in regression models.
- It provides simplicity, interpretability, and robustness, making it widely adopted in economic analysis.
- The historical emergence of OLS traces back to early developments in statistical methods and the pioneering work of various economists.
- The OLS equation mathematically minimizes the sum of squared differences between observed and predicted values of the dependent variable.
- OLS plays a pivotal role in policy evaluation, enabling economists to assess the effectiveness of policies by discerning relationships between variables.
- Its modeling capability allows economists to model historical data and predict future economic trends, aiding strategic planning.
- OLS can contribute to market analysis and pricing strategies by estimating how changes in variables impact market behavior.
- In labor market studies, OLS can unravel relationships between variables like education levels and earnings, informing human capital investment decisions.
- The method empowers business decision-making by identifying key drivers of outcomes, such as the relationship between advertising expenditure and sales.
- Despite its wide application, OLS has limitations, including sensitivity to outliers and various assumptions.

Revision Questions

1. What is the role of Ordinary Least Squares (OLS) regression in Economics?
2. Describe briefly the historical emergence of OLS and its key contributors.
3. Explain the mathematical foundation of the OLS equation in Econometrics.
4. How does OLS contribute to policy evaluation in Economics?
5. What is the forecasting capability of OLS, and how is it applied in economic analysis?
6. Discuss OLS's role in market analysis and pricing strategies, providing examples.
7. In labor market studies, how does OLS contribute to understanding relationships between variables?
8. How does OLS empower business decision-making, particularly in resource allocation?
9. What are the limitations of OLS, and how do they impact its application in economic analysis?
10. Summarize the key points highlighting the transformative influence and versatility of OLS in Economics.

CHAPTER 4

Production Function and Total Factor Productivity

Learning Objectives

- Understand the Concept of the Production Function
- Apply the Cobb-Douglas Production Function in Economics
- Explore Total Factor Productivity (TFP) in Economic Growth
- Identify the Limitations of the Production Function Framework
- Analyze the Broader Economic Context of Production Functions

4.1 Introduction

In the web of economic interactions that drive societies, the process of production orchestrates the transformation of raw materials and inputs into the array of commodities that fuel human progress. This process is underpinned by a fundamental procedure that most economists term the 'production function.' This notion lies at the heart of Economics, offering a structured lens through which the interaction of factors and outcomes can be dissected and understood. The production function serves as a conceptual bridge between the tangible inputs and outputs of economic

P. G. Michaelides, *21 Equations that Shaped the World Economy*,
https://doi.org/10.1007/978-3-031-76140-9_4

activity. It encapsulates the process of production, unraveling the underlying mechanisms that guide the transformation of labor, capital, and technology into tangible outputs that enhance societal welfare. It is a mathematical construct that illuminates the critical relationship between these inputs and the resultant goods and services, offering insights into the forces that shape the productive landscape.

At its core, the production function is akin to a mathematical expression, capturing the essence of how inputs interact to yield outputs. It provides a framework that aids economists in deciphering the dance of resource allocation, technological innovation, and efficiency optimization. By breaking down the production process into its constituent parts, the production function allows us to examine the impact of various factors and their contributions. Furthermore, the production function is not static; it changes over time, mirroring the dynamic nature of economies and societies. Technological progress, innovation, and shifts in resource availability all influence the shape and parameters of the production function. As such, the concept is not confined to the dusty pages of economic textbooks; it finds practical application in diverse arenas. Policymakers utilize production functions to design strategies for economic growth, resource management, and poverty reduction. Business leaders leverage these insights to optimize production processes. In the pages that follow, we will embark on a brief analysis of the production function. We will examine its mathematical underpinnings, present its most popular form, and set out the implications of its key features.

4.2 Production Function and Total Factor Productivity in Economics

The evolution of economic thought is a fascinating journey marked by the development and refinement of key concepts that shed light on the inner workings of economies. Among these foundational ideas, the emergence and evolution of the production function stand out as a critical turning point that changed the way economists conceptualize and analyze the complex process of producing goods and services.

The roots of the production function can, very loosely speaking, be traced back to the writings of classical economists. In the late eighteenth century, as industrialization took hold and economies underwent transformative shifts, economic thinkers were captivated by the factors driving economic growth and the mechanisms behind the creation of wealth. Adam Smith's famous work *An Inquiry into the Nature and Causes of the Wealth of Nations* introduced, among other notions, the concept of division of labor, emphasizing the role of specialization and labor in driving production. While Smith's insights laid the groundwork, this can be seen, very loosely, as the beginning of the journey toward the production function.

The nineteenth century witnessed further investigations into the relationships between inputs and outputs. For instance, John Stuart Mill contributed to this development. Mill's recognition of diminishing returns to labor paved the way for a deeper understanding of how additional units of inputs impact output levels. Although the mathematical formalization was still in its infancy, these ideas were instrumental in shaping the conceptual landscape of the production function.

However, it was not until the neoclassical era that the production function truly began to take shape as a formal mathematical construct. Broadly speaking, economists like Alfred Marshall, Vilfredo Pareto, and Léon Walras helped refine the mathematical framework that underpinned the quantification of economic relationships. Their work established a mathematical foundation for helping understand how changes in inputs, such as labor and capital, influence changes in output. The term 'production function' itself gained prominence probably through the efforts of the economists of the so-called Chicago School. Their work in the early twentieth century established it as a central pillar of Economic Science. A significant leap in the application of production functions came with the works of Robert Solow and Trevor Swan in the mid-twentieth century. The Solow (or Solow-Swan) model, building upon the neoclassical framework, integrated technological progress and capital accumulation as key determinants of long-term economic growth. This marked a pivotal moment where the production function became an essential tool for studying not only resource allocation but also the dynamic process of development.

In the modern era, the production function continues to evolve and adapt to the changing landscape of Economics. With the advent of sophisticated computational tools, data science, and econometric techniques, economists and engineers can analyze complex production relationships with greater precision and realism. The production function's application extends beyond traditional economic analysis; it finds applications in understanding issues ranging from optimal resource allocation and business management to environmental sustainability and policy formulation. Nowadays, the production function remains a tool that guides the understanding of how societies and economies transform inputs into outputs.

4.3 The Equation

In the aforementioned framework, where relationships between inputs and outputs govern the dynamics of production, the Cobb-Douglas (CD) production function is a construct of mathematical elegance. Named after its originators, the mathematician Charles Cobb and the economist Paul Douglas who introduced the functional form, this mathematical formulation has etched its mark on the landscape of Economics, offering a quantifiable framework to dissect the interaction of labor, capital, technology, and output in the process of economic production.

Of course, the CD production function is not merely an abstract mathematical construct; it serves as a powerful tool that unlocks the quantitative patterns and interdependencies within production processes. By its nature, the CD production function invites us to study the relationships between inputs and outputs in a manner that blends mathematical precision with real-world implications. Hence, in what follows, we briefly examine the CD production function and contribute to our understanding of how societies and economies transform inputs into the commodities that define modern existence.

Technically speaking, the CD production function describes the relationship between multiple inputs and the level of output produced by a firm, industry, or economy, under the assumption that they have only one output. Strictly speaking, the production function expresses the maximum level of output that can be produced for a given level of input. Here, we assume that capital and labor are the two (2) inputs, and that technological progress is, as we say, Hicks-neutral. The general form of such a production function at time *t* is thus given by:

$$Y = A(t) \cdot L(t)^{a} \cdot K(t)^{\beta} \tag{4.1}$$

or, for simplicity:

$$Y = A \cdot L^{a} \cdot K^{\beta} \tag{4.2}$$

where:

- *Υ* represents the level of output produced
- *A* denotes the technological level, satisfying $A>0$
- *L* expresses the labor input
- *K* expresses the capital input
- α, β are the so-called elasticities of labor and capital, respectively, typically satisfying $0<\alpha<1$, $0<\beta<1$

By taking the natural logarithm in Eq. (4.2), we obtain:

$$lnY = lnA + a \cdot lnL + \beta \cdot lnK \tag{4.3}$$

Now, the total differential (Sect. 23.2, Appendix B) of *lnΥ*, based on Eq. (4.3), is as follows:

$$d(lnY) = \frac{\partial(lnY)}{\partial(lnA)} \cdot d(lnA) + \frac{\partial(lnY)}{\partial(lnL)} \cdot d(lnL) + \frac{\partial(lnY)}{\partial(lnK)} \cdot d(lnK) \tag{4.4}$$

But, based on Eq. (4.3), we obtain:

$$\frac{\partial(lnY)}{\partial(lnA)} = 1, \ \frac{\partial(lnY)}{\partial(lnL)} = a, \ \frac{\partial(lnY)}{\partial(lnK)} = \beta \tag{4.5}$$

Thus, plugging Eq. (4.5) in Eq. (4.4), we get:

$$d(lnY) = d(lnA) + a \cdot d(lnL) + \beta \cdot d(lnK) \tag{4.6}$$

Taking the derivatives with respect to time:

$$\frac{d(lnY)}{dt} = \frac{d(lnA)}{dt} + a \cdot \frac{d(lnL)}{dt} + \beta \cdot \frac{d(lnK)}{dt} \tag{4.7}$$

Applying the chain rule (Sect. 23.2, Appendix B) in Eq. (4.7), we obtain:

$$\frac{d(lnY)}{dY}\cdot\frac{dY}{dt}=\frac{d(lnA)}{dA}\cdot\frac{dA}{dt}+a\cdot\frac{d(lnL)}{dL}\cdot\frac{dL}{dt}+\beta\cdot\frac{d(lnK)}{dK}\cdot\frac{dK}{dt} \quad (4.8)$$

But:

$$\frac{d(lnY)}{dY}=\frac{1}{Y},\ \frac{d(lnA)}{dA}=\frac{1}{A},\ \frac{d(lnL)}{dL}=\frac{1}{L},\ \frac{d(lnK)}{dK}=\frac{1}{K} \quad (4.9)$$

Plugging Eq. (4.9) in Eq. (4.8), we get:

$$\frac{1}{Y}\cdot\frac{dY}{dt}=\frac{1}{A}\cdot\frac{dA}{dt}+a\cdot\frac{1}{L}\cdot\frac{dL}{dt}+\beta\cdot\frac{1}{K}\cdot\frac{dK}{dt}$$

Rearranging, we obtain:

$$\frac{1}{A}\cdot\frac{dA}{dt}=\frac{1}{Y}\cdot\frac{dY}{dt}-a\cdot\frac{1}{L}\cdot\frac{dL}{dt}-\beta\cdot\frac{1}{K}\cdot\frac{dK}{dt} \quad (4.10)$$

By definition, $\text{TFP}\equiv\frac{dln\text{A}}{dt}=\frac{1}{A}\cdot\frac{dA}{dt}$.

Applying this definition of TFP in Eq. (4.10) we get:

$$\text{TFP}=\frac{1}{Y}\cdot\frac{dY}{dt}-a\cdot\frac{1}{L}\cdot\frac{dL}{dt}-\beta\cdot\frac{1}{K}\cdot\frac{dK}{dt} \quad (4.11)$$

In other words, this quantity indicates that a significant portion of the growth in the output of an economic unit is not due to the growth of capital and labor factors, but to what we called Total Factor Productivity (TFP), which is equal to the residual of the production function, also known as the 'Solow residual,' as estimated econometrically.

In practice, the key assumptions and/or considerations typically made in the CD production function are the following:

1. The inputs (here: capital and labor) are typically assumed to be non-negative. This is because negative quantities of inputs would not make sense in most production contexts.

2. The output is typically assumed to be positive. While negative output could technically be included in the function, it would not have meaningful economic interpretation in most cases.
3. The Cobb-Douglas production function is continuous and differentiable with respect to its inputs. This allows for smooth analysis and mathematical operations.
4. The production function assumes that the combinations of capital and labor inputs used in production are technologically feasible. In other words, it assumes that the specified inputs can be combined to produce the specified output.
5. The inputs and output are often aggregated measures, representing the total quantities used or produced over a given period, rather than individual units.

The CD production function exhibits several characteristics, such as 'homogeneity.' Typically, economists assume about the exponents α and β that $0<\alpha<1$ and $0<\beta<1$. Also, the sum of the exponents α and β is equal to unity, i.e., $\alpha + \beta = 1$. Therefore, the production function is said to exhibit constant returns to scale (CRS). This implies that if all inputs are increased proportionally, output will also increase proportionally. For example, doubling both labor and capital will double the output. In other words, the CD production function is 'homogeneous.'

Lastly, the CD production function has implications for income distribution. The distribution of income between labor and capital is determined by the values of α and β. A higher α implies a larger share of income going to labor, while a higher β implies a larger share going to capital.

Let's consider a typical Hicks-neutral Cobb-Douglas production function to demonstrate the computation of TFP, using a very simple numerical example, and the following values:

- $A = 2$ indicating a certain level of technology
- $L = 10$ units of labor
- $K = 5$ units of capital
- $\alpha = 0.5$
- $\beta = 0.5$

Plugging the numbers in Eq. (4.1) we get:

$$Y_t = 2 \cdot 10^{0.5} \cdot 5^{0.5} \approx 14.14$$

Thus, the output is approximately 14.14 units.

Now, to compute TFP, suppose that, over time, output Y, labor L, and capital K_t grow at the following annual growth rates, respectively:

- $\frac{1}{Y} \cdot \frac{dY}{dt} = 5\%$ (output growth rate)
- $\frac{1}{L} \cdot \frac{dL}{dt} = 2\%$ (labor growth rate)
- $\frac{1}{K} \cdot \frac{dK}{dt} = 3\%$ (capital growth rate)

Plugging the aforementioned numbers in Eq. (4.11), we get:

$$\text{TFP} = 0.05 - (0.5 \cdot 0.02) - (0.5 \cdot 0.03) = 0.025 = 2.5\%$$

Thus, the TFP growth rate is 2.5%. A TFP growth rate of 2.5% means that the economy's output is increasing by 2.5% per year due to improvements in technology, and other productivity-enhancing factors, independent of changes in the amount of labor and capital employed. This growth rate is crucial because it represents how much more productive the economy can become over time. It indicates that the same amount of input, i.e., labor and capital, can produce 2.5% more output each year due to better use of resources.

For instance, suppose an economy produces \$1 trillion worth of goods and services in a given year. With a TFP growth rate of 2.5%, the next year the economy can produce \$1.025 trillion worth of goods and services with the same amount of labor and capital. This increase is due to better management practices, or other factors (excluding labor and capital) that make the production process more efficient.

In this context, TFP holds a central role in understanding economic growth, especially in the context of technological advancements. Robert Solow, and other pioneering economists, harnessed the CD production function to scrutinize growth dynamics. Through their analyses, they revealed empirically, based on Econometrics, that a substantial portion of per capita output growth stems not solely from capital and labor, but also from Total Factor Productivity (TFP). This framework, the so-called

Growth Accounting methodology, embraced for its reliance on robust statistical data and relative avoidance of highly arbitrary assumptions, remains a cornerstone in economic analysis.

4.4 Insights and Consequences

The CD production function transcends theoretical constructs to find robust empirical applications across a spectrum of economic inquiries. Through its lens, economists decipher the complex patterns of economic growth, responsiveness of production, and the dynamics of various industries, enriching our understanding of the complex interplay between inputs, outputs, technology, and productivity.

One of the most prominent empirical applications of the CD production function lies in economic growth and development. By employing historical data and leveraging statistical techniques, as shown earlier, economists estimate the parameters α, β and A. These estimations express the relative contributions of labor, capital, and technological progress to economic expansion. This empirical analysis enables policymakers and researchers to discern the engines propelling growth, facilitating the design of targeted strategies to enhance each factor's impact. Moreover, the CD framework permits cross-country comparisons, shedding light on how different nations' economies harness inputs to achieve varying levels of development.

The CD production function also serves as a compass guiding the analysis of specific industries and sectors. By applying the model to the unique attributes of each industry, researchers estimate its parameters. This approach unveils the relative significance of labor and capital inputs within different sectors, uncovering their impact on overall economic performance. Such insights empower policymakers to develop targeted interventions, allocate resources efficiently, and foster the growth of industries that hold substantial potential.

Consider a manufacturing firm seeking to enhance its productivity. By leveraging the insights offered by the CD production function, the firm can assess the impact of adjusting the mix of labor and capital inputs. Should it invest in hiring more workers or acquiring additional machinery? The function's estimations can shed light on the marginal contribution of each input to the output. If, for instance, the function reveals that capital has a higher marginal contribution, the firm might prioritize capital investment to achieve an optimal balance and boost overall productivity.

Moreover, as we have seen, the parameter A in the CD production function encapsulates technological change, in the broad sense of the term. Consequently, the Total Factor Productivity (TFP) embodies the cumulative effect of innovation, new technical advancements, managerial efficiency, and other intangible factors that enhance the transformation of inputs into output, except for the inputs already explicitly included in the CD production function. An increase in the TFP signifies a leap in technological prowess or a surge in overall efficiency. This implies that the same input, be it labor, capital, or both, can now generate higher levels of output.

The TFP also underlines the potential of total economies to achieve higher levels of output while effectively managing resource constraints. Policymakers and businesses alike can use this understanding to prioritize investments in research and development, foster innovation, and cultivate an environment conducive to technological progress. In essence, the CD production function renders tangible the abstract concept of technological advancement, offering a quantitative lens through which the impact of innovation on economic growth becomes tangible and actionable.

4.5 Conclusion, Limitations, and Critiques

The CD production function is mathematically derived from neoclassical economic theory, which emphasizes rational decision-making, efficient resource allocation, and market equilibrium. Meanwhile, the CD production function thrives as an empirical workhorse, bridging the gap between theory and real-world dynamics. Its applications extend far beyond the confines of academia, influencing policy decisions, shaping business strategies, and informing economic forecasts.

Policymakers, too, find the CD framework indispensable in crafting effective resource allocation strategies. In economic development, the function guides decisions about how to allocate public investments and resources between labor-intensive and capital-intensive sectors. By tailoring input combinations to the unique characteristics of industries and economies, policymakers harness the function's insights to steer growth trajectories and boost overall economic welfare.

However, the application of production functions is not without limitations. To begin with, simplistic assumptions underpin production functions, rendering them mathematically tractable but potentially detached from the realities of actual production processes. For instance, assumptions like constant returns to scale (CRS) offer analytical convenience but may overlook the complexity of technology adoption, the impact of external factors, and the interplay of inputs.

It thereby neglects the qualitative aspects of labor and the social relations of production. This view does not account for how different types of labor can have varying productivity levels, depending on their social context and the specific conditions of production. Moreover, some economists argue that the reliance on mathematical formulations like the Cobb-Douglas function can obscure the true dynamics of most production systems, as it tends to focus on aggregate outputs without addressing the underlying class and power relations as well as the inequalities that shape production processes.

Moreover, production functions tend to confine their scope to immediate inputs and outputs, disregarding the broader externalities that production can trigger. The ripple effects on the environment, society, and other external factors often remain unaccounted for, potentially painting an incomplete picture of the true impact of production processes. While the CD model excels in picturing immediate resource allocation and output levels, it might fall short in capturing the evolving dynamics that unfold over longer time frames. Economic growth, shifts in technology, and evolving consumer preferences can induce changes in production relationships that escape the grasp of traditional production function analysis.

Economists also raise thought-provoking critiques that expand the dialogue surrounding production functions. Contextual complexity, involving institutions, and historical contingencies often shape outcomes but tend to be sidelined in these models. For instance, the assumption of perfect competition implied by many production functions seems unreal. It could be argued that actual markets are often characterized by imperfect competition and the sway of market power, resulting in income inequality and skewed resource allocation. The dynamics of labor markets and oligopolistic structures further muddy the waters of these mathematical relationships.

Additionally, critics highlight the need to acknowledge historical specificity, an aspect often marginalized in production functions. These models abstract away from the rich historical and cultural contexts that mold economic phenomena. Economic Science needs a more holistic approach that accommodates the unique historical trajectories shaping production outcomes. Emphasizing the social and environmental dimensions, critics advocate for a broader perspective that encompasses the wider impacts of production. Traditional production functions may miss the mark by omitting the potential negative externalities, social costs, and environmental repercussions that production can entail. By incorporating an array of factors beyond labor, capital, and technology, including class or power dynamics, social relations, non-market interactions, and the influence of culture and institutions, we could offer a more encompassing lens.

In sum, production functions guide firms, industries, economies, and policymakers. Their insights permeate decisions that shape economic landscapes, from the factory floor to the halls of policy formulation, ensuring that the interplay between labor, capital, and technological progress propels economies toward higher levels of production. However, while production functions remain useful tools, the aforementioned limitations and critiques underscore the necessity of a more balanced approach. Merging the insights of production functions with a broader and more holistic understanding of economic dynamics equips policymakers, researchers, economists, and engineers with enhanced insight and precision.

Chapter Takeaways

- The production function is a useful tool in Economics, expressing the transformation of inputs into commodities that drive economic progress.
- Very loosely rooted in Classical economics, the production function gained mathematical rigor through neoclassical economists.
- The Cobb-Douglas (CD) production function is an expression in mathematical terms that quantifies the relationships between labor, capital, technology, and output.
- The CD production function demonstrates constant returns to scale when $\alpha + \beta = 1$.
- A higher value of α implies a larger share of income going to labor, while a higher value of β implies a larger share going to capital.
- The 'homogeneity' assumption implies that if all inputs are increased proportionally, output will also increase proportionally.
- Total Factor Productivity (TFP) in the CD function captures technological progress and efficiency gains beyond explicit inputs.

- CD production function empowers economic growth and development analysis by quantifying contributions of labor, capital, and TFP.
- Industry analysis benefits from the CD function's tailored insights into labor-capital dynamics and their impact on specific sectors.
- While powerful, production functions have limitations sparking numerous critiques.

Revision Questions

1. What is the production function and how does it contribute to understanding economic processes?
2. How did the CD production function revolutionize empirical economic analysis?
3. Explain the concepts of returns to scale and homogeneity.
4. How does the CD production function capture Total Factor Productivity (TFP) and technological progress?
5. What role does TFP play in economic expansion?
6. In what ways does the production function inform economic growth and development analysis?
7. Describe the significance of estimating labor and capital elasticities using the production function.
8. How does the CD production function guide industry analysis and sector-specific insights?
9. What are the limitations of production functions, and how do they prompt critiques?
10. How can a holistic understanding of Economics, beyond production functions, enhance decision-making?

CHAPTER 5

The Profit Rate

Learning Objectives

- Get Familiar with the Classical and Marxist Versions of the Profit Rate
- Analyze the Role of the Profit Rate in Technological Innovation
- Evaluate the Impact of Profit Rate on Economic Stability
- Identify the Critiques of Profit Rate Theory
- Apply Profit Rate Insights to Policymaking

5.1 Introduction

The examination of the profit rate, which originated from Classical and Marxist traditions, remains relevant in contemporary Economics due to several compelling factors. The study and analysis of profit rate dynamics provide helpful insights into the operation and inherent contradictions of modern economies. By focusing on profit rates, we gain a deeper understanding of how economies function and uncover the underlying tensions and conflicts that inherently shape them. Hence, there are several motivating factors for studying the profit rate.

P. G. Michaelides, *21 Equations that Shaped the World Economy*,
https://doi.org/10.1007/978-3-031-76140-9_5

Firstly, the analysis of the profit rate provides a useful perspective on the workings of the economic system. By examining the tendencies and fluctuations in the profit rate, we gain a deeper understanding of certain contradictions and inherent limitations of economic systems. This knowledge allows us to evaluate the functioning of the economies and look for ways of improvement, if any. Secondly, the profit rate sheds light on the inherent instability of modern economies. The tendency of the rate of profit to fall under certain conditions and the subsequent implications provide insights into the recessionary nature of the economic system. By studying the profit rate, we can better comprehend the factors that contribute to economic instability, crises, and their impact on society.

Thirdly, the analysis emphasizes the relationship between technological innovation, capital accumulation, and the profit rate. By analyzing how technological advancements impact the rate of profit, we gain valuable insights into the dynamics of technological change, and their implications for production and profitability. Fourthly, the profit rate is also linked to the distribution of income in modern economies. Understanding the determinants of the profit rate allows us to examine the allocation of wealth and income between capital and labor. This analysis could provide a framework for studying income inequality and its implications for social and economic justice. Finally, studying the profit rate can inform policy debates and discussions. By analyzing the factors influencing the profit rate, policymakers can better comprehend the potential consequences of various policy interventions for the profitability of firms. This knowledge aids in formulating policies aimed at achieving sustainable economic development. In conclusion, by focusing on the dynamics of the profit rate, we acquire a better understanding of the complexities and challenges associated with modern economic systems, paving the way for informed policy discussions and potential alternatives.

5.2 The Profit Rate in Economics

The theory of the falling rate of profit was developed primarily by Karl Marx, who sought to analyze the dynamics and contradictions inherent in capitalist economies. Marx's analysis seems to be initially inspired by eminent economists of the Classical School, such as Adam Smith and David Ricardo, who recognized the tendency of profits to decline over time, but in the end Marx's theoretical scheme differed significantly.

Adam Smith and David Ricardo were influential economists who made contributions to the development of the theory of the falling rate of profit before Karl Marx. Adam Smith, often regarded as the father of Political Economy or modern Economic Science, analyzed the dynamics of the capitalist economic system in his work. Smith recognized that in a profit-driven economy, entrepreneurs strive to maximize their profits and continually improve their positions. Meanwhile, Smith also observed a long-term tendency for profits to decline. He believed that competition would drive down prices and profits, leading to a situation where capitalists would earn meager returns. Smith's emphasis on the nature of markets and the long-term decline in profitability laid the foundation for the theory of the falling rate of profit.

Subsequently, David Ricardo, another prominent economist and member of the Classical School, built upon Smith's ideas. Ricardo introduced the concept of 'differential rent,' which highlighted the role of landlords in extracting higher rents due to diminishing returns in agriculture. As landlords earned increasing rents, it put pressure on the profits of capitalists, thereby contributing to the declining profit. Ricardo viewed landlords as a hindrance to capitalist development, as their increasing share of income impeded capital accumulation and led to a slowdown in economic growth. By highlighting the distributional conflicts between landlords and capitalists, Ricardo's work added another layer to Smith's understanding of the falling rate of profit.

Finally, it was Karl Marx who developed a comprehensive theory of the falling rate of profit in his *magnum opus Capital.* Marx expanded the analysis beyond the distributional conflicts between landlords and capitalists to focus on the fundamental contradictions within the economic system. He emphasized the exploitative relationship between capital and labor, where capitalists extract profits from the labor of workers. In brief, Marx argued that as capital accumulates and technological advancements increase labor productivity, the ratio of fixed capital to variable capital rises. This, in turn, could lead—under certain circumstances–to a decline in the rate of profit. Marx's theory incorporated the role of competition, the dynamics of technological change, and the class struggle between capitalists and workers, providing a framework for understanding the falling rate of profit.

5.3 The Equation

In this section, we will examine the equation of the rate of profit. According to Marx, capitalism aims at maximizing profit and, in that context, expansion of production represents an end in and of itself. Due to competition between firms to increase their production to make profits at the expense of competitors, wages rise and profits fall as a result of increased demand for workers. Marx argued that firms would reduce their costs by using machinery that required less labor in their production processes, thus leaving some workers unemployed. Labor-saving machines are used by firms as they attempt to overcome the contraction of profits caused by an increase in wages due to an increase in the demand for labor. Due to the intense competition in the market, soon all firms will do the same by laying off workers and replacing them with machines, as is increasingly the case today (e.g., growth of artificial intelligence). Thus, entrepreneurs are seeking to reduce the cost of their goods so as to reduce their selling prices even lower than their competitors' prices and thus drive them into bankruptcy. By increasing technological progress and mechanizing production, that is, substituting physical capital for human labor, average production costs can be reduced.

The rate of profit r is defined by Marx as the ratio of surplus value s to the total capital, i.e., fixed capital C and variable capital v. This implies:

$$r = \frac{s}{C + v} \tag{5.1}$$

or

$$r = \frac{\frac{s}{v}}{\frac{C}{v} + 1} \tag{5.2}$$

Also, surplus value s refers to the additional value produced by workers beyond what is necessary to cover their wages and is equal to:

$$s = TR - v, \tag{5.3}$$

where TR expresses the firm's total revenue.

As a result, from Eq. (5.2) we see that the rate of profit r increases as the so-called 'rate of exploitation' s/v increases, while it decreases as the 'organic (or value) composition of capital' C/v increases.

The process of mechanization driven by technological advancement often becomes evident as variable capital v is replaced by fixed capital C. This transformation leads to an increase in the C/v ratio, since fixed capital integrates novel technologies that enhance productivity. Assuming all other factors remain constant, i.e., *ceteris paribus*, this alteration contributes to a decline in the profit rate, which is anticipated to decrease over the long term according to the aforementioned mathematical equation. This is the 'law of the falling tendency of the rate of profit.'

It's important to mention that the C/v ratio can be very loosely interpreted as the monetary representation of the ratio between physical capital K and human labor l, expressed as K/l, in terms of tangible units like machines and workers. Alternatively, it signifies the 'technical composition of capital' K/l. Consequently, in connection with the 'law of the falling tendency of the rate of profit,' one could contend that the emergence of technological innovation within competitive environments might potentially be the underlying factor driving this phenomenon.

Here is a very simple numerical example:

- Variable capital: \$100
- Constant capital: \$300
- Surplus value: \$200

Plugging the numbers in Eq. (5.1) we get:

$$r = \frac{200}{300 + 200} = 0.5$$

So, the rate of profit r in this example is equal to 0.5, or 50%.

Now, let's see what could happen with an increase in constant capital, i.e., mechanical equipment, relative to variable capital, i.e., laborers. Assume the firm invests in more machinery, increasing constant capital while reducing the reliance on labor, which might slightly affect the surplus value generated.

- Variable capital: \$80, i.e., reduced due to less reliance on labor
- Constant capital: \$500, i.e., increased due to more machinery
- Surplus value: \$180, i.e., a slight reduction due to less labor input

Now, we calculate the new rate of profit r_{new}:

$$r_{new} = \frac{180}{500+80} \approx 0.31$$

So, the new rate of profit in this scenario is approximately 0.31, or 31%. This very simple example illustrates how an increase in constant capital relative to variable capital could potentially lead to a falling rate of profit.

Consequently, it becomes evident that the 'law of the falling tendency' in the profit rate encompasses several aspects. Initially, it holds true when the increasing rate of exploitation is unable to counterbalance the repercussions stemming from the rise in the organic composition of capital. However, the 'law' doesn't rule out the potential absence of these conditions, thereby permitting the containment or reversal of the declining tendency in the profit rate. Secondly, it operates under the premise of 'all other factors remaining constant,' denoted as *ceteris paribus*. Among these additional factors are alterations in the length of the workday and the operating pace of machinery, fluctuations in the prices of raw materials affecting the 'organic composition of capital,' advancements in the skill levels of the workforce, and so forth.

Nonetheless, numerous scholars construe the 'law of the falling tendency' in the profit rate as an all-encompassing trait of the economic framework, asserting its relevance as long as capitalism endures. Moreover, they perceive it as an inflexible 'law' outlining the progression of the profit rate, without necessitating an understanding of the myriad 'other factors' or the relative pace at which the rate of exploitation intersects with the organic composition of capital. This embodiment forms the basis of the 'fallacy of the falling tendency of the rate of profit.'

5.4 Insights and Consequences

The study of the equation of the profit rate carries significant policy implications that can assist policymakers in their pursuit of stability, income equality, and sustainable development. For instance, while almost totally ignored, one important implication is in the field of income distribution. The analysis of profit rates provides insights into the distribution of income between firms and employees. Policymakers can leverage this understanding to design policies that promote a more equitable distribution of wealth. Relevant taxation measures could be implemented to ensure that a fair share of profits is allocated for public goods and services. Additionally, and most importantly, policymakers may consider minimum wage regulations to protect workers' rights and prevent exploitation, along with social welfare programs to provide a safety net for those at the lower end of the income spectrum.

Technological innovation is another area where the study of the profit rate theory could guide policymaking. The theory highlights the impact of technological progress on the profit rate. Policymakers can utilize this knowledge to create an environment that fosters technological advancement, followed by relevant increases in wages. Policies supporting research and development initiatives, protecting intellectual property rights, and investing in education and skill-building programs could encourage technological innovation.

The analysis of profit rate dynamics also informs policies related to investment and economic growth. Policymakers can use this knowledge to create an attractive investment climate by implementing stable macroeconomic policies, improving infrastructure, and providing access to financing. By facilitating investment, policymakers could stimulate economic growth, and create sustainable employment opportunities.

Of course, the understanding of profit rate dynamics also plays a crucial role in promoting stability and preventing crises. Policymakers can monitor profit rate fluctuations to identify potential vulnerabilities in the economic system. This knowledge enables them to implement measures to promote stability. This can include regulatory frameworks to address imbalances, and the use of counter-cyclical fiscal and monetary policies to mitigate the effects of economic downturns. By proactively managing the profit rate dynamics, policymakers can strive to maintain a more stable economic environment.

Lastly, the study of the profit rate theory has implications for sustainable development. Policymakers can incorporate environmental considerations into their policies by recognizing the impact of profit-seeking activities on the environment. Implementing regulations to reduce pollution, providing incentives for investments in renewable energy, and supporting sustainable agriculture and resource management practices could contribute to sustainable development goals. By considering the long-term implications of profit rate dynamics for the environment, policymakers can work toward achieving economic growth while minimizing ecological harm.

5.5 Conclusion, Limitations, and Critiques

In conclusion, the study of the profit rate in Economics offers a lens through which to examine the complexities of modern economies. By analyzing profit rate dynamics and the factors that influence it, we gain helpful insights into the functioning, contradictions, and vulnerabilities of economic systems. This understanding has far-reaching implications for policy discussions and even decision-making, spanning areas such as income distribution, technological innovation, economic stability, and sustainable development. Policymakers can leverage this knowledge to design measures that promote equitable income distribution, protect workers' rights, and ensure a fair share of profits for public welfare. Technological progress, a key driver of economic growth, can be nurtured through policies supporting research, education, and innovation. Additionally, an understanding of profit rate dynamics equips policymakers with tools to foster a more stable economic environment, attempt to prevent crises, and advance sustainable development goals.

However, it's important to acknowledge the limitations and critiques associated with the study of the profit rate. One critique is that the profit rate theory, particularly the notion of a falling tendency of the rate of profit, has a deterministic outlook. Critics argue that it may oversimplify the complexity of economic dynamics by focusing solely on the interaction between the rate of exploitation and the organic composition of capital. Economic systems are influenced by a multitude of factors, including political, social, and institutional forces, which are not fully accounted for in the profit rate equation.

Another criticism revolves around the assumption of *ceteris paribus*, which implies that all other factors remain constant. In reality, economic variables are interconnected and subject to change simultaneously, making it challenging to isolate the effects of a single factor like the profit rate. Moreover, the equation itself is based on certain assumptions that might not hold universally, such as the assumption that technological progress leads to a rise in the organic composition of capital. Furthermore, some scholars argue that the profit rate theory's focus on internal contradictions within the economic system might not fully capture the complexities of economic development and global interdependencies. The theory's applicability to different historical and geopolitical contexts is a subject of ongoing debate.

In conclusion, while the study of the profit rate offers helpful insights into the dynamics of modern economies and informs policy discussions, it should be approached with a critical perspective. While the profit rate equation provides a framework for analysis, it should not be viewed as an all-encompassing 'law' governing economic outcomes. To fully comprehend the inherent workings of economic systems, it is essential to integrate diverse perspectives, consider broader socio-political factors, and recognize the limitations of any single theory. As such, the study of the profit rate stands as a vital tool within the larger toolkit of economic analysis and policy formulation.

Chapter Takeaways

- The theory of the falling rate of profit originated with the works of Adam Smith and David Ricardo.
- Marx expanded on Smith's and Ricardo's ideas, incorporating exploitation, class dynamics, and technological progress into an entirely new theoretical framework.
- The rate of profit equation considers the ratio of surplus value to total capital and highlights the impact of technological advancements and labor exploitation.
- The 'falling rate of profit theory' suggests that the rate of profit tends to decline due to the increase in the organic composition of capital.
- The study of the profit rate provides valuable insights into the functioning of modern economies, technological progress, and policy formulation.
- Profit rate dynamics help understand patterns in profitability, business cycles, and the occurrence of economic crises.
- Factors influencing the profit rate include technological changes, labor market conditions, and economic policies.
- The profit rate is linked to income distribution, allowing analysis of wealth and income disparities.
- The study of the profit rate has practical policy implications for income distribution, technological innovation, investment, economic stability, and sustainability.
- Understanding the profit rate informs policymakers about the cyclical nature of economies and helps promote stability.

Revision Questions

1. What insights does the study of the profit rate provide about modern economies?
2. How does the profit rate help us understand economic recessions and crises?
3. Who were the key economists who contributed to the theory of the falling rate of profit and how?
4. What did Adam Smith and David Ricardo contribute to the understanding of the profit rate?
5. How did Karl Marx expand upon the theories of earlier economists into a new theoretical framework?
6. What are the factors that influence the profit rate?
7. How is the profit rate linked to income distribution?
8. How does understanding the profit rate inform policymakers about economic stability?
9. What potential factors are not explicitly considered in the profit rate equation?
10. What does the falling rate of profit theory suggest, and why is it important for understanding the economic system?

CHAPTER 6

General Equilibrium

Learning Objectives

- Trace the Historical Development of General Equilibrium Theory
- Understand the Fundamental Concepts of General Equilibrium
- Analyze the Role of Consumer Utility and Profit in GE
- Evaluate the Mathematical Structure of General Equilibrium Models
- Examine the Limitations and Extensions of General Equilibrium Theory

6.1 Introduction

In modern Economics, the concept of 'equilibrium' stands as a neoclassical cornerstone of understanding how markets operate. The interaction between supply, demand, and prices is said to form the basis for the functioning of economies, guiding the allocation of resources and the distribution of goods and services. Among the various states, one of the most profound and significant is the General Equilibrium (GE). The notion of GE represents a state where all markets within an economy simultaneously achieve an 'equilibrium.' The concept holds immense importance for

P. G. Michaelides, *21 Equations that Shaped the World Economy*,
https://doi.org/10.1007/978-3-031-76140-9_6

economists, and stakeholders, as it offers insights into market dynamics and the efficient allocation of resources. This chapter focuses on the complexities of GE, dissecting its underlying principles and shedding light on its role in shaping modern Economics. We will analyze the theory, model, and evidence that underpin this concept, to uncover its relevance in real-world scenarios.

The journey begins by revisiting the fundamental tenets, i.e., the building blocks of market forces. By examining how these forces interact and influence one another, we lay the groundwork for comprehending the dynamic nature of markets and the emergence of equilibrium states. Understanding how consumers and producers make decisions allows us to grasp the mechanisms that drive market equilibrium. The works of Alfred Marshall and, especially, Léon Walras laid the groundwork for a mathematical understanding of resource allocation in GE. The latter's contribution paved the way for modern economic analysis, demonstrating how multiple interdependent markets can achieve a state of equilibrium, simultaneously. In conclusion, this chapter will highlight the relevance of GE in Economic Science.

6.2 General Equilibrium in Economics

The concept of GE represents a revolutionary milestone in neoclassical economic theory, transforming the way most economists perceive and analyze market dynamics. Before its emergence, Economic Science was largely dominated by other schools of economic thought. However, with the advent of GE theory, economists acquired some mathematical tools to study the interconnections and interdependencies among markets, paving the way for a new understanding of how economies function as a whole. For instance, early economic theorists, such as Adam Smith, David Ricardo, and Karl Marx, primarily focused on the study of labor theory of value and its specific components and driving forces. These economists laid the groundwork for understanding economic forces and trade but in general avoided using a strict mathematical framework to analyze the economy as an integrated system. A breakthrough in mathematical economic theory came in the late nineteenth century, when the work of French economist Léon Walras introduced the concept of a GE system.

Léon Walras, born in 1834 in France, as well as Carl Menger and Stanley Jevons independently reached similar conclusions, marking them as trailblazing economists within the Neoclassical School which dominated Economics. Walras is probably the 'architect' behind the contemporary GE theory. While the investigation of interdependencies among economic actors had previously engaged economists like Condorcet and Cournot through mathematical avenues, the synthesis of a comprehensive analytical framework uniting diverse economic agents had remained elusive. Notably, this period witnessed economists turning their gaze toward Physics, embracing a broader integration of mathematical tools into Economics. The famous ***École Polytechnique***, i.e., the Engineering School of Paris, had twice rejected Léon Walras for admission. As a result, he eventually studied Engineering, but at the Paris ***École des Mines***, until his father encouraged him to pursue Economics.

Léon Walras introduced new concepts about price determination, transaction processes, and the attainment of GE through his work. Alongside Menger and Jevons, his insights from the 'marginal revolution' were assimilated into economic theory, evolving over subsequent decades to shape the foundation of what we recognize today as Neoclassical Economics. Léon Walras extensively employed Mathematics to dissect economic phenomena and advocated for Economics to embrace the methodologies and tools of Physics. This inclination led him to draw analogies between physical processes (like friction) and economic dynamics (such as free competition). He posited that the market operates under perfect competition, analogous to the frictionless functioning of the system in Mechanics. Consequently, Walras provided an alternative perspective for scrutinizing the pivotal significance that the competitive market model occupies within contemporary Microeconomic Analysis.

Central to Walras's General Equilibrium Theory was the notion of a hypothetical 'Walrasian Auctioneer.' This auctioneer acted as an intermediary, adjusting prices across all markets until a state of equilibrium was reached, where all markets cleared simultaneously. This so-called tâtonnement or trial-and-error process, a series of price adjustments, was a 'thought experiment' used by Walras to illustrate how markets would converge to equilibrium.

Following Walras, Italian engineer Vilfredo Pareto made significant contributions to GE theory. Pareto, who was educated as an engineer at the Polytechnic of Turin, worked initially in the Italian railways, before moving to the University of Lausanne, where he succeeded Walras. In his works, Vilfredo Pareto further refined and extended the concept of GE. He introduced the concept of 'Pareto optimality,' wherein no reallocation of resources could make one individual better off without making another individual worse off. Pareto efficiency became a key criterion for assessing the optimality of an allocation in a General Equilibrium setting. The seminal works of Kenneth Arrow and Gérard Debreu in the mid-twentieth century led to the formalization of GE theory. In their famous research in neoclassical Microeconomic Analysis, Arrow and Debreu provided a mathematical proof for the existence of a competitive equilibrium in a GE system. They extended Walras's and Pareto's ideas, demonstrating the conditions under which a competitive market economy could achieve a state of GE.

6.3 The Equation

As mentioned earlier, GE takes into account the interdependencies among markets, providing an understanding of how prices and quantities are determined across the entire economic system. For instance, a change in the price of a commodity can affect the demand for related goods and the incomes of resource suppliers. This section focuses on the essence of GE, analyzes its foundational concepts, and introduces a fundamental equation that underpins this theory.

Walras's groundbreaking theory introduces a novel framework where diverse economic agents engage in market activities, assuming roles as (i) producers, (ii) consumers, or (iii) entrepreneurs, thereby fostering complex interactions within the market. This complex interplay involves the conversion of labor into products which entrepreneurs may acquire to further fuel the production of other goods, while final consumers may opt to consume them directly. These ultimate consumers, having contributed their labor to entrepreneurs, subsequently utilize the income earned to acquire the products crafted from their own labor efforts. As they pursue their distinct interests, these various actors naturally cultivate exchange relationships within the market environment.

Walras's theory aimed to showcase how deliberate exchanges among economically engaged agents, characterized by being (i) well informed, (ii) attuned to their interests, and (iii) driven by goal maximization, can culminate in a mode of production and income distribution. This objective was realized through the formulation of the GE model by Walras, which underscored that economic agents, guided by their self-interest, possess the capacity, under specific circumstances, to attain a state of market 'equilibrium.' This pioneering contribution led to the establishment of the theory of GE, subsequently named 'Walrasian Equilibrium' in recognition of his pivotal role. A key assumption of GE theory is that all markets 'clear' meaning that the quantity demanded equals the quantity supplied for every good and service. In other words, there are no persistent shortages or surpluses in any market. Market 'clearing' ensures a state of equilibrium, where demand and supply are balanced. A system of equations serves as the foundation of GE theory and represents the core principle upon which the system rests.

GE analysis is an economic framework that analyzes how countless individual decisions, seemingly separate from each other, interact and coordinate to achieve efficient resource allocation in an economy. From the work of Walras, and beyond, economists have emphasized the role of the price system in this coordination process. The basic idea is that a known set of prices provides the necessary information to 'synchronize' diverse individual decisions. The price mechanism serves as a vital force that brings balance between the desires of buyers and sellers in a market. At a prevailing price, all willing buyers can purchase the goods they desire, and all willing sellers can sell their products, leading to a state of equilibrium without any excess supply or shortages. However, this equilibrium is often confined to individual markets, and as we expand our analysis to encompass the entire economy, the concept of partial equilibrium becomes insufficient.

In GE analysis, we acknowledge that the equilibrium of a single market is interconnected with other markets, as supply and demand in one market can be influenced by the prices prevailing in other markets. Thus, it becomes essential to study the simultaneous equilibrium of all markets in the economy to gain a comprehensive understanding of the interconnections among commodities. It follows from this analysis that a coherent theory of the price system and the coordination of economic activity must take into account the simultaneous GE of all markets within an economy.

Walras made the following fundamental assumptions as part of the GE approach at a given price level:

- Consumers are driven by the pursuit of utility maximization, while firms endeavor to optimize profits. In simple terms, an agent's utility function measures the level of satisfaction or happiness that the agent derives from consuming a bundle of commodities. The utility function is a mathematical representation of an agent's preferences over different bundles of goods. For each bundle of goods, the utility function assigns a real number, indicating the level of satisfaction or happiness the agent gets from consuming that bundle, compared to other bundles.

- Consumers exhibit diminishing marginal utility, meaning that as they consume more of a particular good, the additional satisfaction from each extra unit decreases. For example, while the first slice of pizza is highly satisfying, the fourth and fifth slices add much less satisfaction. This principle leads to a pattern where consumers diversify their consumption rather than saturate it, continually seeking a variety of goods and services to maximize overall utility. Thus, their consumption remains 'unsaturated' as they pursue different products to maintain higher satisfaction levels.
- A competitive market prevails, characterized by a multitude of consumers and producers whose individual actions lack the potency to impact product prices.
- Homogeneous products are produced by firms that have similar costs and technology.
- Economic actors base decisions on full information about the prevailing prices.
- Scarcity applies to both inputs and outputs, with positive prices and finite availability.
- Price dependency governs the demand and supply of inputs and outputs.
- The dynamics of supply and demand exhibit continuity, devoid of abrupt fluctuations.
- Each product's production function is uniquely aligned with a static composition of production factors, resisting substitution within prevailing technological constraints.
- A selected product serves as the reference point for gauging the values of other goods and production factors, i.e., acts as *numéraire*.
- A predetermined distribution characterizes the initial allotment of products, and in a simplified Walrasian GE framework, we focus on a pure exchange economy, where production is absent. The economy comprises a finite number of agents and commodities. Each agent possesses a specific bundle of commodities, and they are destined to consume these commodities. However, before this event, there is an opportunity for trade to take place at designated prices.

The primary goal of the Walrasian approach is to determine whether there exist prices in the market that would lead to a state where the quantities demanded by all agents perfectly match the quantities supplied. In other words, we seek to find 'equilibrium prices' that ensure that all willing buyers can purchase exactly what they desire, and all willing sellers can sell their goods at these prices, resulting in no excess supply or shortages.

Let us consider an economy which has I agents $i \in I = \{1, \ldots, I\}$ and K commodities $k \in K = \{1, \ldots, K\}$. A so-called bundle of commodities is a vector $x \in R_+^K$ where all quantities are non-negative. Each agent i has an endowment $e^i \in R_+^K$, and a u^i: $R_+^K \to R$. For this exchange economy ε, and its endowments and utilities, we can write $\varepsilon = ((u^i, e^i)_{i \in I})$.

Agents are assumed to be price-takers. The vector of prices is $p \in R_+^K$, meaning that all prices are non-negative. Considering the constraints imposed by the agent's budget, each agent chooses consumption in order to maximize their utility. Consequently, each agent i solves the following problem:

$$\begin{aligned} &\max_{x \in R_+^K} u^i(x) \\ &\text{s.t. } p \cdot x \leq p \cdot e^i \end{aligned} \tag{6.1}$$

The consumer's wealth $p \cdot e^i$ is the amount they could get if they sold their entire endowment.

We now define an equilibrium for this exchange economy. In this context, we will define a Walrasian equilibrium, which occurs when a vector of prices and consumption bundles satisfy two (2) conditions: (a) each agent's consumption maximizes their utility given the prices and (b) the aggregate endowment equals the total demand for each commodity.

A Walrasian equilibrium for the economy ε is a vector $(p, (x^i)_{i \in I})$ such that:

(a) Agents maximize their utilities:

$$x^i \in \arg\max_{x \in B^i_{(p)}} u^i(x) \, \forall i \in I \tag{6.2}$$

In the context of the described exchange economy, $B^i_{(p)}$ represents the budget set for agent i given the price vector p. The budget set consists of all possible consumption bundles $\text{x} \in R_+^K$ that agent i can afford given their initial endowment and a given price vector. Mathematically, the budget set $B^i_{(p)}$ is defined as:

$$B^i_{(p)} = \left\{ x \in R^K_+ \mid p \cdot x \leq p \cdot e^i \right\}$$

(b) Markets 'clear,' meaning that the total demand for each commodity just equals the aggregate endowment for all $k \in K$.

$$\sum\nolimits_{i \in I} x^i_k = \sum\nolimits_{i \in I} e^i_k \forall k \in K \tag{6.3}$$

This framework assumes the existence of a hypothetical Walrasian auctioneer who adjusts prices in response to excess demand or supply until all markets clear. The auctioneer, acting as an intermediary, continuously iterates price adjustments until the equation is satisfied, signifying the attainment of the hypothesized GE. More precisely, under the oversight of a central auctioneer, the relative prices of goods are communicated based on a designated unit's value. Participants, informed by the stated prices, declare their selling and buying intentions for different goods. These intentions are then collected by the auctioneer. By detecting disparities between demand and supply for specific goods, the auctioneer revises prices, i.e., raising those with excess demand and lowering those with excess supply. Individuals adjust their intentions in response to the new prices. The iterative process of adjustment, known as 'tâtonnement' or 'trial-and-error,' ensues as the auctioneer reevaluates the market. This iterative process persists until 'equilibrium prices' are attained. Until these equilibrium prices are determined, transactions are withheld. In essence, Walras's approach centered on an auction-driven exchange economy, guided by the iterative pursuit of equilibrium through price adjustments.

Walras employed the aforementioned assumptions to unveil, through systems of linear interdependent equations, the existence of prices that usher in equilibrium markets. These prices ensure parity between aggregate demand and aggregate supply. Furthermore, it's imperative to note that GE does not preclude the presence of excess demand on the side of consumers or surplus supply on the side of sellers. Certain markets might witness a scenario where supply outpaces demand, or vice versa. This observation illuminates a significant facet: the summation of excess demand and excess supply yields an equilibrium where this total equals zero. This intriguing insight underscores that even in the face of individual market disequilibrium, Walras's law retains its relevance. Ultimately, Walras contends that the imbalance between supply and demand can be resolved by the fluctuation of the good's price, thereby triggering reverberating effects across other interconnected markets within the system.

From this perspective, it is apparent that a coherent theory of the pricing system and the coordination of economic activity must consider the simultaneous equilibrium of all markets in the economy. As a result, the following questions arise: (i) Does a general equilibrium exist? and (ii) What are its characteristics? An economy attains GE when a set of conditions materializes: (a) across each market, demand aligns harmoniously with supply, (b) each economic agent effortlessly transacts as per their intended buy and sell plans, and (c) firms and consumers alike seamlessly exchange goods in quantities that optimize their utility and profits, respectively.

The journey toward this equilibrium destination requires knowledge of several factors: the count of consumers and firms, initial resource endowments, consumer preferences, and accessible production technologies. Beyond these prerequisites, the remaining trajectory is shaped by the economy's maximizing behavior and the orchestration of the competitive market mechanism. Yet, in practice, two pivotal elements steer this equilibrium. The first, as previously analyzed, is the distinctive role of the auctioneer. The second involves the equally distinct role assumed by firms. Within this context, Walras, employing mathematical tools, endeavored to address a fundamental query: Can prices be determined to guide all markets in an economy toward GE? His analysis yielded affirmative results, contingent upon two conditions: (a) transactions remaining 'concealed' until the central auctioneer 'discovers' GE, and (b) firms operating at zero profits within this equilibrium state. In fact, within his analytical framework, Walras postulated that firms would achieve zero profits in an equilibrium state due to competitive pressures. Consequently, in the Walrasian GE framework, the onus of objective maximization rests solely on one group: consumers. In this schema, entrepreneurs and the auctioneer assume a role of coordination and facilitation, working with pre-established prices and production technologies.

Walras fashioned a system to encapsulate the interaction between consumers and entrepreneurs. This framework entailed equations for demand, supply, and equilibrium in each market, spanning goods, their production factors, and services. However, the challenge lay in the necessity for the number of unknowns to match the number of equations. Unique solutions were not guaranteed; they could be (i) inexistent, (ii) infinite, or even (iii) ambiguous in economic interpretation. This dilemma persisted for nearly a century until neoclassical economists formulated the famous Arrow-Debreu Theorem. This groundbreaking contribution, subject to numerous specific bounding constraints, revealed the potential for a unique solution within the GE framework.

Let's see a very simple example. Consider an economy populated by two (2) agents, A and B, with a utility function of the form: $U(x, y) = x \cdot y$. Agent A is endowed with two (2) units of x and one (1) unit of y, and agent B is endowed with one (1) unit of x and five (5) units of y. If the two (2) agents in the economy are price-takers, we need to find the general equilibrium of the economy.

So, let i=A, B be the consumers. The dimension is two (2) since we have (2) two goods x and y with prices p_x and p_y, respectively. Therefore, using vector notation, we have the vector of products $z^i = (x, y)$ and the vector of prices $p = (p_x, p_y)$. The relative price of good x with respect to good y is then defined as $p' = p_x/p_y$, so the vector of relative prices is expressed as $p = (p', 1)$.

The budget constraint for agent A, by plugging the numbers in Eq. (6.1), based on her initial endowment, is:

$$z^A \cdot p^T \leq (2,1) \cdot p^T \Leftrightarrow p_x \cdot x_A + p_y \cdot y_A \leq 2 \cdot p_x + 1 \cdot p_y,$$

where exponent T denotes transposition. This equation can now be transformed, by dividing by p_y and using the relative price p' of the two goods, as:

$$p' \cdot x_A + y_A \leq 2 \cdot p' + 1$$

Similarly, for agent B, her budget constraint in relative prices is:

$$p' \cdot x_B + y_B \leq p' + 5$$

The utility that agent A has, due to her initial endowment, is:

$$U^A(x = 2, y = 1) = 2$$

whereas for agent B we have:

$$U^B\left(x=1,\, y=5\right)=5$$

The maximization problem for agent A, by plugging the numbers and the relevant function in Eq. (6.1), is:

$$\left.\begin{array}{l}\max\limits_{z\in R_+^2} u^A\left(z\right)\\ p\cdot z\le p\cdot e^A\end{array}\right\}\text{or}\left.\begin{array}{c}\max_{x_A,y_A} U\left(x_A,y_A\right)=\max_{x_A,y_A}\left\{x_A\cdot y_A\right\}\\ s.t.\, p'\cdot x_A+y_A\le 2\cdot p'+1\end{array}\right\}$$

Similarly, the maximization problem for agent B is:

$$\left.\begin{array}{l}\max\limits_{z\in R_+^2} u^B\left(z\right)\\ p\cdot z\le p\cdot e^B\end{array}\right\}\text{or}\left.\begin{array}{c}\max_{x_B,y_B} U\left(x_B,y_B\right)=\max_{x_B,y_B}\left\{x_B\cdot y_B\right\}\\ s.t.\, p'\cdot x_B+y_B\le p'+5\end{array}\right\}$$

The solution of the maximization problem for consumers A and B is given by Eq. (6.2):

$$z^{A*}=\left(x_{A,}^{\ *}y_A^{\ *}\right)=\arg\max_{z\in B_{(p)}^A} u^A\left(z\right)$$

$$z^{B*}=\left(x_{B,}^{\ *}y_B^{\ *}\right)=\arg\max_{z\in B_{(p)}^B} u^B\left(z\right)$$

For agent A, the constraint typically becomes an equality at the optimal point, i.e., the agent expedites her whole budget. This is because the agent is assumed to prefer more of both goods to less, given that more is better, i.e., the so-called assumption of non-satiation in utility theory mentioned before. For instance, intuitively, if agent A did not spend her entire budget, she could increase her utility by purchasing more of at least one good, given the budget constraint. Hence, under the assumption of 'rational behavior' and 'non-satiation,' agent A will spend the entire budget to maximize her utility. So, the constraint becomes an equality and we can solve for y_A:

$$\left.\begin{array}{c}\max_{x_A,y_A}\left\{x_A\cdot y_A\right\}\\ s.t.\, p'\cdot x_A+y_A=2p'+1\end{array}\right\}\text{or}\left.\begin{array}{c}\max_{x_A,y_A}\left\{x_A\cdot y_A\right\}\\ s.t.\, y_A=p'\cdot\left(2-x_A\right)+1\end{array}\right\}$$

or

$$\max_{x_A} \left\{ x_A \cdot \left[p' \cdot (2 - x_A) + 1 \right] \right\}$$

We take the first-order condition (FOC) for maximization (Sect. 23.3, Appendix C) that yields:

$$\frac{d\left(x_A \cdot \left[p' \cdot (2 - x_A) + 1 \right]\right)}{dx_A} = 0$$

$$\frac{d\left(\left[\left(2 \cdot p' \cdot x_A - p' \cdot x_A^{\ 2}\right) + x_A\right]\right)}{dx_A} = 0$$

$$2 \cdot p' - 2 \cdot p' \cdot x_A + 1 = 0$$

$$x_A = \frac{2 \cdot p' + 1}{2 \cdot p'}$$

To check the second-order condition (SOC), we need to find the second derivative of the objective function with respect to x_A and ensure that it is negative, indicating a local maximum (Sect. 23.3, Appendix C). Therefore, taking the second derivative yields:

$$\frac{d^2\left(x_A \cdot \left[p' \cdot (2 - x_A) + 1 \right]\right)}{dx_A^{\ 2}} = \frac{d(2 \cdot p' - 2 \cdot p' \cdot x_A + 1)}{dx_A} = -2 \cdot p' < 0$$

Since, 2 and p' are positive, the second derivative is also negative. Therefore, the second-order condition (SOC) indicates that our solution indeed maximizes utility.

So, the maximum amount demanded by consumer A is:

$$\left.\begin{aligned} x_A^{\ *} &= \frac{2 \cdot p' + 1}{2 \cdot p'} = 1 + \frac{1}{2 \cdot p'} \\ y_A^{\ *} &= p'(2 - x_A) + 1 \end{aligned}\right\}$$

$$\left.\begin{aligned} x_A^* &= 1+\frac{1}{2\cdot p'} \\ y_A^* &= 2\cdot p' - p'\cdot x_A + 1 \end{aligned}\right\}$$

$$\left.\begin{aligned} x_A^* &= 1+\frac{1}{2\cdot p'} \\ y_A^* &= 2\cdot p' - p'\cdot\left(1+\frac{1}{2\cdot p'}\right) + 1 \end{aligned}\right\}$$

$$\left.\begin{aligned} x_A^* &= 1+\frac{1}{2\cdot p'} \\ y_A^* &= 2\cdot p' - p' - \frac{1}{2} + 1 \end{aligned}\right\}$$

$$\left.\begin{aligned} x_A^* &= 1+\frac{1}{2\cdot p'} \\ y_A^* &= p' + \frac{1}{2} \end{aligned}\right\}$$

Now, for agent B, we have:

$$\left.\begin{aligned} \max_{x_B,y_B} U(x_B,y_B) = \max_{x_B,y_B}\{x_B\cdot y_B\} \\ s.t.\, p'\cdot x_B + y_B = p' + 5 \end{aligned}\right\} \Leftrightarrow \left.\begin{aligned} \max_{x_B,y_B}\{x_B\cdot y_B\} \\ s.t.\, y_B = p'\cdot(1-x_B)+5 \end{aligned}\right\}$$

Similarly, by solving the maximization problem for agent B, we get:

$$\left.\begin{aligned} x_B^* &= \frac{5}{2\cdot p'} + \frac{1}{2} \\ y_B^* &= \frac{1}{2}\cdot p' + \frac{5}{2} \end{aligned}\right\}$$

Next, we plug these expressions in the market clearing condition in Eq. (6.3) to get:

$$z^{A*} + z^{B*} = (2+1, 1+5)$$

$$z^{A*} + z^{B*} = (3,6)$$

$$\left.\begin{aligned} x_A^* + x_B^* &= 3 \\ y_A^* + y_B^* &= 6 \end{aligned}\right\}$$

By plugging the x_A^* and x_B^* in either of the above equations, we get:

$$\begin{gathered} x_A^* + x_B^* = 3 \\ 1 + \frac{1}{2 \cdot p'} + \frac{5}{2 \cdot p'} + \frac{1}{2} = 3 \\ \frac{6}{2 \cdot p'} = \frac{3}{2} \\ \frac{6}{p'} = 3 \\ p' = 2 \end{gathered}$$

Therefore, by plugging the value of the relative price p' in the maximum demanded quantities, for agents A and B, we get:

$$\left.\begin{aligned} x_A^*\Big|_{p'=2} &= 1 + \frac{1}{2 \cdot p'} = \frac{5}{4} \\ y_A^*\Big|_{p'=2} &= p' + \frac{1}{2} = \frac{5}{2} \end{aligned}\right\}$$

$$\left.\begin{aligned} x_B^*\Big|_{p'=2} &= \frac{5}{2 \cdot p'} + \frac{1}{2} = \frac{7}{4} \\ y_B^*\Big|_{p'=2} &= \frac{1}{2} p' + \frac{5}{2} = \frac{7}{2} \end{aligned}\right\}$$

Finally, since $p = (p', 1)$, we get: $p = (2, 1)$.

Consequently, the general equilibrium for the economy is

$$\varepsilon = \left\{ p = (2,1); \left(\frac{5}{4}, \frac{5}{2}\right); \left(\frac{7}{4}, \frac{7}{2}\right) \right\}.$$

In other words, given two consumers A and B, and two goods x and y, the economic intuition is that for the given vector of relative prices $((p_x/p_y), 1) = (2, 1)$, the equilibrium quantities $(x_A^*, y_A^*) = ((5/4), (5/2))$ and $(x_B^*, y_B^*) = ((7/4), (7/2))$ represent the amounts of the two goods for each consumer that clear the market at these prices, with supply equaling demand, while ensuring that consumers' utility maximization conditions are satisfied. Under certain conditions, this GE state ensures a Pareto efficient allocation of resources, where no individual can be made better off without making someone else worse off.

6.4 Insights and Consequences

The GE framework encompasses several pivotal elements of modern Economic Science. A prominent feature involves a shift away from broader socio-economic aggregates and a focus on resource allocation optimization. This is epitomized by the mathematical maximization of utility within the constraints of available resources, a principle that lies at the heart of conventional economic problem-solving.

Another aspect is the incorporation of the calculus of variations, a method that facilitates the identification of 'optimal' solutions. This concept is intertwined with the notion of 'marginal utility,' denoting the incremental satisfaction gained from an additional unit of a good. The adoption of the utilitarian approach, championed by figures like Bentham, stresses the idea of human action guided by the pursuit of maximum utility. This perspective replaces notions of innate human 'nature' with a focus on pleasure and pain as motivational forces.

Before the emergence of GE, Economics was largely dominated by other schools of economic thought. Consequently, based on GE, a shift emerged in Economic Science, pivoting from an 'objective' perspective such as the labor theory of value, to a 'subjective' one based on the utility derived from an object. This implies that an object's value hinges on individual desire rather than being derived, e.g., from labor input. The GE viewpoint emphasizes 'individualism,' casting various economic actors as agents driven by their own interests. This individual-centric approach, spanning consumers, producers, and entrepreneurs, contrasts with notions of a broader macroeconomic, societal, or even synergetic context.

This individualistic lens extends to the transformation of the economy into a more Physics-like laboratory, characterized by strict laws and Mathematical theorems. Walras's advocacy for this transformation aimed to establish Economics as a field governed by universal, timeless principles, akin to Physics and Engineering. However, factors like imperfect information, market structure, class, and power dynamics can disrupt the delicate balance, leading to deviations from equilibrium.

GE theory finds applications in some economic contexts, such as trade policy and welfare analysis. It helps economists understand how policy changes can have spillover effects and how market 'distortions' can affect overall economic efficiency. GE theory aims to offer an understanding of the interdependencies among markets within an economy. The basic GE equation lies at the heart of this theory, embodying the principle of market clearing and equilibrium. While its application is subject to countless limitations and restrictive assumptions, GE remains a vital tool for neoclassical economists to analyze economic systems.

6.5 Conclusion, Limitations, and Critiques

In Economic Science, the concept of 'equilibrium' serves as a neoclassical guiding light that shapes market dynamics. The journey through GE unveils a complex web of interconnected markets, where the pursuit of individual interests culminates in a harmonious balance of demand and supply. At the center of GE is the concept of 'market clearing,' where the equilibrium price prevails as the point of convergence between demand and supply. Walras, a pioneer of this theory, introduced the notion of a Walrasian auctioneer who orchestrates price adjustments until all markets achieve equilibrium. This iterative process, known as 'tâtonnement' or 'trial-and-error,' encapsulates the dance between consumers and producers, in their quest for equilibrium. While GE theory rests upon a foundation of numerous restrictive assumptions, it offers insights into economic phenomena. The so-called market mechanism, driven by consumer preferences and producer profits, yields a balance that is believed to ensure the efficient allocation of resources. The utility-maximizing behavior of consumers and the profit-seeking motives of firms are supposed to converge in a symphony of interactions that shape market dynamics.

The implications of GE theory extend far beyond theoretical concepts. It is supposed to offer a lens through which policymakers can assess the impacts of interventions, technological advancements, and globalization on market outcomes. By embracing the myriad of complexities of GE, economists unlock a toolbox of analytical tools to address real-world challenges such as unemployment, trade imbalances, and economic crises.

The emergence of GE theory marked a *paradigm shift* in Economic Science, providing economists with a mathematical framework to study the interdependencies among markets. From the pioneering work of Walras to the rigorous formalization by Arrow and Debreu, GE theory has remained a cornerstone of neoclassical economics. Furthermore, the emergence of computational methods and advances in empirical analysis have allowed economists to test the implications of GE theory with real-world data. While challenges and fierce critiques persist, the evolution and extensions of GE continue to drive some parts of economic research, in an attempt to enrich our understanding of how economies function as interconnected systems.

General Equilibrium (GE) theory, while a cornerstone of neoclassical economics, has faced various limitations and critiques over time. One significant limitation is its reliance on the assumption of perfect competition, which includes numerous small firms and consumers, homogeneous products, and no single market participant having the power to influence prices. Real-world markets usually exhibit imperfect competition, with monopolies, oligopolies, and differentiated products. Furthermore, GE theory assumes that all economic agents have perfect information about prices and can instantly respond to changes. In reality, information is often imperfect, costly to acquire, and asymmetrically distributed among participants. Another critique is the static nature of traditional GE models, which analyze equilibrium at a single point in time, failing to account for dynamic changes and adjustments in the economy over time, such as technological progress, changing preferences, and the evolution of industries. The mathematical complexity of GE models can also be a barrier to practical application, as the necessary simplifications for mathematical tractability may lead to models that do not accurately represent real economic systems. Additionally, GE theory typically ignores the role of institutions, transaction costs, and market frictions, which can significantly affect market outcomes. Institutions like banks, governments, and legal systems play crucial roles in the functioning of real economies.

While Arrow and Debreu proved the existence of an equilibrium under certain conditions, the uniqueness and stability of that equilibrium are not guaranteed. Multiple equilibria or unstable equilibria can arise, complicating the predictive power of GE models. GE models may also fail to fully capture the interdependencies between different markets and the presence of externalities that affect third parties not directly involved in a transaction, leading to an incomplete analysis of the overall economy. Furthermore, GE theory assumes that consumer preferences and production technologies can be represented by 'well-behaved' utility and production functions, but actual preferences and technologies can be more complex and less predictable. The policy implications derived from GE models can be unrealistic if the underlying assumptions do not hold, and policymakers need to consider the limitations of GE when using it as a basis for economic policy decisions.

Finally, GE theory does not incorporate insights from behavioral economics, which shows that real human behavior often deviates from the rational agent model assumed in traditional Economics. Factors such as bounded rationality, biases, and heuristics are not accounted for. Additionally, GE models often assume an initial endowment of resources and usually do not account for how income and wealth distribution evolves over time, inadequately addressing inequality and its effects on economic dynamics. Overall, while GE theory provides a foundational neoclassical framework for understanding the interdependencies of markets, its limitations necessitate careful consideration. As the economic landscape continues to evolve, GE remains a compass for neoclassical economists. It informs economic discourse, policy formulation, and the pursuit of market outcomes. Its legacy endures, inspiring economists to study the inherent characteristics of market dynamics.

Chapter Takeaways

- 'Equilibrium' is a foundational concept in neoclassical Economics, revealing the interplay between supply, demand, and prices.
- General Equilibrium (GE) is a pivotal state where all markets within an economy achieve equilibrium, simultaneously.
- Léon Walras, a famous neoclassical economist and the 'architect' of GE, introduced the concept of an auctioneer who adjusts prices to achieve market equilibrium.
- In GE theory, interconnected markets interact, and changes in one market can trigger ripple effects, leading to a state of balanced supply and demand.
- Market 'clearing,' where quantity demanded equals quantity supplied, is a fundamental assumption, ensuring equilibrium prevails across all goods and services.
- GE underscores the complex nature of markets, where consumers and producers engage in utility maximization and profit optimization, respectively.
- GE theory departs from earlier analyses, attempting to study the interdependencies among markets.
- The original Walrasian equilibrium model postulates that firms achieve zero profits due to competitive pressures.
- GE's legacy lies in its ability to inform economic policy and address real-world challenges.
- As Economics evolves, GE remains a neoclassical guiding compass, providing insights into market dynamics and resource allocation.

Revision Questions

1. What is the fundamental role of equilibrium in Economics, and how does it relate to the interaction between supply, demand, and price?
2. Define General Equilibrium (GE) and explain its significance in understanding market dynamics and resource allocation.
3. Who is Léon Walras, and what role did he play in introducing the concept of GE?
4. How does the idea of the Walrasian auctioneer contribute to this concept?
5. How does GE theory differ from previous analyses, and why is it important?
6. Explain the concept of market 'clearing' in the context of GE theory and its role in achieving equilibrium across different markets.
7. In the Walrasian GE framework, how do consumers and producers interact to achieve equilibrium outcomes?
8. What role does the pursuit of utility maximization and profit optimization play?
9. Describe the assumptions and conditions under which GE is achieved in an economy, including the role of the Walrasian auctioneer and zero profits for firms.
10. Discuss the limitations and critiques of GE theory.

CHAPTER 7

Input-Output Analysis

Learning Objectives

- Understand the Core Concepts of Input-Output Analysis
- Apply Input-Output Analysis to Evaluate Multiplier Effects
- Explore the Applications of Input-Output Models in Economics
- Assess the Role of Input-Output Analysis in Economic Dynamics
- Identify the Limitations of Traditional Input-Output Models

7.1 Introduction

Input-Output (IO) Economics, developed by the pioneering economist Wassily Leontief, represents an important milestone in our understanding of economic systems. This framework goes beyond traditional macro- or microeconomic analysis by emphasizing the interdependence and inherent connections between industries, revealing the complex interaction of production, consumption, and resource allocation that defines modern economies. At the heart of the Leontief model is the concept of an input-output table, a meticulously constructed matrix that captures the flow of goods and services between sectors. This matrix encapsulates the myriad ways in which industries rely on one another's outputs as inputs, forming a web of

P. G. Michaelides, *21 Equations that Shaped the World Economy*,
https://doi.org/10.1007/978-3-031-76140-9_7

relationships that transcend sector boundaries. By quantifying these interactions, economists analyze economic phenomena.

A key advantage of the Leontief model is its capacity to illuminate the indirect and induced effects of changes within an economy. For instance, imagine a scenario where consumer demand for cars increases. Using the input-output table, economists can trace how this spike in demand not only affects the car industry directly but also triggers a chain reaction throughout the supply chain. Steel manufacturers experience a surge in orders for raw materials, while rubber producers see heightened demand for tires. This 'domino effect' showcases the hidden mechanisms that define economic systems.

Furthermore, the Leontief model plays a pivotal role in policy analysis and decision-making. Policymakers can employ the model to assess the potential consequences of various policy interventions before implementation. For instance, a government considering an infrastructure investment can use the model to estimate the ripple effects across different sectors, helping to gauge the overall economic impact and optimize resource allocation. In other words, Input-Output Economics is a powerful lens through which we can decipher the complex choreography of economic activities.

7.2 Input-Output Analysis in Economics

The emergence of Leontief's Input-Output Analysis represented a shift in economic analysis, reshaping the landscape of how economists approach and comprehend the workings of economies. Rooted in a desire to capture the holistic essence of economic systems, Wassily Leontief embarked on a journey that would culminate in the creation of this revolutionary framework.

Leontief's motivation sprang from a critical examination of the prevailing economic models of his time. Traditional economic theories, while insightful, often focused on individual markets in isolation, or even on the total economy, failing to account for the interdependencies and complex relationships that pervade real-world economies. Leontief recognized the need for a more comprehensive approach that would uncover the hidden connections between an economy's sectors and examine the dynamic flow of inputs and outputs that fuel economic activity.

The input-output table emerged as the cornerstone of Leontief's groundbreaking approach. This matrix, meticulously constructed through detailed data collection and analysis, provided a comprehensive overview of the flows of goods and services between industries. Each cell of the matrix quantified the inputs required by an industry from other sectors and the resulting outputs that fed into other industries. This visual representation of economic interactions transcended the narrow confines of sectoral analysis, offering a panoramic view of production, consumption, and resource allocation in the economy.

Practical applications of Leontief's methodology came to the forefront, particularly during times of economic upheaval. World War II served as a testing ground for the framework's potential, as governments sought to optimize resource allocation for war production. Leontief's input-output analysis played a critical role in guiding policy decisions, ensuring efficient utilization of scarce resources during times of crisis. Post-war reconstruction and economic planning further elevated the significance of Leontief's approach. Nations ravaged by conflict turned to the IO model to chart their paths to recovery, leveraging its ability to project the potential outcomes of policy choices. The framework's predictive capabilities allowed governments to assess the economic consequences of different strategies and prioritize investments accordingly.

The ripple effects of Leontief's IO framework extended beyond Economics. Its success spurred interdisciplinary interest, inspiring scholars from various fields to analyze its potential applications. Sociologists, urban planners, and environmental scientists started to recognize the use of IO analysis in understanding the interconnectedness of social systems, urban development, and resource utilization.

7.3 The Equation

We will dive into the example of increased consumer demand for cars presented earlier and analyze the detailed chain of effects, stage by stage, using the Leontief IO framework. Imagine that there is a sudden surge in consumer demand for cars, i.e., *'Initial Demand Increase.'* People want to buy more cars due to, for instance, favorable economic conditions or a new model release. This results in an increase in the final demand vector X for the car industry. The car industry experiences a direct increase in production to meet the higher demand. More cars are manufactured, leading to a rise in car outputs, *Ycar*, i.e., '*Direct Impact on Car Industry.*'

However, the effects do not stop there, as is the case in conventional models. The car industry relies on inputs from various sectors, such as steel, rubber, and electronics. The Leontief model allows us to quantify these interdependencies. As car production increases, the car industry demands more inputs from these sectors, i.e., *'Indirect Effects on Suppliers.'*

For instance, steel is a crucial input in car manufacturing. The increased demand for cars leads to higher demand for steel from the steel industry, i.e., *'Increased Demand for Steel.'* This triggers a chain reaction: steel manufacturers produce more steel to meet the demand, which requires additional inputs such as iron, coal, and energy. Similarly, the increased car production requires more tires, driving up demand in the rubber industry, *i.e., 'Higher Tire Demand.'* Rubber producers respond by producing more tires, which, in turn, requires additional inputs such as rubber materials and energy.

The effects continue to cascade through the supply chain. As the demand for tires and steel increases, their respective industries expand production, leading to higher demand for their inputs. This process ripples through the entire economy, affecting various sectors and creating a 'domino effect' of increased economic activity, i.e., *'Spillover Effects.'* The increased production in steel, rubber, and other related industries leads to higher employment levels as these sectors hire more workers to meet the rising demand. This, in turn, generates higher incomes for workers, potentially boosting consumer spending further across various sectors, i.e., *'Employment and Income Effects.'* The increased consumer spending in various sectors can lead to a feedback loop. As more people are employed and earn income, their purchasing power rises, which can further stimulate demand in other sectors, perpetuating the cycle of increased economic activity, i.e., *'Feedback Loops.'*

In this context, the Leontief Input-Output framework provides a comprehensive tool to trace the chain of effects triggered by changes in final demand. The scenario of increased car demand demonstrates how this framework expresses the interconnected mechanisms within the economy. It showcases how changes in one sector reverberate throughout the supply chain, affecting multiple sectors and generating indirect and induced effects that contribute to the overall economic dynamics.

Therefore, the basic form of the Leontief Input-Output Equation can be expressed as follows:

$$X = A \cdot X + Y, \tag{7.1}$$

where:

- Y represents the vector of final demand for each sector
- A is a square matrix of so-called technical coefficients, where each element a_{ij} indicates the amount of input required from each sector i to produce one unit of output in another sector j
- X is the vector of outputs produced by each sector

The square matrix A consists of the 'technical coefficients,' which quantify the input requirements for each sector. These coefficients capture the direct relationships between industries, reflecting the proportion of outputs from one industry that are used as inputs by another industry. But how are the technical coefficients calculated? The calculation of technical coefficients in the IO framework involves determining the amount of input required from each sector to produce one unit of output in another sector. There are several methods used to calculate these coefficients, each with its own level of detail and complexity. Here's an indicative overview:

(i) Direct Survey Method: In this approach, detailed surveys are conducted within each industry to gather information about the quantities and types of inputs used in production. These surveys collect data on factors such as raw materials, labor, energy, and other resources. By analyzing these data, economists calculate the specific quantities of inputs required to produce a unit of output for each sector.

(ii) Inter-Industry Transactions Data: This method involves analyzing existing data on transactions between industries. Governments, statistical agencies, and organizations often collect data on the value of goods and services exchanged between sectors. By examining these transaction data, economists estimate the relative importance of each input in the production process.

(iii) Input-Output Tables from Previous Periods: Historical input-output tables from previous years can serve as a valuable source of information. By computationally analyzing changes in these tables over time, economists often infer how input requirements have evolved and calculate the technical coefficients accordingly.

It's important to note here that the accuracy and level of detail of technical coefficients depend on the data available and the chosen method. A combination of approaches is often used to derive these coefficients, and the level of sophistication can vary based on the complexity of the economy being analyzed. Regardless of the method used, the goal is to develop a comprehensive input-output table that reflects the relationships between sectors. This table is the foundation for assessing the impact of changes in demand, and understanding the interconnectedness of an economy.

Now, let's focus on Eq. (7.1). The vector Y expresses the final demand for goods and services from each sector including consumption by households, government spending, and investment by businesses. It is an expression of the total demand for output across the economy. The vector X represents the outputs produced by each sector. These outputs serve as inputs for other sectors and contribute to the overall economic activity.

The IO model analyzes the equilibrium between production and demand. To ensure balance, the outputs produced X minus the inputs used by the other sectors of the economy $A \cdot X$ should equal the final demand Y. Or, to put it simply, a sector's production is equal to the inputs provided to other sectors plus the final demand. As mentioned earlier, one of the notable features of the Input-Output model is that changes in final demand for one sector can lead to changes in outputs and inputs throughout the economy, as the effects propagate through the interconnected network of industries.

This is a central concept in Economics, and within the context of the IO model it deals with the case where an initial change in final demand for goods and services in one sector leads to a larger, cumulative impact on the entire economy. This effect arises due to the interconnected nature of industries and the effects that changes in demand create throughout the production chain.

Mathematically, based on Eq. (7.1), we can easily derive the so-called Leontief Equation, which expresses the aforementioned process. Starting from Eq. (7.1):

$$X = A \cdot X + Y$$

Solving for matrix X as follows:

$$X - A \cdot X = Y$$

or

$$I \cdot X - A \cdot X = Y$$

which simplifies to

$$(I - A) \cdot X = Y,$$

where I is the identity matrix.

Assuming $\det(A - I) \neq 0$ we multiply both sides by $(I - A)^{-1}$ from the left to get (Sect. 23.4, Appendix D):

$$(I - A)^{-1} \cdot (I - A) \cdot X = (I - A)^{-1} \cdot Y,$$

where, by definition:

$$(I - A)^{-1} \cdot (I - A) = I.$$

Therefore, we get the Leontief Eq. (7.2):

$$X = (I - A)^{-1} \cdot Y \tag{7.2}$$

The Leontief Equation calculates the total change in output X which results from a change in final demand Y for goods and services. The matrix $(I - A)^{-1}$ represents the inverse of the difference between the identity matrix and the matrix of technical coefficients, often called 'Leontief's Inverse Matrix.' This inverse matrix captures the cumulative impact of changes in demand as they propagate through the production network.

To illustrate the Leontief Input-Output (IO) framework, let's consider a very simple example involving two (2) sectors: the automobile industry (sector 1) and the steel industry (sector 2). Suppose we have the following data:

- For the automobile industry (sector 1)
  - it requires 50 units of steel to produce 100 cars.
  - the final demand for cars is 120 units.
- For the steel industry (sector 2):
  - the final demand for steel is 240 units.

We can represent this information using the Input-Output Eq. (7.1):

For our example, Y is the final demand vector. Since we have only two sectors, it's a 2 × 1 vector representing the final demand for cars and steel. In this context $Y = \begin{pmatrix} 120 \\ 240 \end{pmatrix}$.

Since we have only two sectors, it's a 2 × 2 matrix representing the input-output relationships between sectors. In our case, the coefficient a_{21} of steel (sector 2) required to produce cars (sector 1) is 0.5, i.e., 50 units of steel per 100 cars, or:

$$a_{21} = \frac{50\,\text{units of steel}}{100\,\text{cars}}$$

Since there's no direct input requirement from the automobile industry (sector 1) to the steel industry (sector 2), the coefficient a_{12} for that entry is 0, i.e., $a_{12} = 0$.

In this example, we assume that $a_{11} = a_{22} = 0$, implying that the input from sector 1 (cars) used by sector 1 (cars) to produce one unit (car) of its output is equal to zero(0) and similarly for sector 2. Therefore:

$$A \equiv \begin{pmatrix} a_{11} & a_{12} \\ a_{21} & a_{22} \end{pmatrix} \text{ or } A = \begin{pmatrix} 0 & 0 \\ 0.5 & 0 \end{pmatrix}$$

Please note that sectors often require some of their own outputs for production processes. This reflects the recursive nature of production where intermediate goods and services are often needed to produce final goods and services within the same sector.

Next, X is the vector of outputs produced by each sector. Since we have only two sectors, it's a 2 × 1 vector representing the outputs of cars and steel $X = \begin{pmatrix} X_1 \\ X_2 \end{pmatrix}$.

Now, we can plug these values into the Leontief Input-Output Eq. (7.1):

$$\begin{pmatrix} X_1 \\ X_2 \end{pmatrix} = \begin{pmatrix} 0 & 0 \\ 0.5 & 0 \end{pmatrix} \cdot \begin{pmatrix} X_1 \\ X_2 \end{pmatrix} + \begin{pmatrix} 120 \\ 240 \end{pmatrix}$$

Simplifying this equation, we get:

$$\begin{pmatrix} X_1 \\ X_2 \end{pmatrix} = \begin{pmatrix} 0 \\ 0.5 \cdot X_1 \end{pmatrix} + \begin{pmatrix} 120 \\ 240 \end{pmatrix}$$

$$\begin{pmatrix} X_1 \\ X_2 \end{pmatrix} = \begin{pmatrix} 0 + 120 \\ 0.5 \cdot X_1 + 240 \end{pmatrix}$$

$$\begin{pmatrix} X_1 \\ X_2 \end{pmatrix} = \begin{pmatrix} 120 \\ 60 + 240 \end{pmatrix}$$

$$\begin{pmatrix} X_1 \\ X_2 \end{pmatrix} = \begin{pmatrix} 120 \\ 300 \end{pmatrix}$$

This result shows the equilibrium state where the final demand for cars and steel matches the total outputs produced by each sector, considering the input requirements specified by the technical coefficients.

Alternatively, we can calculate the Leontief input-output inverse matrix, by plugging numbers in Eq. (7.2). For our example, we need to compute $(I - A)^{-1}$.

Therefore:

$$(I - A) = \begin{pmatrix} 1 & 0 \\ 0 & 1 \end{pmatrix} - \begin{pmatrix} 0 & 0 \\ 0.5 & 0 \end{pmatrix} = \begin{pmatrix} 1 & 0 \\ -0.5 & 1 \end{pmatrix}$$

And (Sect. 23.4, Appendix D):

$$(I - A)^{-1} = \begin{pmatrix} 1 & 0 \\ -0.5 & 1 \end{pmatrix}^{-1} = \frac{1}{\det(I - A)} \cdot \begin{pmatrix} 1 & 0 \\ 0.5 & 1 \end{pmatrix} = \begin{pmatrix} 1 & 0 \\ 0.5 & 1 \end{pmatrix},$$

Since $\det(I - A) = 1 \cdot 1 - (-0.50) \cdot 0 = 1$

Finally, we plug these numbers into Eq. (7.2) to get:

$$X = \begin{pmatrix} 1 & 0 \\ 0.5 & 1 \end{pmatrix} \cdot \begin{pmatrix} 120 \\ 240 \end{pmatrix}$$

$$X = \begin{pmatrix} 1 \cdot 120 + 0 \cdot 240 \\ 0.5 \cdot 120 + 1 \cdot 240 \end{pmatrix}$$

$$X = \begin{pmatrix} 120 \\ 60 + 240 \end{pmatrix}$$

$$X = \begin{pmatrix} 120 \\ 300 \end{pmatrix}$$

The resulting vector X represents the total outputs produced by each sector due to the final demand of 120 units for cars and 240 units for steel, taking into account the inter-industry dependencies.

7.4 Consequences and Insights

Leontief's IO framework has far-reaching implications that span various economic, social, and policy domains. It serves as a versatile and powerful tool, offering insights and analytical capabilities. One significant application of the framework is in conducting economic impact assessments. It facilitates the evaluation of major events or policy changes, enabling economists to assess the effects of new infrastructure projects or estimate the consequences of, e.g., hosting events like the Olympic Games. By comprehensively analyzing how different sectors are affected, the IO framework provides a more holistic understanding of the economic implications.

In the meantime, in an era of global supply chains, the framework's relevance extends to analyzing supply chain resilience. It aids in identifying critical sectors and potential vulnerabilities within supply networks. This insight is invaluable for policymakers and businesses striving to enhance the robustness of supply chains and effectively deal with disruptions. Furthermore, the input-output model can be adapted to analyze financial flows and investment strategies. It enables the assessment of changes in investment patterns, capital flows, and financial policies, shedding light on their impacts on various sectors and the broader economy. The diffusion of technology and innovation across sectors is another area where the framework excels. By tracing the channels through which technological advancements spread, input-output analysis provides insights into how innovation influences productivity, competitiveness, and overall economic growth.

The framework also contributes to understanding inequality and income distribution. By tracing income flows and expenditures, it offers insights into how changes in one sector can impact income distribution, contributing to a more comprehensive understanding of these complex dynamics. Investments in education and human capital can also be analyzed using the input-output model to quantify their effects on various sectors. This aspect highlights how improvements in skills and knowledge translate into enhanced productivity and economic growth across the economy. In trade and economic integration, the IO framework proves invaluable for assessing the potential effects of trade agreements and regional integration. It allows economists to estimate the impacts of tariff reductions, changes in trade policies, and cross-border investments on different sectors and regions.

During times of crisis, such as natural disasters, the input-output framework aids in disaster recovery and planning. By mapping sector interdependencies, policymakers can strategically allocate support to sectors crucial for rebuilding and mitigating long-term economic damage. Economists and policymakers can utilize the framework for scenario analysis and sensitivity testing. By simulating changes in various sectors under different scenarios, they can analyze potential outcomes and evaluate the robustness of policy decisions.

7.5 Conclusion, Limitations, and Critiques

The IO framework pioneered by Wassily Leontief has revolutionized our understanding of economic systems, offering a comprehensive lens through which we can unravel the web of interdependencies and relationships that define modern economies. By emphasizing the connections between industries and tracing the flow of goods, services, and resources, this approach has proven indispensable in diverse fields, from policy analysis to disaster recovery planning. It provides a comprehensive tool for economists, policymakers, and researchers to analyze the dynamics of an economy and make educated decisions. The model's strengths are evident in its ability to capture the multiplier effects of changes in demand, its practical applications in policy analysis and economic impact assessments, and its relevance in understanding supply chain dynamics and innovation diffusion.

However, like any analytical tool, the traditional IO approach framework is not without limitations and criticisms. Several key considerations merit attention. For instance, the IO model assumes constant technical coefficients for some years, implying that the IO relationships remain unchanged regardless of shifts in demand or production techniques. This assumption does not hold true in rapidly evolving sectors or during periods of technological disruption. Also, the traditional IO framework relies on linear relationships between sectors and does not account for nonlinear effects or feedback loops that might arise from complex interactions. Furthermore, the traditional IO model is static and does not capture dynamic changes over time. Economic systems are inherently dynamic, and the traditional model's inability to account for evolving behaviors and structural shifts limits its predictive accuracy in rapidly changing environments. Additionally, the model treats sectors as homogenous entities, overlooking variations within sectors. It assumes uniformity in production processes, technology adoption, and input requirements, which may oversimplify the complexities of real-world industries.

Finally, the model assumes a uniform capital good, neglecting variations in capital quality and its impact on production processes and efficiency, constructs IO tables often based on incomplete or even outdated data that could introduce errors into the analysis, and, lastly, focuses on physical rather than monetary flows of goods and services, and does not focus on the behavioral aspects of decision-making, such as consumer preferences or firms' strategic choices. Despite these limitations, the input-output framework remains a powerful tool that enriches our understanding of economic systems and offers valuable insights into the dynamics of interdependent sectors. Its contributions to policy analysis and supply chain management are undeniable.

Chapter Takeaways

- Input-Output (IO) Analysis, pioneered by Wassily Leontief, unveils complex relationships within economic systems.
- The IO framework emphasizes interdependence, revealing connections between sectors.
- The IO approach traces the flow of goods, services, and resources across sectors.
- The model captures effects of changes in demand, yielding far-reaching impacts.
- It has practical applications in policy analysis and understanding supply chains.
- Despite its strengths, the traditional model assumes constant technology over a period of time, and linear relationships limiting accuracy.
- The traditional framework's static nature hinders capturing dynamic changes and nonlinear effects over time.
- Homogeneity assumption oversimplifies real-world complexities within sectors.
- The IO model neglects behavioral aspects of decision-making and variations in capital quality.
- Limitations notwithstanding, the framework remains an invaluable tool for understanding economic systems.

Revision Questions

1. Who pioneered the IO framework, and what is its main contribution to Economic Science?
2. How does the input-output model emphasize the interdependencies between sectors?
3. What practical applications does the IO framework have in policy analysis?
4. Explain the Leontief inverse matrix in the IO model and its significance.
5. What are some limitations of the IO framework in capturing real-world economic dynamics?
6. How does the traditional model's assumption of constant coefficients affect its accuracy?
7. Why is the IO framework considered 'static,' and how does this affect its applicability?
8. What is the homogeneity of capital assumption within the IO model, and how might it oversimplify reality?
9. How does the IO framework contribute to understanding supply chain dynamics and innovation diffusion?
10. Despite its limitations, why is the IO framework still considered a valuable tool for economists and policymakers?

CHAPTER 8

Break-Even Point

Learning Objectives

- Understand the Concept of the Break-Even Point
- Analyze the Equation Underlying the Break-Even Point
- Apply the Break-Even Analysis to Different Cases
- Evaluate the Role of Break-Even Analysis in Risk Management
- Identify the Limitations and Critiques of Break-Even Analysis

8.1 Introduction

The Break-Even Point is a notion that extends beyond the numerical intersection of costs and revenue. It serves as a motivator for businesses to examine their financial structure, fostering a culture of financial literacy and strategic thinking. One of the key motivations for examining the Break-Even Point is its role in risk management. In an era marked by economic uncertainties and market volatility, businesses must operate in landscapes fraught with challenges. The Break-Even Point acts as a financial 'safety net' allowing companies to assess the level of risk associated with their operations, and proactively identify potential pitfalls, enabling them to fortify their financial positions and weather economic storms.

P. G. Michaelides, *21 Equations that Shaped the World Economy*,
https://doi.org/10.1007/978-3-031-76140-9_8

Furthermore, the Break-Even Point becomes a dynamic tool for setting achievable targets. As businesses set their sights on growth and expansion, the Break-Even Point provides a baseline for goal-setting. Managers can leverage this information to establish sales targets, production levels, and pricing strategies that go beyond mere survival. The Break-Even Point becomes a motivational benchmark, inspiring teams to exceed the minimum threshold and strive for profitability.

In pricing strategies, the Break-Even Point plays a pivotal role in ensuring that products and services are priced competitively while covering costs. Businesses armed with a good understanding of their Break-Even Point make educated decisions, striking a balance between attracting customers and generating profits. This knowledge becomes particularly crucial in industries with thin profit margins, where precise pricing can make the crucial difference between success and failure.

Moreover, the Break-Even Point is a crucial tool in resource allocation. By identifying the point at which costs are recouped, businesses can optimize their use of resources, minimizing waste and inefficiencies. This not only contributes to cost control but also fosters a culture where every resource is strategically deployed.

8.2 The Break-Even Point in Economics

The emergence of the Break-Even Point in Economics and Finance signifies an evolution in the way businesses and economists approached financial analysis. The concept gained prominence during a transformative period in economic history marked by industrialization, changing business models, and a growing need for more sophisticated tools to assess financial viability. At the heart of this emergence was a recognition of the complexities in managing costs and revenues, particularly as businesses transitioned from small-scale enterprises to larger, more complex organizations. The Industrial Revolution, which spanned the late eighteenth to early nineteenth century, brought about a shift in production methods. Mass production became the norm, and businesses faced new challenges in understanding the financial implications of scaling their operations.

Accountants studied the principles of cost accounting, providing insights into the idea of finding a point at which total costs would equal total revenue. This marked an early attempt to formalize the concept that would later become known as the Break-Even Point. This initial attempt witnessed further contributions from economists and management theorists who sought to refine and expand the applications of Break-Even analysis. In fact, the mid-twentieth century proved to be a turning point for the Break-Even Point as it gained widespread recognition. The advent of more sophisticated computing technologies allowed businesses to handle large datasets efficiently, paving the way for more accurate break-even calculations. This technological advancement democratized access to Break-Even analysis, making it a practical tool for firms.

The Break-Even Point's emergence also reflects a broader shift in economic thinking toward a more quantitative and analytical approach. As businesses faced increased competition and market dynamics became more complex, there was a growing need for tools that could help tackle these complexities. Businesses could use Break-Even Analysis to evaluate their financial position, make informed decisions about pricing and production, and assess the risks and rewards that have to do with different strategies using a more systematic approach than before.

Today, the Break-Even Point remains a helpful tool for financial planning and strategic management. Its continued relevance underscores its adaptability to different economic contexts and its enduring value in guiding businesses toward financial sustainability and success. The evolution of the Break-Even Point mirrors the ongoing quest for practical and insightful tools in the fascinating terrain of modern Economics.

8.3 The Equation

The Break-Even Point is a metric that helps firms determine the level of sales at which total costs equal total revenue, which results in zero profit. The derivation of the Break-Even Point (BEP) equation involves understanding the relationship between costs, revenue, and profit. Assuming a linear relationship between costs and production levels, here's a step-by-step derivation.

Initially, we define the variables:

- **Fixed Costs (*FC*) are the** costs that practically do not change with the level of production or sales (e.g., rent, equipment, insurance).
- **Variable Costs (*VC*) are the** costs that vary directly with the level of production (e.g., materials, labor).
- **Selling Price per Unit (*SPU*)** is the price at which each unit is sold.

- **Variable Cost per Unit (*VCU*)** is the cost incurred for producing each unit.
- **Quantity (*Q*)** is the number of units produced and sold, assuming no stock.

Next, we define the basic equations.

- **Total Costs (*TC*)** consist of Fixed Costs and Variable Costs, equal to:

$$TC = FC + (VCU \cdot Q)$$

- **Total Revenue (*TR*)** is the income from selling the product, equal to:

$$TR = SPU \cdot Q$$

- **Break-Even Point** (BEP) **is the point at which** Total Revenue (TR) equals Total Costs (TC), meaning the firm makes no profit or loss, namely:

$$TR = TC$$

Now, we set up the Equation:

$$SPU \cdot Q = FC + (VCU \cdot Q)$$

Finally, we must solve for *Q*.

To find the Break-Even Point in terms of units (*Q*), isolate *Q* in the equation:

$$SPU \cdot Q - VCU \cdot Q = FC$$

Factor out *Q* on the left side:

$$Q \cdot (SPU - VCU) = FC$$

Divide both sides by the contribution margin ($SPU - VCU$), assuming $SPU - VCU \neq 0$:

$$Q = \frac{FC}{SPU - VCU}$$

So, the Break-Even Point (BEP) in units is:

$$\text{Break Even Point}(\text{BEP}) = \frac{\text{Fixed Costs}(\text{FC})}{\text{Selling Price per Unit}(\text{SPU}) - \text{Variable Cost per Unit}(\text{VCU})} \tag{8.1}$$

The Break-Even Point in units expresses the quantity of products or services a firm must sell to cover its total costs. Once this point is reached, the firm neither makes a profit nor incurs a loss. After that point, a firm starts making profits assuming a linear relationship between costs and units produced/sold. It acts as a reference point for managers to evaluate the viability of different production levels and pricing strategies.

Let's see a very simple numerical example. With a linear relationship between costs and production levels, let's assume:

- Fixed Costs: \$1000
- Selling Price per Unit: \$10
- Variable Cost per Unit: \$5

Now, we can plug these values into Eq. (8.1):

$$\text{Break Even Point} = \frac{1000}{10-5} = \frac{1000}{5} = 200\,\text{physical units}$$

So, in this example, the Break-Even Point for the firm is 200 physical units. This means that the company needs to sell at least 200 physical units of its product to cover its costs and break even, before starting to make profits.

8.4 Consequences and Insights

In Economics and Finance, the Break-Even Point is a compass for businesses trying to balance between costs and revenue. It is a strategic tool that guides pricing decisions, helping firms set prices that contribute to profitability. Beyond pricing, Break-Even Analysis becomes a critical element in risk management. By computing the minimum level of activity required to avoid losses, firms can identify vulnerabilities and implement strategies to mitigate financial risks. Operational efficiency is enhanced through Break-Even Analysis, which aids in resource allocation and cost control. It enables businesses to optimize their operations, minimizing waste and inefficiencies. Moreover, the Break-Even Point is integral to strategic decisions related to market entry, expansion, and product lifecycle management. It assists businesses in evaluating the feasibility of new ventures, determining optimal product mixes, and making decisions about when to introduce, maintain, or phase out products.

In Finance, the Break-Even Point is a linchpin for professionals engaged in various facets of corporate finance and investment analysis. It forms the foundation for financial planning and budgeting, enabling finance teams to set realistic targets aligned with expected revenues. Cash flow management benefits significantly form Break-Even insights, as businesses can forecast the timing and level of production or sales required to cover costs, making sure that liquidity needs are met. Capital structure decisions are influenced by Break-Even Analysis, as finance professionals weigh the mix of debt and equity required to support projects or expansions. In investment analysis and valuation, the Break-Even Point is a key metric, offering insights into the time required for investments to generate positive returns. It is particularly relevant in mergers and acquisitions, where understanding the Break-Even dynamics of target companies informs strategic decisions.

Risk management takes on a financial lens with Break-Even insights, helping finance professionals identify and address vulnerabilities. Debt servicing capacity is assessed using Break-Even Analysis, providing lenders with a crucial metric to evaluate a company's ability to meet financial obligations. Financial forecasting gains precision with Break-Even calculations, allowing finance teams to project future scenarios and anticipate challenges and opportunities.

Ultimately, the Break-Even Point is a dynamic tool with numerous practical applications for businesses and financial professionals alike in a rapidly evolving economic environment. For instance, consider a software company which plans to launch a new product. The Break-Even Point becomes a pivotal metric in determining the minimum number of software licenses it needs to sell to cover the fixed costs related to the development, marketing, and operational expenses. By computing the Break-Even Point, the company can set a competitive yet profitable price per license, ensuring that each sale contributes significantly to covering costs and, eventually, generating profits. In the context of risk management, let's examine an event planning company organizing a concert. The Break-Even Point helps determine the minimum number of tickets that must be sold to cover fixed costs, such as venue rental, artist fees, and promotion. By conducting Break-Even Analysis, the firm can assess the financial risk associated with the event, allowing for strategic adjustments in ticket pricing, marketing efforts, and overall event planning to avoid losses.

For a manufacturing firm, Break-Even Analysis becomes a crucial tool in optimizing operational efficiency. Suppose the company produces widgets, and Break-Even insights reveal the production level at which it covers all costs. This information allows the firm to streamline production processes, negotiate better deals with suppliers, and identify opportunities for cost savings, contributing to increased efficiency and competitiveness. In investment analysis, let's examine a cryptocurrency startup seeking funding for a new crypto project. The Break-Even Point becomes a pivotal metric for investors to assess the startup's sustainability and the time it will take to achieve profitability. This information influences investment decisions, as investors seek ventures that not only have promising products but also demonstrate a clear path to financial viability. In the financial sector, a lending institution requires businesses to demonstrate an understanding of their Break-Even Point when applying for a loan. For instance, a manufacturing company seeking funds for equipment upgrades can use Break-Even Analysis to showcase its ability to cover fixed costs and repay the loan through projected sales, providing assurance to lenders about the business's financial health.

8.5 Conclusion, Limitations, and Critiques

The Break-Even Point is a pivotal concept in Economics and Finance. Its practical utility is profound, influencing decision-making in areas such as pricing, production levels, risk mitigation, and financial planning. By understanding the Break-Even Point, businesses gain insights into the dynamics between fixed costs, variable costs, and revenue, enabling them to make informed choices that contribute to financial sustainability and profitability. The very simple examples offered earlier illustrate the diverse applications of Break-Even Analysis across industries. From software development to event planning, manufacturing, retail, and beyond, businesses leverage the Break-Even Point to tailor their strategies. It becomes a guiding metric in setting prices, optimizing operational efficiency, and making crucial decisions about market entry, expansion, and product lifecycle management.

While the Break-Even Point is a powerful tool, it is not without its limitations. In the previous analysis, one very crucial assumption involves linearity, implying a consistent linear relationship between costs and production levels. In practice, business environments are sometimes highly nonlinear and dynamic, challenging the accuracy of linear models. Additionally, the static nature of fixed costs assumed by Break-Even Analysis may not capture the dynamic complexities of industries where fixed costs are 'not so fixed' anymore and evolve over time. The simplicity of the model, while making it accessible, may oversimplify the complexities of certain businesses, particularly those with multifaceted cost structures.

Critiques, particularly from the standpoint of behavioral economics, shed light on the limitations of traditional economic models, including Break-Even Analysis. These critiques emphasize that human behavior, biases, and market dynamics are often more substantial than the rational assumptions made in this model. Moreover, in industries characterized by innovation and uncertainty, predicting the Break-Even Point becomes challenging, as the model may struggle to account for unpredictable factors.

Another aspect of critique involves the consideration of social and environmental externalities. Traditional economic models, including Break-Even Analysis, may not comprehensively address the broader impacts that businesses have on society and the environment. This critique highlights the need for a more holistic approach that integrates social and environmental considerations into economic and financial analyses.

To conclude, the Break-Even Point remains a practical tool, but its application requires a good understanding of its strengths and limitations. Businesses and financial professionals should view it as part of a broader toolkit, incorporating alternative perspectives and accounting for the complexities of real-world economic environments. The continuous evolution of business dynamics demands an adaptive approach, and while the Break-Even Point is a valuable guide, practical wisdom lies in recognizing its place within a more comprehensive framework of economic and financial analysis.

Chapter Takeaways

- The emergence of the Break-Even Point constitutes a milestone in economic and financial practice.
- The Break-Even Point extends beyond numerical calculations to foster financial literacy and strategic thinking within businesses.
- It acts as a risk management tool, allowing firms to proactively assess the level of risk associated with their operations in dynamic economic landscapes.
- The Break-Even Point is a dynamic tool for setting practical and achievable goals, motivating businesses to exceed minimum thresholds and strive for profitability.
- In pricing strategies, it plays a pivotal role in ensuring competitive pricing that covers costs, especially crucial in industries with thin profit margins.
- The Break-Even Point is instrumental in resource allocation, optimizing the use of resources and fostering operational excellence within businesses.
- The Break-Even Point equation involves fixed costs, selling price, and variable cost per unit, providing a clear benchmark for assessing financial health.
- It is a powerful tool for decision-making, risk assessment, financial planning, and scenario analysis, enabling businesses to deal with complexities.
- Practical examples across industries illustrate the Break-Even Point's application.
- Acknowledging limitations and addressing critiques ensures a better understanding, guiding businesses and professionals in practical decision-making.

Revision Questions

1. What was the context of the development of the Break-Even Point?
2. What is the Break-Even Point, and how does it extend beyond numerical calculations to influence strategic thinking within businesses?
3. How does the Break-Even Point act as a risk management tool, and why is it crucial in dealing with economic uncertainties?
4. In what ways does the Break-Even Point motivate firms to set practical goals and strive for profitability beyond mere survival?
5. How does the Break-Even Point contribute to resource allocation and operational excellence within businesses?
6. Explain the role of the Break-Even Point in pricing strategies, particularly in industries with thin profit margins.
7. Break down the components of the Break-Even Point equation and explain how it provides a benchmark for assessing financial health.
8. Discuss the practical applications of the Break-Even Point in decision-making, risk assessment, financial planning, and scenario analysis.
9. Provide practical examples across industries to illustrate how businesses leverage the Break-Even Point for strategic decision-making.
10. What are the limitations of the Break-Even Point, and how can businesses address these challenges to ensure a more comprehensive understanding?

CHAPTER 9

The Fisher Equation

Learning Objectives

- Understand the Fundamentals of the Fisher Equation
- Analyze the Relationship Between Nominal and Real Interest Rates
- Examine the Role of the Fisher Equation in Monetary Policy
- Evaluate the Implications of the Fisher Equation
- Identify the Limitations and Critiques of the Fisher Equation

9.1 Introduction

In the early twentieth century, Irving Fisher, an eminent economist, conceived the Fisher equation. At its core, the equation appears deceptively simple: nominal interest rate equals real interest rate plus expected inflation. Yet, beneath this elegant expression lies a deeper insight into the decision-making processes of individuals, the strategies of investors, and the strategies of policymakers. The tumultuous economic landscape of Fisher's era, punctuated by the aftermath of World War I and the Great Depression, provided fertile ground for the emergence of theories that could provide clarity in times of uncertainty. Fisher's equation offered a fresh perspective on the link between interest rates and inflation, reshaping how we understand the dynamics of monetary policy.

P. G. Michaelides, *21 Equations that Shaped the World Economy*,
https://doi.org/10.1007/978-3-031-76140-9_9

The trajectory of the Fisher equation through time has been a testament to its resilience and adaptability. The equation's endurance has been due to its capacity to adapt to the changing economic landscapes and technological advancements that have shaped our globalized world. This chapter will introduce the Fisher equation. We will discuss the practical examples of this equation, understanding its role in shaping the financial decisions of individuals and corporations. We will trace how the equation has been utilized to deal with economic challenges and foster growth. We will examine the equation's role in policy decisions, as central banks grapple with the delicate balance between fostering economic expansion and averting destabilizing inflation.

However, a comprehensive understanding of the Fisher equation requires a critical lens that acknowledges its limitations and complexities. In this context, we will question its assumptions and examine its deviations from reality.

9.2 The Fisher Equation in Economics

The early twentieth century ushered in an era of profound upheaval and uncertainty. As we know, the reverberations of World War I were felt across continents, leaving nations grappling not only with the physical devastation of conflict but also with the economic aftershocks that reverberated through societies. The webs of global trade were disrupted, currencies fluctuated wildly, and economies struggled to find their footing amid the wreckage of war. As nations attempted to rebuild, the effects of war debts and shattered industries cast a shadow over prospects for economic recovery.

It was within this chaotic milieu that Irving Fisher's idea emerged as an expression of innovative thought. Driven by a desire to understand the fundamental drivers of economic development, Fisher approached his studies with a sense of urgency. The conventional economic theories of the time struggled to grapple with the challenges posed by the post-war environment. Fisher recognized that a more accurate perspective was needed, one that could provide insights into the complex interplay of economic forces in a world undergoing transformation.

Fisher's approach to Economics was nothing short of visionary. He refused to be confined by disciplinary boundaries, drawing inspiration from a diverse array of fields. This interdisciplinary approach endowed him with a unique capacity to view economic phenomena from multiple angles, enabling him to spot connections and patterns that others might have overlooked. For Fisher, Economics was not a standalone discipline but rather a complex mosaic woven from the threads of various intellectual pursuits. This mindset positioned him at the forefront of a 'new wave' of economic thought, one that sought to marry theory with empirical analysis to create a more complete understanding of economic dynamics.

Fisher's quest for understanding led him to a pivotal question: How do interest rates, inflation, and the value of money interrelate to shape economic outcomes? It was this question that spurred him to embark on a journey of synthesis, a process of weaving together insights from various fields to construct a comprehensive framework. This framework eventually crystallized into what is now known as the Fisher equation. The Fisher equation, though elegant and extremely simple in its formulation, provides a conceptual bridge between the macroeconomic world of aggregate price levels and the microeconomic world of individual financial decisions. Fisher's equation demonstrates that these seemingly disparate economic forces are intimately intertwined, and changes in one could ripple through the entire economic system.

Upon its introduction, the Fisher equation was met with a mix of excitement and skepticism. Economists recognized the equation's potential to shed new light on the complexities of monetary policy, inflation dynamics, and investment decisions. However, some questioned the equation's assumptions and its ability to express the complexity of real-world economic scenarios. Nevertheless, as time unfolded, the equation's significance became increasingly apparent.

9.3 The Equation

To derive the Fisher equation, we need to understand the relationship between nominal interest rates, real interest rates, and expected inflation. Let's define the following variables:

i expresses the nominal interest rate, the visible cost of borrowing or the return on investments, before taking inflation into account.

r denotes the real interest rate, a measure of the actual cost of borrowing or lending after accounting for inflation, exactly adjusted for the effect of inflation.

π denotes the expected inflation rate, an estimation of how the general price level is projected to change over a specific period.

Now, let's assume an amount of money today, say P. In one year, the nominal value of this money will grow to $P \cdot (1 + i)$. However, the real value of money after one year should account for the inflation rate. If P grows at the real interest rate r, it will become $P \cdot (1 + r)$ in real terms. Considering the effect of inflation, the purchasing power of $P \cdot (1 + r)$ in terms of nominal value is adjusted by the expected inflation rate. Thus, the nominal equivalent of $P \cdot (1 + r)$ would be $P \cdot (1 + r) \cdot (1 + \pi)$.

So, we can equate the two expressions for the future value:

$$P \cdot (1+i) = P \cdot (1+r) \cdot (1+\pi)$$

Since P is the same on both sides, it can be canceled out, leaving us with:

$$(1+i) = (1+r) \cdot (1+\pi) \tag{9.1}$$

This equation shows how the nominal interest rate is a combination of the real interest rate and the expected inflation rate, reflecting the Fisher effect. Of course, there is a mathematical approximation of the Fisher equation that is commonly used to simplify its application and calculations. We can derive a simplified version of the Fisher equation by making an approximation for small values of the interest rates and inflation rate. We start from the full Fisher Eq. (9.1):

$$(1+i) = (1+r) \cdot (1+\pi)$$

We expand the right-hand side:

$$1+i = 1+\pi+r+r \cdot \pi \tag{9.2}$$

However, for small values of r and π, the product $r \cdot \pi$ becomes very small and can be approximated as negligible. This is because the product of two small numbers is even smaller, making the term $r \cdot \pi$ very close to zero.

Mathematically:

$$r \cdot \pi \approx 0 \tag{9.3}$$

By plugging Eq. (9.3) in Eq. (9.2), we get:

$$1 + i \approx 1 + \pi + r$$

Now, we subtract 1 from both sides to isolate i:

$$i \approx \pi + r$$

Therefore, for small values of the real interest rate and the expected inflation rate, the Fisher equation simplifies to:

$$i \approx \pi + r \tag{9.4}$$

This simplified version is often used for ease of calculations and to provide a quick estimate of the nominal interest rate given the real interest rate and expected inflation. It's important to note that this approximation holds when the nominal interest rate is relatively low and the time period under consideration is short. Keep in mind that while this approximation is convenient for quick calculations, it may not adequately capture the increased complexity of economic reality, especially when interest rates are higher or when longer time periods are involved. For more precise calculations, using the full Fisher Eq. (9.1) may be necessary.

Let's see a very simple example. A prospective entrepreneur seeks capital to fund a new venture. This entrepreneur has secured a business loan at a nominal interest rate of 8%, spanning a loan term of five years. Economists' projections suggest that inflation will rise at an annual rate of 3% during this period. The Fisher equation, with its mathematical elegance, provides a means to dissect the situation. With $i = 0.08$ (8%) and $\pi = 0.03$ (3%), the entrepreneur can plug these numbers in Eq. (9.1) to unravel the real interest rate r, i.e., the actual cost of borrowing factoring in inflation:

$(1 + 0.08) = (1 + r) \cdot (1 + 0.03)$

When solving for r, this calculation yields a real interest rate r of approximately 0.048 (4.8%). The revelation is profound. While the nominal interest rate stands at 8%, the true cost of borrowing, considering the erosive effects of an anticipated 3% inflation, is close to 4.8%. This insight empowers the entrepreneur to make an informed decision, evaluating the borrowing cost against inflation.

9.4 Consequences and Insights

The Fisher equation reverberates with profound implications that span the fields of finance, investment, monetary policy, and individual decision-making. Firstly, the equation sheds light on the crucial distinction between nominal and real values in the world of Economics. Nominal interest rates, often quoted and observed, fail to account for the erosive impact of inflation on the purchasing power of money. By introducing the concept of real interest rates adjusted for inflation, the Fisher equation illuminates the true cost of borrowing and lending, fostering a more accurate understanding of economic dynamics. Furthermore, the Fisher equation serves as a compass for investors in a landscape full of uncertainty. Investors' ultimate goal is to preserve and potentially grow their wealth. However, this task is complicated by the unpredictable fluctuations of inflation. By incorporating expected inflation into the equation, investors can recalibrate their expectations and make decisions that safeguard their returns against the effects of rising prices.

From a macroeconomic perspective, the Fisher equation finds profound utility in shaping the trajectories of monetary policy. Central banks, tasked with steering economies toward stability, use this equation's insights to calibrate interest rates. By considering expected inflation, central banks strive to set nominal interest rates that correspond with real economic conditions. This equilibrium-seeking approach aims to ensure that borrowing costs are reflective of the true cost of borrowing, ultimately promoting economic stability. Consider the context of lending and borrowing. Lenders set nominal interest rates based on their desired returns, but these returns are intimately linked to the prevailing rate of inflation. The equation underscores the necessity for lenders to consider both nominal and real interest rates to avoid eroding their purchasing power when lending money over extended periods.

9.5 Conclusion, Limitations, and Critiques

As we have seen, the Fisher equation stands as a sentinel in the vast expanse of economic theory, deciphering the interplay of money, interest rates, and inflation. Its significance extends beyond its seemingly modest formulation since it illuminates the pathways of economic decisions, policies, and forecasts.

Yet, even as we celebrate its insights, it is essential to shine a light on the equation's main limitations and acknowledge the critiques. The assumption that individuals possess foresight into future inflation can falter in turbulent times, undermining the equation's applicability. Furthermore, the equation's reliance on a risk-free real interest rate simplifies the risk profiles of financial markets, potentially leading to misrepresentations in complex scenarios. The Fisher equation, while invaluable, offers a simplified snapshot that might not encompass the full spectrum of economic reality.

In conclusion, the Fisher equation is another expression of the synergy between theory and application, offering insights that ripple from individual choices to global economic strategies. As economic landscapes evolve and new paradigms emerge, the Fisher equation's legacy endures. By embracing its insights while critically examining its limitations, we empower ourselves to dive into the complex currents of the financial world with greater understanding.

Chapter Takeaways

- The Fisher equation is a cornerstone concept that bridges the gap between nominal and real values, by factoring in the effects of inflation.
- Conceived by Irving Fisher, the equation emerged from a desire to comprehend the fundamental connections between money, interest rates, and inflation.
- The equation's formulation highlights the interrelation between nominal interest rates, real interest rates, and expected inflation.
- The Fisher equation helps individuals to make educated financial choices by revealing the inflation-adjusted costs of investments.
- Investors leverage the equation to recalibrate expectations and safeguard returns against the corrosive impact of inflation.
- Central banks utilize the equation's insights to set nominal interest rates that consider expected inflation.
- The equation bridges the gap between macroeconomic aggregate price levels and microeconomic individual financial decisions.
- The equation assumes individuals possess foresight into future inflation and relies on a simplified risk-free real interest rate, which can be critiqued in the face of uncertainty and real-world complexities.
- Some critics challenge the equation's linear framework and its ability to capture nonlinear economic dynamics.
- The Fisher equation endures as a tool that unites theory and application.

Revision Questions

1. What fundamental relationships does the Fisher equation uncover in Economics?
2. What role did Irving Fisher play in the emergence of the Fisher equation?
3. Explain the difference between nominal and real interest rates as revealed by the Fisher equation.
4. How does the Fisher equation empower individuals to make informed financial decisions?
5. What guidance does the Fisher equation offer to investors in dealing with uncertain economic landscapes?
6. How do central banks utilize the insights of the Fisher equation in formulating monetary policies?
7. How does the Fisher equation bridge the macro–micro gap in economic analysis?
8. What are some of the limitations associated with the Fisher equation?
9. How do economists critique the Fisher equation's framework?
10. In what ways does the Fisher equation's legacy endure in modern Economics?

CHAPTER 10

Net Present Value

Learning Objectives

- Understand the Concept of Net Present Value
- Analyze the Components of the NPV Equation
- Apply NPV in Various Cases
- Evaluate the Role of NPV in Decision-Making
- Identify the Limitations and Critiques of NPV

10.1 Introduction

In Economics and Finance, there is a continual search for tools that enhance precision in assessing the economic viability of investments. At the forefront of this pursuit lies the concept of Net Present Value (NPV). NPV, grounded in the fundamental principle of the time value of money, serves as a powerful tool for assessing projects over time. The narrative of Net Present Value (NPV) within Economic Science mirrors the discipline's pursuit of precision and sophistication in assessing investment feasibility. The genesis of NPV represents a seminal chapter, drawing from centuries of acknowledging the time value of money and culminating in a formalized methodology that changes the way economists evaluate the economic viability of projects.

P. G. Michaelides, *21 Equations that Shaped the World Economy*,
https://doi.org/10.1007/978-3-031-76140-9_10

This chapter examines NPV's theoretical foundations, practical applications, and profound implications within the broader economic landscape. It emerges as an indispensable metric, offering a quantitative approach to decipher the economic merit of diverse projects. The journey will uncover its mathematical expression and the principles that underlie its computations. Very simple examples will be provided to illustrate how NPV transcends mathematical abstraction to become a dynamic and pivotal tool for businesses, policymakers, and investors.

10.2 Net Present Value in Economics

As we know, the mid-twentieth century marks a watershed moment when economists and financial analysts, confronted with the complexities of investment appraisal, sought better mathematical tools. While the idea of the time value of money had lingered in economic discussions, it was the formalization of NPV that marked a substantial step forward. In particular, NPV framed the relationship between risk, return, and project valuation. The realization that future flows should be discounted to their present value became the center of NPV methodology.

The application of NPV permeated various branches of Economics and Finance, finding utility in public finance, environmental economics, and development economics. Its versatility as a tool for evaluating the economic worth of investments across diverse scenarios underscored its adaptability and universality. The latter part of the twentieth century witnessed a confluence of NPV with computational advancements. The emergence of powerful computing technologies enhanced economists' ability to conduct calculations efficiently. This not only facilitated a deeper understanding of the economic implications of projects but also made it accessible to a broader audience of decision-makers.

As NPV became integrated into economic analyses, its influence extended beyond academia and corporate boardrooms to shape policy decisions. Governments, businesses, and international organizations recognized the significance of NPV as a guiding metric for project evaluation, appreciating its capacity to account for the temporal element in resource allocation. The adoption of NPV by policy circles reflects its practical utility in informing decisions with long-term consequences. Furthermore, the evolution of NPV has been intertwined with advancements in financial theory and risk management. The incorporation of risk-adjusted discount rates and considerations for uncertainty broadened the applicability of NPV, enabling its use in scenarios where future cash flows are subject to varying degrees of risk. This expansion of NPV's scope aligns with the evolving landscape of economic dynamics, where risk and uncertainty are inherent features.

Therefore, the emergence of Net Present Value in Economics was not merely a historical event but a dynamic response to the evolving demands of decision-makers and economists. Just like other tools, the historical trajectory of NPV reveals not only its mathematical foundations but also its transformative impact on how economists operate in the terrain of investment evaluation in the ever-changing landscape of economic dynamics.

10.3 The Equation

To calculate NPV, we need to determine the expected cash inflows and outflows for a particular investment, e.g., project or business opportunity. Then, we discount each net cash flow (i.e., the inflows minus the outflows) to its present value, using a specific discount rate, which reflects the time value of money and the risk associated with the investment.

To derive the NPV equation, we start with the concept that a future net cash flow C_t at time t is the net cash flow present value $PV(C_t)$ grown by the interest rate r over t periods. For a period of, say, one (1) year, the net cash flow present value $PV(C_1)$ grown by the interest rate r is equal to C_1, namely:

$$PV(C_1)\cdot(1+r)=C_1$$

Solving for $PV(C_1)$, we get:

$$PV(C_1)=\frac{C_1}{(1+r)}$$

For a future cash flow C_2 at time 2, the Net Present Value $PV(C_2)$ grown by the interest r over two periods is equal to C_2:

$$\left[PV(C_2)\cdot(1+r)\right]\cdot(1+r)=C_2$$

since $PV(C_2)$ is grown by the interest rate r over *2* periods. This is equal to:

$$PV(C_2)\cdot(1+r)^2 = C_2$$

Solving for $PV(C_2)$, we get:

$$PV(C_2) = \frac{C_2}{(1+r)^2}$$

Similarly, the present value $PV(C_t)$ of a future cash flow C_t at time t can mathematically be expressed as:

$$PV(C_t) = \frac{C_t}{(1+r)^t}$$

Now, the *NPV* is equal to the sum of the present values of all future net cash flows, minus the initial investment I at time 0. Assume we have net cash flows C_0, C_1, C_2, ..., C_T in periods 0 through T. The initial investment I is often considered separately from C_0.

To calculate the *NPV*, we sum the present values of all future net cash flows and subtract the initial investment. This is mathematically expressed as:

$$NPV = \left[PV(C_0) + PV(C_1) + PV(C_2) + \ldots + PV(C_T)\right] - I \qquad (10.1)$$

Or, by plugging the aforementioned equations in Eq. (10.1), we get:

$$NPV = \left[\frac{C_0}{(1+r)^0} + \frac{C_1}{(1+r)^1} + \frac{C_2}{(1+r)^2} + \ldots + \frac{C_T}{(1+r)^T}\right] - I \qquad (10.2)$$

We often consider C_0 to be 0 if the initial investment I is treated separately.

Thus, the NPV can be expressed as:

$$NPV = \sum_{t=0}^{T} \frac{C_t}{(1+r)^t} - I \qquad (10.3)$$

In summary, NPV is the difference between the total present value of all future net cash inflows and the initial investment.

However, we have to note the following:

1. The choice of the discount rate r is crucial and requires careful consideration. It expresses the rate of return required to justify an investment, reflecting the cost of capital or the opportunity cost of investing in a particular project instead of an alternative. The discount rate depends on various factors like the prevailing interest rates, the project's risk, and the firm's cost of capital.
2. The heart of the NPV equation lies in the estimation of cash flows C_t, *in time* $t = 0, \ldots \ldots T$, which can include both inflows and outflows. These cash flows should be carefully forecasted, considering revenues, operating expenses, taxes, and any other financial implications related to the investment. Accuracy in projecting cash flows is paramount for the reliability of NPV analysis.
3. The NPV equation also depends on factors in the initial investment I, which encompasses all upfront costs associated with starting the investment project. This includes capital expenditures, working capital requirements, and any other costs related to the initiation of the project.
4. The NPV equation considers the entire time horizon of the investment, in periods 0 through T, usually measured in years. The choice of the time horizon is crucial as it determines the duration over which the project's performance is assessed.

The decision rule associated with NPV is straightforward. If the resulting NPV is positive ($NPV > 0$), it implies that the investment will generate more value than its cost, signaling its economic viability. A negative NPV ($NPV < 0$), on the other hand, may indicate that the project fails to achieve the desired rate of return. Given the inherent uncertainty in predicting future cash flows and selecting an appropriate discount rate, sensitivity analysis is often conducted. This involves assessing how variations in factors such as (1) cash flows, (2) discount rate, and (4) duration of the project impact NPV, providing investors with insights into the robustness of their financial projections.

Let's see a very simple numerical example. Imagine a small bakery owned by Vivian and Evina, who are considering investing \$1000 in a new piece of equipment for their shop. They expect this equipment to boost their bakery's earnings over the next three (3) years. They anticipate the following additional net cash inflows: \$300 in the first year, \$400 in the second year, and \$500 in the third year. To determine if this investment is worthwhile, they use a discount rate of 5%, reflecting the time value of money. By calculating the NPV of these expected net cash inflows, they can decide if purchasing the equipment will be beneficial for their shop's financial health.

Since $C_0 = 0$, substituting these values into Eq. (10.2), we get:

$$NPV = \frac{0}{(1+0.05)^0} + \frac{300}{(1+0.05)^1} + \frac{400}{(1+0.05)^2} + \frac{500}{(1+0.05)^3} - 1000$$

$$NPV = 0 + 285.71 + 362.81 + 431.92 - 1000 \approx 80.44$$

So, in this example, the Net Present Value (NPV) of the investment is approximately \$80.44. Since the NPV is positive, it implies that the investment would generate more value for Vivian and Evina than its cost, suggesting it should be undertaken.

10.4 Insights and Consequences

NPV carries profound implications, influencing decision-making processes, shaping investment strategies, and contributing to the broader understanding of the economic environment. NPV is a compass for strategic decision-making in both corporate finance and public sector investments. Companies utilize NPV to evaluate the financial viability of potential projects or acquisitions. For instance, consider an automobile company planning to install a new production line. NPV analysis would compare the present value of expected increased revenue from the new production line against the initial investment and relevant operating costs, guiding the company in deciding whether the investment aligns with its strategic objectives. Moreover, by incorporating sensitivity analysis, decision-makers can evaluate how changes in key variables, such as discount rates or cash flow projections, influence NPV. This aids in identifying potential vulnerabilities. In this context, a real estate developer assessing a new project in a relatively unstable macroeconomic environment might conduct sensitivity analysis to gauge the project's NPV under different interest rate scenarios, ensuring resilience against market fluctuations.

In capital budgeting, NPV guides organizations in allocating resources efficiently. In the context of public finance, government agencies employ NPV to assess the economic viability of public projects, such as infrastructure development. Consider a city government deciding whether to invest in a new public transportation system. NPV analysis would weigh the long-term benefits against the upfront and operational costs, aiding in the optimal allocation of public funds. NPV plays a pivotal role in financing decisions by providing information on the economic return on investment. Lenders and investors often rely on NPV analysis to assess the creditworthiness of a project.

For instance, a renewable energy project seeking financing would present NPV calculations to demonstrate the long-term economic benefits of clean energy generation compared to the initial investment, influencing investor decisions. In the world of mergers and acquisitions, NPV guides decisions on potential acquisitions or mergers. Companies assess the NPV of merging with or acquiring another business to determine whether the investment aligns with their growth objectives. For example, a technology firm considering the possibility of acquiring a smaller competitor would conduct NPV analysis to evaluate the combined entity's future cash flows and assess the acquisition's impact on shareholder value.

Even governments employ NPV to evaluate the economic impact of public policies. Whether it's a healthcare initiative or education reform, NPV allows policymakers to quantify the expected benefits and costs over time. For instance, a government considering a healthcare intervention might use NPV analysis to weigh the long-term societal benefits, like improved public health and productivity in the economy, against the associated costs. Finally, individual investors use NPV to evaluate the potential returns on different investment opportunities. A retail investor considering real estate investments, for instance, might utilize NPV to compare the expected cash flows and appreciation of various properties, helping them make educated decisions aligned with their financial goals.

10.5 Conclusion, Limitations, and Critiques

Based on our analysis of NPV within Economics and Finance, it becomes apparent that it plays a pivotal role in decision-making. Its significance lies in its ability to systematically assess the present value of future cash flows, thereby offering a quantitative basis for determining the economic viability of projects.

While NPV is a powerful metric, it is based on a number of assumptions that do not always align perfectly with the complexities of the real world. One notable limitation is the assumption of a constant discount rate over the project's life. In dynamic economic environments, where interest rates fluctuate, this assumption oversimplifies the evaluation process. NPV is also sensitive to the accuracy of net cash flow projections. Forecasting future net cash flows involves inherent uncertainties, and small errors in these projections could lead to significant variations in NPV outcomes. Moreover, the traditional NPV calculation doesn't account for qualitative factors such as managerial flexibility, brand value, or the impact of strategic options.

Critiques of NPV also go beyond its technical limitations and focus on other theoretical perspectives. Some critics argue that NPV gives priority to short-term profit over long-term sustainability. The focus on maximizing present value may lead to decisions that undervalue projects with extended payback periods but substantial long-term benefits. Also, in environmental economics, scholars question NPV's effectiveness in incorporating the full scope of environmental impacts. Furthermore, traditional NPV may not adequately capture the externalities associated with projects, such as ecological damage or social consequences. Moreover, NPV may perpetuate a narrow economic perspective, often neglecting societal well-being and equity considerations. The exclusive emphasis on cash returns may overlook other impacts of projects on communities, minorities, employment, and inequality.

In conclusion, while NPV stands as a pivotal tool, its limitations and critiques highlight the need for a context-aware approach. Decision-makers should complement NPV analyses with qualitative assessments, consider uncertainties in projections, and be attuned to the broader societal implications of their choices. By acknowledging these complexities, NPV can be wielded as a more holistic tool, contributing to sound decision-making in the ever-evolving landscape of Economics and Finance.

Chapter Takeaways

- NPV is a pivotal metric in Economics and Finance, aiding in decision-making, resource allocation, and financial valuation.
- We analyze the evolution of NPV, highlighting its transformative impact on economic analysis.
- NPV's influence extends to diverse economic applications, spanning corporate finance.
- The NPV equation incorporates the time value of money, discount rates, cash flows, and initial investments.
- NPV can assist in strategic decision-making, guiding firms, policymakers, and investors in assessing the projects.
- Sensitivity analysis is crucial in evaluating NPV, offering insights into the robustness of financial projections under varying conditions.
- We emphasize the limitations of NPV, such as assumptions of constant discount rates, sensitivity to cash flow projections, and the neglect of qualitative factors.
- Critiques of NPV highlight its potential bias toward short-term gains, overlooking long-term sustainability and societal well-being.
- NPV's exclusive focus on financial returns may neglect broader impacts on communities, minorities, employment and inequality.
- Decision-makers are urged to complement NPV analyses with qualitative assessments, consider uncertainties in projections, and be attuned to the societal implications of their choices.

Revision Questions

1. What role does NPV play in Economics and Finance?
2. Analyze the emergence and evolution of NPV.
3. Break down the NPV equation, highlighting the significance of discount rates, cash flows, and initial investments.
4. How does NPV guide strategic decisions in corporate finance and public sector investments?
5. How does NPV contribute to risk management in financing decisions?
6. Discuss the significance of sensitivity analysis in evaluating NPV.
7. Examine the diverse applications of NPV, providing real-world examples.
8. What are the limitations of NPV, and how do they impact its reliability?
9. Analyze the critiques of NPV, focusing on its potential biases and oversights.
10. Why is a context-aware approach necessary when using NPV in decision-making?

CHAPTER 11

The Income Accounting Equation

Learning Objectives

- Understand the Income Accounting Identity
- Analyze the Variables Within the Income Accounting Equation
- Evaluate the Concept of Equilibrium Income
- Apply the Income Accounting Identity to Real-World Scenarios
- Identify Critiques and Limitations of the Income Accounting Identity

11.1 Introduction

In Economics, understanding the patterns and relationships that define an economy is akin to deciphering a complex puzzle. The Income Accounting Identity, a cornerstone of Economic Science, offers a systematic and structured approach to uncovering this puzzle. Among other theoreticians, the roots of the Income Accounting Identity can be traced back to the pioneering work of economist John Maynard Keynes. Over time, it has evolved into an indispensable tool for economists, providing a robust framework for studying the ebbs and flows of income within an economy. The identity encapsulates the fundamental notion that every transaction in an economy involves an exchange of income.

P. G. Michaelides, *21 Equations that Shaped the World Economy*,
https://doi.org/10.1007/978-3-031-76140-9_11

At its core, the Income Accounting Identity embodies a set of relationships that highlight the interconnectedness of key economic variables. By examining how these elements interact, economists can paint a comprehensive picture of the factors driving economic activity. Beyond its theoretical foundations, the practical applications of the Income Accounting Identity are vast. Policymakers leverage its insights to formulate effective economic policies, businesses use it to assess market trends and consumer behavior, and researchers employ it to conduct empirical studies. Its adaptability makes it an invaluable tool in addressing contemporary economic challenges.

11.2 Income Accounting Identity in *Economics*

The emergence of the Income Accounting Identity in Economics represents a very important moment in the evolution of economic thought, marked by a departure from traditional, microeconomically founded models toward a more comprehensive understanding of macroeconomic dynamics. The intellectual landscape of the early to mid-twentieth century was shaped by the aftermath of the Great Depression, a period that necessitated a reevaluation of economic theories in light of unprecedented economic challenges.

John Maynard Keynes, a central figure in this intellectual creation, challenged classical economic doctrines with his revolutionary work. Keynes shifted the focus from individual markets to the broader concept of aggregate demand, urging economists to consider the economy as a unified whole. This *paradigm shift* laid the foundation for a more holistic view of economic analysis, setting the stage for the emergence of the Income Accounting Identity. Amid the practical challenges of post-Depression economic recovery, economists and policymakers needed tools that could capture the interconnected nature of economic activities.

The formalization of the Income Accounting identity found expression in the field of national income accounting. The identity, in its equation form, encapsulated the essential relationships between various economic components, asserting that the total income of an economy is equal to the total expenditures within that economy. This equation provided a framework for studying income generation, distribution, and utilization. The significance of the Income Accounting Identity lies in its versatility and adaptability. As economies became more complex and interconnected, the identity became a crucial tool for understanding the dynamics of modern economic systems. Today, the Income Accounting Identity stands as a foundational concept in economic analysis.

11.3 The Equation

The Income Accounting Identity encapsulates the core relationships in an economy. Its equation is as follows:

$$Y \equiv C + I + G + (X - M) \tag{11.1}$$

where:

Consumption expenditure *C* represents the spending on goods and services. It's a crucial component dependent on a variety of factors such as disposable income, consumer confidence, and interest rates. Understanding consumption patterns is vital for predicting economic trends and gauging the impact of various policy measures.

Investment expenditure *I* expresses the spending by firms on capital goods such as machinery and buildings. It also portrays the level of firm confidence, and expectations about future economic conditions. Investment is a critical driver of growth, as it contributes to the expansion of productive capacity and job creation.

Government spending *G* covers all expenditures by the public sector on goods, services, and infrastructure. It is a powerful tool for policymakers to influence economic activity. Changes in government spending, often driven by fiscal policy decisions, can impact overall demand, employment, and the well-being of citizens.

Net exports *X–M* denote the difference between a country's exports *X* and imports *M*. This term highlights the role of international trade in shaping an economy. A positive net export value contributes to economic growth, while a negative value implies that a country is importing more than it is exporting, potentially affecting its overall economic situation.

The Income Accounting Identity also provides a comprehensive method for calculating the so-called equilibrium income. For the economy to be in 'equilibrium,' the total output (income) produced by the economy must equal the total demand (aggregate spending) on that output. So, based on the Income Accounting Equation, we can derive the 'equilibrium income' in an open economy with government spending, in a Keynesian framework. In this context, the economy's total output *Y* is determined by aggregate demand, which includes consumption *C*, investment *I*, government spending *G*, and net exports *X–M*, as we have seen earlier.

In an open economy, i.e., one with international trade, aggregate demand is the sum of consumption, investment, government spending, and net exports, namely:

$$AD = C + I + G + (X - M)$$

However, the consumption function can be expressed as:

$$C = C_0 + c \cdot Y_d$$

where:

- C_0 is the autonomous consumption, i.e., consumption when income is zero
- c is the marginal propensity to consume
- Y_d is the disposable income equal to $Y - T$
- T is the total taxes

Therefore:

$$C = C_0 + c \cdot (Y - T)$$

Meanwhile, Investment is assumed to be autonomous, namely $I = I_0$, where I_0 is autonomous investment. Government spending is also assumed to be autonomous, namely $G = G_0$, where G_0 is autonomous government spending. Net exports are also assumed to be autonomous for simplicity, namely $(X - M) = NX_0$, where NX_0 is autonomous net exports.

Now, we substitute the expressions for consumption, investment, government spending, and net exports into the aggregate demand equation:

$$AD = C_0 + c \cdot (Y - T) + I_0 + G_0 + NX_0$$

In equilibrium, aggregate demand (AD) equals total output (Y):

$$Y = AD$$

Substituting the aggregate demand equation:

$$Y^* = C_0 + c \cdot \left(Y^* - T\right) + I_0 + G_0 + NX_0$$

Now, we solve for the equilibrium income Y^*:

$$Y^* = C_0 + c \cdot Y^* - c \cdot T + I_0 + G_0 + NX_0$$
$$Y^* - c \cdot Y^* = C_0 - c \cdot T + I_0 + G_0 + NX_0$$
$$Y^* \cdot \left(1 - c\right) = C_0 - c \cdot T + I_0 + G_0 + NX_0$$
$$Y^* = \frac{C_0 - c \cdot T + I_0 + G_0 + NX_0}{1 - c} \tag{11.2}$$

The derived formula highlights how the autonomous consumption, investment, government spending, taxes, and net exports are associated with the overall equilibrium income in the economy.

Let's use the derived formula and a very simple numerical example to illustrate the equilibrium income in an open economy with government spending. Let's assume:

- Autonomous consumption: $100
- Marginal propensity to consume: 0.8
- Taxes: $50
- Autonomous investment: $150
- Government spending: $200
- Net exports: $50

To calculate the equilibrium income Y^*, we will substitute the given values into Eq. (11.2). We plug in the numbers to calculate the equilibrium income:

$$Y^* = \frac{100 - 0.8 \cdot \left(50\right) + 150 + 200 + 50}{1 - 0.8} = \frac{460}{0.2} = 2300$$

The equilibrium income Y^* is $2300. Of course, relevant scenario analysis could be conducted.

11.4 Consequences and Insights

The Income Accounting Identity provides a lens through which economists and policymakers operate in the world of economic interactions. Consider consumption *C* as a prime mover in economic dynamics. Beyond the aggregate level, the identity prompts an analysis of individual and demographic variations. For instance, during periods of economic expansion, where consumer confidence is high, one might witness not only an overall increase in consumption but also shifts in spending patterns. Luxury goods and experiences may see a surge as discretionary incomes rise, offering insights not only into economic health but also into the social and cultural dimensions of spending behavior.

The investment component *I*, entwined with the pulse of businesses, extends beyond numerical fluctuations. Suppose an economy experiences a technological breakthrough, sparking innovation and increasing the efficiency of capital. In this context, the Income Accounting Identity anticipates a potential surge in investment as businesses strive to capitalize on this innovation, exemplifying how the identity is not just a formula but a dynamic notion reflecting the evolution of industries.

Government spending *G* is a policy variable, especially when analyzed through the prism of the Income Accounting Identity. During times of economic recession, where consumption and investment are sluggish, the identity suggests that an increase in government spending can act as a counterbalance. This could manifest in large-scale infrastructure projects, social welfare programs, or public sector initiatives, stressing the identity's role in guiding policy decisions.

The international trade dimension $X-M$ emphasizes the importance of global economic interdependence. Imagine a scenario where a country experiences a surge in imports, due to increased consumer demand for foreign goods. This import-driven spike is decoded by the identity, prompting a closer examination of trade policies, currency dynamics, and global economic linkages. It shows how changes in one part of the world can reverberate through the identity, impacting economic landscapes elsewhere.

Practically, the identity's implications also ripple through industries and sectors. In the renewable energy sector, for instance, considerations of government spending on green initiatives, consumer preferences affecting consumption of sustainable products, and potential investments in clean technologies collectively form a narrative that shapes the trajectory of environmental sustainability. In essence, the Income Accounting Identity is not merely a formulaic expression; it provides a lens through which to analyze not just the numerical values but the stories they tell about societal trends, and the interconnectedness of economies on a global scale.

11.5 Conclusion, Limitations, and Critiques

In conclusion, the Income Accounting Identity stands as a pivotal concept in economic analysis, providing a comprehensive framework for understanding the relationships within an economy. From one perspective, the Income Accounting Identity serves as a foundational tool for calculating Gross Domestic Product (GDP) and assessing the overall health of an economy. Moreover, the identity's application extends beyond theoretical frameworks into real-world scenarios. The simplicity of the identity makes it an invaluable asset in the economist's toolkit.

The Income Accounting Identity, while widely employed and acknowledged in economic analysis, faces several limitations that have been scrutinized and critiqued. These critiques go beyond the conventional use of the identity and also refer to its assumptions, oversimplifications, and the broader implications of its application. One central critique revolves around the assumption of full employment. The identity, as conventionally presented, operates within the context of an economy where output is equated with income and expenditures. However, this assumption ignores the persistent challenges of underemployment and unemployment. Economists argue that in real-world scenarios where labor markets are not operating at full capacity, the identity fails to accurately reflect the complexities of the employment landscape.

The treatment of government spending G within the identity has also drawn criticism. While the identity implies that an increase in government spending can stimulate economic activity, it may not consider the composition and quality of that spending. Some perspectives emphasize that the impact of government expenditure depends on a variety of factors like the nature of the spending (e.g., infrastructure, social programs, defense) and its distribution throughout the economy.

The identity's handling of the financial sector is another area of contention. Some economists, particularly those in the post-Keynesian and Marxist tradition, argue that the identity does not account for the complexities of financial intermediation and credit creation. In reality, the financial system plays a pivotal role in influencing investment decisions, interest rates, and overall economic dynamics, aspects that are not fully captured by the identity.

Moreover, the assumption of an international trade term $X-M$ is often criticized for overlooking the complexities and inequities immanent in global trade relationships. Critics argue that the identity's treatment of net exports assumes equal access to markets and a fair distribution of benefits, neglecting issues such as trade imbalances, currency fluctuations, and the unequal power dynamics among nations in the global economy.

The Income Accounting Identity is also faulted for its neutrality toward income distribution. While the identity treats all income as equal, critics argue that this overlooks the substantial disparities in wealth and income distribution within societies. Economists contend that the identity should incorporate considerations of inequality, as it is integral to understanding the social implications of economic policies and their potential impacts on overall economic stability.

In essence, the critiques of the Income Accounting Identity highlight the need for a more context-specific approach to economic analysis. They emphasize the importance of acknowledging real-world complexities, structural imbalances, and distributional considerations to enhance the accuracy and relevance of economic models. As the field of Economics evolves, these critiques contribute to ongoing discussions on refining analytical tools and frameworks for a more comprehensive understanding of economic systems.

Chapter Takeaways

- The Income Accounting Identity is a foundational concept in Economics, offering a systematic approach to understanding economic patterns.
- It traces its roots to economists like John Maynard Keynes, evolving into a useful tool for studying income dynamics.
- The identity encompasses relationships between the key macroeconomic variables.
- Its macro and micro perspectives enable a better understanding of aggregate economic performance and sector-specific trends.
- Policymakers leverage the identity to formulate effective economic policies, and businesses use it to assess market trends.
- The equation represents the equilibrium between total income and expenditures in an economy.
- Consumption, investment, government spending, and net exports each play a crucial role in shaping economic trajectories.

(*continued*)

(continued)

- The identity's implications extend to real-world scenarios, influencing decisions in areas like international trade, and fiscal policy.
- Critiques focus on assumptions of full employment, the treatment of government spending, oversimplification of savings, and the neutrality toward income distribution.
- Despite critiques, the Income Accounting Identity remains a powerful and adaptable tool, guiding economic analysis and decision-making.

Revision Questions

1. What are the origins of the Income Accounting Identity, and how has it evolved?
2. How did John Maynard Keynes contribute to the development of the Income Accounting Identity?
3. Explain the components of the Income Accounting Identity and their roles in shaping economic activity.
4. How does the Income Accounting Identity contribute to the computation of Gross Domestic Product (GDP)?
5. Analyze the practical applications of the Income Accounting Identity.
6. Elaborate on the implications of consumption patterns and investment dynamics within the Income Accounting Identity.
7. Discuss the emergence of the identity in response to economic challenges.
8. Analyze the critiques and limitations of the Income Accounting Identity, particularly regarding assumptions of full employment and income distribution.
9. In what ways does the Income Accounting Identity influence decision-making in renewable energy and international trade sectors?
10. Evaluate the significance and adaptability of the Income Accounting Identity in contemporary economic landscapes.

CHAPTER 12

The Nash Equilibrium

Learning Objectives

- Analyze the Strategic Behavior of Rational Actors
- Understand the Concept of Nash Equilibrium
- Apply Nash Equilibrium to Real-World Contexts
- Examine the Prisoner's Dilemma as a Key Example
- Evaluate the Challenges and Limitations of Nash Equilibrium

12.1 Introduction

Within the complex landscape of strategic interactions, where supply and demand are tightly interwoven with human decision-making, the Nash Equilibrium, crafted by John Nash and other brilliant minds, has revolutionized the way economists analyze outcomes in scenarios where individual actors must operate with self-interest, while considering the actions of others. In its essence, the Nash Equilibrium equation encapsulates the equilibrium point at which rational decision-makers, each driven by their own objectives, arrive when engaged in a situation involving strategic choices. Picture, for instance, a scenario where nations negotiate trade

P. G. Michaelides, *21 Equations that Shaped the World Economy*, https://doi.org/10.1007/978-3-031-76140-9_12

agreements while guarding their own economic interests. The Nash Equilibrium enables us to uncover the stable outcome that emerges when each participating country optimizes their choices given the decisions made by others, creating a harmonious convergence of interests.

To comprehend the mechanics of this concept, one must dive into the heart of Game Theory, a field of study that dissects strategic interactions. The Nash Equilibrium concept materializes from the principle that, in a strategic environment, individuals will adjust their choices only when it serves their best interests. Any deviation from their current strategy would lead to a less favorable outcome. Thus, equilibrium is attained when no one has a reason to unilaterally change their course of action, thus creating a state of balance.

The implications of the Nash Equilibrium equation are far-reaching. This equilibrium state serves as a compass for understanding not only market dynamics and competition but also cooperation, conflict, and negotiation. It uncovers the logic behind pricing strategies, cartel behavior, and the formation of alliances between nations, industries, firms, etc. Furthermore, its applications ripple across diverse disciplines, enriching political analysis and the social sciences' analysis of human behavior.

12.2 Nash Equilibrium in Economics

The application of the Nash Equilibrium concept in Economics finds its origins in the pioneering work of mathematician Antoine-Augustin Cournot. Cournot introduced a theory of oligopolistic competition, encompassing scenarios ranging from monopoly to perfect competition. He revealed the interdependence of economic outcomes among firms, a theme later analyzed by John Nash. While Cournot laid the groundwork for game analysis, he did not fully develop its comprehensive methodology in his research.

The path to Nash's theory commenced with Emile Borel's investigation of solving two-person games. Borel sought superior methods for game solution and introduced the concept of 'strategies,' which specify 'optimal' actions for each player in various circumstances. Building on Borel's foundational work, John von Neumann presented a model for sequential games with imperfect information, defining strategies as complete plans based on available information. Von Neumann emphasized that players should choose strategies prior to observing others' moves, and he outlined the essential elements of a competitive game: players, strategies, expected payoffs, and independent strategy selection, which he termed the 'normal form'.

Von Neumann's contribution marked a crucial step toward formalizing Game Theory, culminating in the establishment of the Nash Equilibrium. The Nash Equilibrium illuminates the stable point where rational actors make decisions in consideration of others' choices. This concept, rooted in Cournot's insights and nurtured through the works of Borel and von Neumann, has emerged as a cornerstone in understanding strategic interactions across various disciplines, shaping economic models, management strategies, and diverse fields like *Finance* and Political Science.

Until the era of John Nash, Economics primarily focused on production and distribution. Nash's work initially seemed confined to mathematical contexts with limited relevance to Economics as traditionally defined. However, by embracing a more 'behavioral' approach, which views *Economics* as the study of behavior within a broader social context, his theory assumed a pivotal role. This shift broadened the scope of Economics beyond concepts like market price determination and resource allocation in perfect competition. Game Theory emerged as a crucial analytical framework to study situations where decision-makers consider others' choices, especially in conflicting scenarios, without being fully dependent on those choices. This perspective is valuable for modeling conflicts among rational decision-makers, seeking to maximize utility, in a microeconomic setup.

A foundational work on game theory and economic behavior, *Game Theory and Economic Behavior*, was written in 1944 by von Neumann and Morgenstern. This groundbreaking work introduced concepts like cooperative games and formalized Game Theory's application to diverse economic problems. Nash's pivotal contributions include defining the equilibrium of non-cooperative games, exemplified by his historic 1950 article establishing the existence of equilibrium in normal form games. His realization of the non-cooperative equilibrium notion, coupled with von Neumann's normal form, offered a comprehensive methodological framework for analyzing a wide spectrum of games. Furthermore, Nash's work shed light on the concept of Pareto efficiency, where an equilibrium is optimal if no player can benefit without causing harm to another. This idea was influenced by Vilfredo Pareto, the founder of Pareto efficiency. In essence, Nash's groundbreaking insights transformed Economics into a study of rational behavior within social contexts, paving the way for the rigorous analysis of various strategic interactions.

12.3 The Equation

A Nash Equilibrium refers to a collection of strategies adopted by players in a manner where no player gains by altering their chosen strategy. In essence, this implies that even if a player were fully aware of the strategies employed by all other participants, they would still opt to stick with their initial approach. The Nash Equilibrium serves as a valuable tool for dissecting outcomes in competitive scenarios, particularly those relating to conflict. Similarly, it finds utility in dissecting economic elements such as markets, currencies, and auctions. These equilibria also facilitate the establishment of cooperation driven by self-interest, achieved by designing relative incentives that lead each actor to independently choose the desired action. The classic example of the Prisoner's Dilemma to be presented later on exemplifies this concept. Although, there is not one very specific formula to calculate the 'Nash Equilibrium' in all contexts, we will now slightly formalize the aforementioned analysis.

Let S_i express the set of all strategies for the i-th player, and S be the Cartesian product of the strategy sets for each player $S = S_1 \times S_2 \times \ldots \times S_n$. Essentially, the elements of S encompass all conceivable combinations of individual strategies. In other words, this means that S includes all possible combinations of strategies that players can choose from.

Furthermore, let $f_i(s)$ denote the payoff or return for player i given a strategy profile $s \in S$; it's important to note that a player's payoff depends not only on their own strategy but also the strategies of the other players. This function captures the interdependence of payoffs on player' i's own strategy and those of the other players.

Consequently, a Nash Equilibrium is defined as a strategy profile $s = (s_1, s_2, \ldots, s_n)$ that satisfies the condition:

$$f_i(s) \geq f_i\left(s_1, s_2, \ldots, s_{i-1}, s_i', s_{i+1}, \ldots, s_n\right) \text{ for all } s_i' \in S_i \tag{12.1}$$

for all players i, where $s_i' \in S_i$ denotes an alternative strategy for player i other than s_i available to them. This implies that a strategy profile $s = (s_1, s_2, \ldots, s_n)$ is indeed a Nash Equilibrium, if no player can improve their payoff or return by changing their strategy.

In cases where this inequality is strict, i.e.,

$$f_i(s) > f_i\left(s_1, s_2, \ldots, s_{i-1}, s_i', s_{i+1}, \ldots, s_n\right) \tag{12.2}$$

the profile s is deemed a *strict* Nash Equilibrium. Otherwise, it is referred to as a *weak* Nash Equilibrium. Nash's theorem assures that at least one Nash Equilibrium exists as long as S_i is finite for all players i and there is a finite number of players, which is derived from the famous Brouwer or Kakutani fixed point theorem, which underpins the existence of equilibrium in such settings.

Let's see now a very famous example. Imagine two individuals, A and B, both detained separately. Law enforcement lacks conclusive evidence to convict them of a murder they are suspected of committing jointly. In an attempt to procure confessions, the police propose an intriguing proposition to each prisoner: If both individuals admit to the murder, both will face a sentence of 10 years in prison. Alternatively, should one prisoner confess while the other denies involvement, the confessor will walk free (0), while the denier will be subjected to a lengthy 25-year prison term. Lastly, if both maintain their innocence regarding the murder charges, both will serve a reduced sentence of one (1) year each for their minor offenses. This set-up, encapsulated in the table below, has earned the name the 'Prisoner's Dilemma' (Table 12.1).

Examining the potential actions of both players reveals the corresponding outcomes enclosed in parentheses. The first number denotes the years of imprisonment for player A, while the second number signifies the imprisonment period for player B. Upon studying the provided table, it might be instinctual to conclude that both players should opt to deny the charges. This choice would seemingly lead to a minimal sentence of one (1) year each in prison. However, the concept of the 'Nash Equilibrium' diverges from this apparent logic. Let's see the reasons.

Given the game table at hand, player B is confronted with a binary decision: to either admit guilt or reject the charges. If player B opts to confess, player A's strategic move aligns with confessing as well, aiming to reduce their respective prison time to 10 years, instead of the threatening 25 years from both denying the charges. Conversely, if player B denies involvement, player A's 'optimal' response is confession, in order to avoid

Table 12.1 The Prisoner's Dilemma

		B	
		Confession	*Denial*
A	*Confession*	(10, 10)	(0, 25)
	Denial	(25, 0)	(1, 1)

imprisonment instead of serving just one (1) year in prison for denying confession. Consequently, regardless of B's choice, player A's most advantageous action is to confess.

Symmetrically, player B finds themselves in an analogous dilemma. Hence, both participants arrive at the rational conclusion of confessing, resulting in a scenario where both incur a 10-year prison sentence. Even if player A initially hoped for player B to deny the charges, allowing them both to serve a shorter one-year term, the rational course for player A would still involve confessing, so as to totally avoid imprisonment. In light of this, both players opt to confess, driven by their individual self-interests. In summary, the Prisoner's Dilemma compels both players to select 'confession' as their rational strategy, culminating in an outcome where both individuals are sentenced to 10 years in prison.

Of course, the concept of Nash Equilibrium reveals that even when one player is about to cooperate, the other may betray them for self-gain. This 'rational' behavior can lead to outcomes that seem counterintuitive, where individual decisions favor an equilibrium that maximizes self-interest, even if it's not collectively optimal just like in our analysis of the so-called Prisoner's Dilemma. A Nash Equilibrium represents a situation where players make choices that are unchanging in light of others' behavior, given their rationality. While this concept is appealing for its simplicity and stability, it doesn't necessarily yield the best outcomes for individuals or the group, and it might even lead to undesirable results. Hence, critiques highlight that the Nash Equilibrium can overlook factors like social norms, moral values, and collective behavior.

The Prisoner's Dilemma highlights the challenge of sustaining cooperation when collective interests clash with individual motives, potentially undermining cooperative efforts. Notably, the Nash Equilibrium may lack uniqueness, requiring alternative criteria for selection. Additionally, experimental results question the assumption of purely rational behavior, and extended gameplay experiences reveal higher cooperation levels, contrary to initial beliefs.

Nash advocated technology and algorithms for problem-solving, yet enthusiasm for Nash Equilibrium application waned due to computational challenges. Finding precise or approximate equilibria in complex games can be infeasible, with no efficient algorithm to compute them. As games involve more players, the practicality diminishes, rendering the task practically impossible, especially in some highly complex scenarios. This computational limitation implies that even markets cannot readily find Nash equilibria, emphasizing the complexity of these solutions.

12.4 Consequences and Insights

Nash Equilibrium carries significant implications in the field of Economics, offering valuable insights into various real-world scenarios and strategic interactions. The concept plays a pivotal role in understanding and predicting behaviors in complex economic environments. In industries characterized by a small number of dominant firms, known as oligopolies, Nash Equilibrium serves as a guiding principle for predicting how these firms set prices. For instance, in the airline industry, where a handful of carriers compete for passengers, the decisions made by each airline regarding ticket pricing have a direct impact on the others. Nash Equilibrium helps anticipate the stable pricing levels that will ultimately emerge as a result of these interactions.

Beyond pricing, Nash Equilibrium provides a framework for comprehending competitive dynamics in broader markets. In the retail sector, for example, multiple sellers may adjust their prices based on the actions of their competitors. By considering the strategic decisions of each player, Nash Equilibrium aids in predicting the eventual equilibrium points of stable pricing in markets with multiple sellers offering similar products. Advertising strategies also fall under the influence of Nash Equilibrium. Firms engaging in advertising campaigns must carefully allocate resources to promotional activities while weighing potential gains in market share. This equilibrium concept is evident in the smartphone market, where large companies strategically determine their advertising budgets based on the actions and reactions of their rivals.

Labor negotiations and agreements can also be modeled using Nash Equilibrium. When unions negotiate with management, both sides make decisions based on the anticipated actions of the other party. Nash Equilibrium helps analyze the equilibrium outcomes of such negotiations, providing insights into the terms of labor agreements. On a global scale, Nash Equilibrium is highly relevant to international trade scenarios. Countries engage in trade negotiations and formulate tariff policies, while considering the actions of their trading partners. This equilibrium concept is instrumental in understanding how nations strategically adjust trade barriers in response to the decisions made by their counterparts.

Environmental policy discussions, particularly those centered around addressing externalities like pollution, can benefit from Nash Equilibrium analysis. When countries attempt to attract firms by ‘relaxing’ environmental standards, a ‘race to the bottom’ could ensue. Nash Equilibrium aids in studying how nations can coordinate their policies to mitigate pollution, as a collective action. Resource allocation problems, such as fisheries management, also fall within the scope of Nash Equilibrium. In such scenarios, multiple stakeholders, like fishermen, make decisions on resource utilization based on the expectations of others. Nash Equilibrium helps identify sustainable harvest levels and offers insights into managing shared resources effectively.

Industries with network effects, like online platforms, showcase the significance of Nash Equilibrium in understanding user patterns. Firms aim to attract users, but individual decisions depend on the choices of others. Nash equilibrium provides a lens through which to analyze and predict the dynamics of user behavior. Even in the highly complex world of financial markets, Nash Equilibrium finds relevance. Investors make decisions based on their expectations of how others will act. In the stock market, for instance, Nash Equilibrium models can be used to anticipate price movements driven by traders' reactions to various factors.

Of course, to further comprehend the significance of the Nash Equilibrium in non-cooperative games, it's crucial to grasp the notion of 'rationality' within Economics. Game Theory places the 'rational player' at the center of economic dynamics, an actor who strategically pursues individual preferences to optimize personal utility, irrespective of collective action. This player is aware of others' potential strategies. However, this concept of a totally rational player is an abstraction, devoid of real-world complexities such as age, gender, emotion, and social context.

However, despite theoretical inconsistencies and empirical challenges, the 'rational behavior' assumption strongly persists in Economic Science for several reasons. It serves as a convenient, albeit imperfect, starting point for analysis. By portraying individuals in an abstract, objectified manner, economists can apply rigorous, strict, mathematical laws to model human and social behavior. Additionally, while empirical findings might deviate from mathematical predictions, such differences are often supposed to stem from individual 'irrationality' rather than a flaw in the theoretical framework.

Nash's contribution to Economics uncovers a crucial insight: the pursuit of relentless self-interest without considering collective well-being can lead to undesirable outcomes. This is evident in scenarios such as the Prisoner's Dilemma, where individualistic choices result in suboptimal collective outcomes. Consequently, it highlights that equilibria considered 'optimal' from an individual perspective may not translate to desirable collective states.

What's more, the practical applicability of Nash's theory faces very serious computational challenges in complex real-world economic problems. Calculating Nash equilibria becomes daunting when numerous players with diverse preferences, multiple moves, and potential outcomes are considered. Hence, this raises doubts about the 'equilibrium' view of the economic system. Consequently, an alternative to strict individualism could emerge through cooperative actions and mutually beneficial relationships. This approach can offer fresh perspectives on tackling social and economic challenges, potentially leading to improved outcomes.

12.5 Conclusion, Limitations, and Critiques

John Nash's revolutionary concept of Nash Equilibrium has left its mark on the world of *Economics*, uncovering dynamics that govern decision-making in competitive scenarios. At its core, the Nash Equilibrium postulates that individuals, acting rationally to maximize their own utility, settle on strategies that remain unaltered when known by all players. While this framework provides invaluable insights into theoretical analyses, its practical implications for Economics are multifaceted.

As we have seen, one of the most significant ramifications lies in the interpretation of individual behavior within economic systems. Nash Equilibrium offers a powerful tool to dissect complex interactions, shedding light on how market participants may arrive at stable outcomes in scenarios ranging from pricing strategies to resource allocation. This lens allows economists to discern patterns of behavior, anticipate market trends, and even formulate policies toward mutually beneficial results. Moreover, Nash Equilibrium provides a lens through which economists can dissect the dynamics of oligopolistic markets, where a limited number of firms dominate an industry. The concept of Nash Equilibrium has also found resonance as we have seen in the analysis of international trade and negotiations. Countries engaged in trade relationships often operate within a complex matrix of incentives and concessions. Nash Equilibrium helps elucidate how nations may position themselves strategically to maximize gains, whether by leveraging tariffs, quotas, or diplomatic moves. This understanding is especially relevant in trade negotiations, where Nash Equilibrium insights could guide diplomats toward mutually advantageous agreements.

Furthermore, the concept of Nash Equilibrium has led to a reevaluation of traditional economic *paradigms*, emphasizing the interplay between self-interest and collective well-being. While most economic theories often assume that rational individuals pursuing their own gain lead to socially optimal outcomes, Nash's work implies scenarios where this assumption breaks down. This and of course several other analyses have prompted the emergence of behavioral economics, a field which studies how psychological and cognitive factors influence decision-making, and may lead to outcomes diverging from traditional patterns.

In the practical world of policymaking, Nash Equilibrium informs the design and evaluation of regulatory frameworks. Understanding how individuals respond to incentives, constraints, and market conditions is crucial for crafting effective policies that align private interests with public goals. For instance, in the domain of environmental policy, Nash Equilibrium insights could inform the implementation of carbon pricing mechanisms or the negotiation of international climate agreements.

However, the limitations of Nash Equilibrium in real-world applications highlight significant areas where the model's assumptions diverge from actual market dynamics and human behavior. For Nash Equilibrium to hold, players must have complete information about the game structure, including payoffs and strategies available to all other players. For example, in markets, buyers and sellers often have different levels of information about the quality and value of goods and services. Traditional economic models, including those based on Nash Equilibrium, assume rational behavior devoid of psychological influences. In this context, Nash Equilibrium assumes that all players in a game are perfectly rational and will always make decisions that maximize their utility. However, behavioral economics has documented numerous biases that affect decision-making.

More precisely, Nash Equilibrium does not consider the impact of emotions on decision-making. Yet, emotions such as fear, anger, and empathy can significantly influence economic choices. For example, fear can lead to panic selling in financial markets, while empathy might drive cooperative behavior in social dilemmas, even when such actions are not predicted by Nash Equilibrium. Nash Equilibrium also assumes static preferences and strategies over time. In reality, preferences and strategies often evolve due to changing circumstances, learning, and adaptation. For instance, repeated interactions and long-term relationships can foster trust and cooperation, altering the strategic landscape and leading to outcomes that differ from the static predictions of Nash Equilibrium.

Despite these limitations, Nash Equilibrium remains a valuable framework for understanding strategic interactions. Its contributions to

Economic Science are profound, as it provides a systematic way to analyze how individuals and firms behave in competitive and cooperative environments. Nash Equilibrium helps economists model competitive markets, and in understanding how firms set prices and output levels and engage in strategic behavior. It provides insights into market structures, such as oligopolies, where firms must consider the reactions of their competitors when making decisions. Additionally, Nash Equilibrium is instrumental in dissecting strategic interactions, offering insights into both cooperative and competitive dynamics. This makes it an indispensable asset in the economist's toolkit, capable of offering profound implications for economic analysis.

Chapter Takeaways

- Nash Equilibrium reveals the strategy of individuals in competitive scenarios, focusing on outcomes where no player benefits from changing their strategy.
- The equilibrium assumes that players are 'rational' and aware of each other's possible strategies, making decisions to maximize their own utility.
- The Prisoner's Dilemma exemplifies the challenge of cooperation versus self-interest, illustrating how rational choices can lead to suboptimal outcomes.
- Nash Equilibrium has practical applications in analyzing markets, auctions, and conflict scenarios, providing insights into how players interact and make decisions.
- The concept challenges 'perfect rationality,' acknowledging that human behavior can deviate due to factors like emotions, biases, and incomplete information.
- Nash Equilibrium's abstraction of the 'rational player' simplifies analyses but does not capture all the complexities of real-world decision-making.
- The equilibrium model informs policymaking by offering insights into incentive structures, regulatory design, and international negotiations.
- While Nash Equilibrium is a powerful tool, its computational feasibility can be limited in complex scenarios with numerous players and strategies.

(*continued*)

(continued)

- Nash's work underscores the tension between individual self-interest and collective well-being, encouraging a holistic approach to understanding economic interactions and their impact on society.
- Ultimately, Nash Equilibrium provides a valuable framework for analyzing strategic interactions, fostering a deeper understanding of economic behavior.

Revision Questions

1. What is Nash Equilibrium, and how does it characterize the strategic behavior of rational players in competitive situations?
2. Explain the concept of the Prisoner's Dilemma and how it expresses the tension between individualism and more collective outcomes.
3. How does Nash Equilibrium apply to real-world scenarios such as markets, auctions, and conflict resolution?
4. Discuss the assumption of perfect rationality in Nash Equilibrium and its limitations in capturing human decision-making complexities.
5. How does behavioral economics challenge the idealized notion of the 'rational player' in Nash Equilibrium?
6. What role does Nash Equilibrium play in informing policy decisions and regulatory design in various economic contexts?
7. In what ways can computational limitations impact the practical applicability of Nash Equilibrium in complex scenarios?
8. How does Nash's work highlight the balance between individual motivations and collective well-being?
9. How has the concept of Nash Equilibrium influenced our understanding of strategic interactions and decision-making processes?
10. Considering the tension between individual and collective interests, how can Nash Equilibrium guide us in achieving socially optimal outcomes in a diverse and interconnected world?

CHAPTER 13

Capital Asset Pricing Model

Learning Objectives

- Understand the Fundamentals of the CAPM
- Analyze the Mathematical Formulation of CAPM
- Apply CAPM to Financial Decision-Making
- Evaluate the Applications of CAPM
- Identify the Limitations and Critiques of CAPM

13.1 Introduction

In the ever-evolving world of Finance, where uncertainty and opportunity intermingle, one indispensable theoretical scheme has redefined how we perceive, assess, and strategize investments: the Capital Asset Pricing Model, also known as CAPM. Rooted in the bedrock of modern finance, CAPM serves as a milestone for investors, analysts, and researchers. A key feature of CAPM is that it provides a framework beyond mere number crunching, elevating investment decisions to a level of informed and 'rational' decision-making.

This chapter will study CAPM, its mathematical underpinnings, and the insights it bequeaths. Through this model, we can envisage the situation wherein investors optimize their portfolios in pursuit of the nexus

P. G. Michaelides, *21 Equations that Shaped the World Economy*,
https://doi.org/10.1007/978-3-031-76140-9_13

between risk and reward. We shall traverse its genesis, tracing its evolution to its present stature as a cornerstone of financial theory. Its elegance in explicating the systematic risk encapsulated in 'beta' cannot be denied, yet its assumptions—such as frictionless markets and rational investors—invite questions in a world often governed by emotions and market imperfections.

We shall decipher how this model's delicate interplay of risk and return finds resonance in portfolio diversification, guiding us to craft balanced portfolios that harness reward while mitigating risk. The very notion of required rates of return takes on new meaning as we grasp CAPM's role. As a result of its relevance, the model enables us to dissect financial phenomena, develop investment strategies, and seize opportunities in the market's dynamic fluctuations.

13.2 CAPM in Economics

To truly appreciate the emergence of the Capital Asset Pricing Model (CAPM) in Finance, one must journey briefly through the historical currents that gave rise to this groundbreaking theory. As we know, the mid-twentieth century was a period of intellectual ferment, characterized by the post-World War II reconstruction, burgeoning financial markets, and a quest for systematic understanding of the world of investments. The aftermath of World War II brought about a pressing need for economic revitalization. As economies sought stability and growth, the question of how to allocate resources and encourage investment took center stage. This environment spurred economists to scrutinize investment decisions, setting the stage for the birth of CAPM.

Central to CAPM's emergence was Harry Markowitz's work on portfolio theory in the 1950s. Markowitz's insight that diversification could mitigate risk resonated deeply. This perspective challenged the prevailing belief that risk could be avoided through careful selection of individual securities. Markowitz introduced a quantitative framework to assess and manage investment risk. This marked a significant departure from the approaches that had previously dominated investment decision-making.

As the 1960s dawned, the convergence of brilliant minds further fueled the development of CAPM. Markowitz's research works were refined and extended. One of these contributions was the introduction of 'beta'—the systematic risk of an asset—as the key determinant of its expected return within a well-diversified portfolio. This marked a watershed moment, as the notion of 'beta' elegantly captured an asset's contribution to the overall risk of a portfolio. The model provided a benchmark, allowing investors to compare the risk-adjusted performance of assets.

In this framework, the historical context of the 1960s was ripe for CAPM's acceptance. Financial markets were rapidly evolving, and the need for a standardized approach to valuing assets and assessing risk became apparent. CAPM's quantitative nature and ability to provide a technical foundation for understanding the risk-return trade-off resonated with academia, practitioners, and regulators. It was a response to the *ad hoc* methods of pricing assets prevalent at the time, methods that usually relied on intuition, trial and error, and market sentiment.

13.3 The Equation

The basic CAPM equation expresses the relationship between risk, expected return, and market equilibrium. Its mathematical formula encapsulates a wealth of insights, empowering investors to make informed decisions within the dynamic landscape of investment opportunities. The CAPM equation is:

$$E(R_i) = R_f + \beta_i \cdot \left[E(R_m) - R_f \right] \tag{13.1}$$

where:

1. Expected Return $E(R_i)$ represents the anticipated future return an investor foresees for a specific asset *i*. It combines both the compensation for risk and the potential for reward.
2. Risk-Free Rate R_f symbolizes the minimum return investors expect for placing their funds in a risk-free asset, usually a government bond. It serves as a reference point against which the returns of riskier assets are measured.
3. Beta β_i is the defining feature of CAPM, which expresses an asset's sensitivity to market movements. Assets with a beta of 1 will move in line with the market, while assets with a beta below 1 will be less volatile, and assets with a beta above 1 will be more volatile. Volatility here measures how much and how quickly the value of an asset rises and falls, indicating the level of risk relative to the market. Securities with negative betas move in the opposite direction of the market,

while securities with a beta of zero are unrelated to the performance of the market. Let's see some very simple examples.

(a) A firm with a β greater than 1 is more volatile than the market. For example, a high-risk cryptocurrency company with an average of 1.75 would have earned 175% of what the market returned in a particular period.
(b) A company with a β lower than 1 is less volatile than the whole market. For instance, a gas utility company with a beta of 0.45 would have returned 45% of what the market returned during the same period.
(c) A firm with a negative β is negatively related to market returns. For instance, a gold company with a factor of −0.2 would have returned −2% in an environment where the market was up 10%.

4. The Market Risk Premium $[E(R_m) - R_f]$ is a term that expresses the 'excess' return that investors expect for investing in the market over a risk-free rate. It captures the additional compensation required for embracing uncertainty and variability inherent in the broader market.

Let's see now another very simple example, to illustrate the CAPM equation's application explicitly. Consider a scenario involving a stock in the technology sector. Let's assume the risk-free rate (R_f) is 3%, the expected return of the overall market ($E(R_m)$) is 10%, and the beta (β) of the technology stock is estimated at 1.5.

Using the CAPM equation, we can compute the expected return for the stock i:

$$E(R_i) = 0.03 + 1.5 \cdot (0.10 - 0.03)$$

or

$$E(R_i) = 0.135 \text{ or } 13.5\%$$

In this hypothetical example, the CAPM estimates that the technology stock should yield an expected return of 13.5%. This figure accounts for the risk-free rate and the stock's higher beta, reflecting its greater volatility compared to the overall market. Investors evaluating the stock's potential return against its associated risk can use this estimate to inform their decisions.

13.4 Consequences and Insights

CAPM resonates across Finance with profound implications that shape the way we understand risk, return, and the dynamics of investment decisions. It stands not merely as a mathematical formula, but as a framework that has left a mark on theory, practice, and policy. One of the main contributions of CAPM is its role in fostering a common language for assessing risk and return. Before its inception, investors and analysts grappled with a disparate array of methods to analyze investment opportunities. CAPM distilled this complexity into a single equation, rendering the trade-offs between risk and expected return tangible. This transformation from subjective intuition to a quantifiable relationship catalyzed a change in investment practices. In the world of portfolio management, the 'beta' became an essential tool for diversification, allowing investors to harmonize assets with different risk profiles. CAPM's prescription for risk reduction through diversification evolved from theory to actionable strategy, guiding investors toward maximizing returns, for a given level of risk.

The relationship between CAPM and asset valuation is symbiotic. The model's equation establishes a coherent link between an asset's inherent risk and its expected return, thus providing a benchmark for pricing. It's a compass for asset allocation, merger evaluations, and capital budgeting decisions. In academia, CAPM's emergence triggered a revolution in financial thought. It inspired a wave of research and empirical testing that sought to validate its assumptions and refine its predictions. This ethos of empirical scrutiny has seeped into all corners of *Finance*, fostering a culture of evidence-based decision-making that seeks to bridge the gap between theory and reality. In summary, the CAPM equation serves as a useful tool in modern finance. Through its application, investors gain insights into the pricing of assets and can make informed decisions in their pursuit of optimal investment portfolios.

13.5 Conclusion, Limitations, and Critiques

As we draw the threads of our analysis of CAPM together, we stand in awe of the profound impact it has cast upon the landscape of Finance. CAPM's introduction wasn't a mere intellectual exercise; it was a pivotal moment that revolutionized how we perceive and analyze the complex relationship between risk and return in investment decisions.

However, while CAPM's legacy is undeniable, it does not stand immune to criticism. Its assumptions of frictionless, efficient markets and rational investor behavior have been challenged by the rise of behavioral finance and the recognition of market anomalies. The model's sensitivity to input assumptions and its inability to account for idiosyncratic risk cast shadows on its predictive accuracy. These critiques remind us that while CAPM's elegance has reshaped the field, it is crucial to acknowledge its limitations. Real-world markets are marred by imperfections, investor biases, and complex interactions that may defy the model's idealized premises. This is where the richness of financial thought comes into play, through dialogue, debate, and the quest to refine and evolve theories to better capture the multifaceted realities of global markets.

In sum, the implications of CAPM encompass a web of insights that span from investor psychology to market structure. It offers a shift, transforming the abstractions of financial theory into actionable strategies. Its historical significance, its role in shaping modern portfolio management and asset valuation, and its influence on academic research collectively paint CAPM as a foundational pillar in Finance. In conclusion, the emergence of CAPM was not merely a result of theoretical musings; it was woven into the historical mosaic of the mid-twentieth century, shaped by the imperatives of post-war economic reconstruction, the complexities of financial markets, and the intellectual endeavors of visionary scholars. CAPM has not only stood the test of time but has also fostered a continuum of analysis and adaptation, enriching our understanding of financial phenomena and challenging us to push the boundaries of financial theory further.

Chapter Takeaways

- The emergence of CAPM was influenced by post-World War II economic imperatives and the need for standardized investment approaches.
- CAPM's original foundation lies primarily in the works of Harry Markowitz.
- CAPM revolutionized investment practices by quantifying the relationship between risk and expected return.
- CAPM redefines asset valuation by linking an asset's inherent risk to its expected return, providing a benchmark for assessing its value in relation to the market.

(*continued*)

(continued)

- CAPM's formula encapsulates risk-free rates, 'beta,' and the market risk premium, enabling investors to make informed decisions.
- The model's implications are far-reaching, transforming portfolio management by advocating diversification strategies that balance risk and reward.
- CAPM's applications extend beyond practical investment decisions to academic research, driving empirical testing and refining financial thought.
- The model's assumptions have been subject to scrutiny by behavioral finance.
- CAPM's limitations remind us of the complexities inherent in real-world markets, and its legacy is enriched by ongoing dialogue and adaptation.
- Ultimately, CAPM's legacy is marked by its enduring impact on the field, transforming financial landscapes and guiding investment strategies.

Revision Questions

1. What does CAPM stand for, and why is it considered a cornerstone in Finance?
2. How did the historical context of the mid-twentieth century contribute to the emergence of CAPM?
3. What role did Harry Markowitz play in CAPM's development?
4. Describe the core components of the CAPM equation and explain the significance of each.
5. How does CAPM transform portfolio management practices? Explain its role in diversification.
6. What is the relationship between CAPM and asset valuation? How does it provide a benchmark for pricing assets?
7. How did CAPM influence academic research in Finance? What is its role in empirical testing?
8. Discuss the assumptions underlying CAPM and explain the critical perspectives.

(*continued*)

(continued)

9. What are the implications of CAPM's limitations in real-world market scenarios?
10. Summarize the legacy of CAPM and its enduring impact on investment decision-making, portfolio management, and financial theories.

CHAPTER 14

Quantity Theory of Money

Learning Objectives

- Trace the Historical Evolution of the QTM
- Understand the Fundamentals of the QTM
- Analyze the Relationship Between Money Supply and Prices
- Evaluate the Applications of the QTM in Monetary Policy
- Identify the Limitations and Critiques of the QTM

14.1 Introduction

The Quantity Theory of Money (QTM) is another fundamental theory in Economics that analyzes the relationship between the quantity of money and certain economic variables, such as prices and output. It is considered one of the oldest theories in Economics, and provides a framework for analyzing the impact of changes in the money supply on the economy. The theory's central proposition suggests that changes in the quantity of money in an economy directly influence the level of prices, assuming other factors remain constant.

P. G. Michaelides, *21 Equations that Shaped the World Economy*, https://doi.org/10.1007/978-3-031-76140-9_14

The motivation for studying the QTM arises from the profound influence that money has on our lives and the functioning of modern economies. In general, money is considered to act as (i) a medium of exchange, (ii) a store of value, and (iii) a unit of account enabling the functioning of transactions and facilitating economic activities. However, money also acts as an end in itself. For instance, very often a commodity, i.e., product or service, is sold to replace this commodity with money. Hence, instead of facilitating commodity circulation, money is an end in itself. As a result, comprehending the factors that determine the quantity of money is important for policymakers, investors, businesses, and individuals alike.

By leveraging the QTM, economists seek to unravel the relationship between the supply of money and the broader economic landscape. They strive to comprehend the implications of monetary policy decisions and fluctuations in the money supply, helping guide policymakers in making educated choices. Furthermore, the QTM plays a crucial role in analyzing long-term economic trends and the dynamics of economic development. It is a lens through which economists study the relationship between changes in the money supply, economic output, and inflation. By examining historical data and evidence, economists can empirically assess the validity of the theory and refine their understanding of how monetary factors impact economic performance.

14.2 Quantity Theory of Money in Economics

The development of Economic Science throughout history has witnessed the emergence of various theories and concepts, aimed at understanding the workings of monetary systems. Among these theories, the QTM stands as a cornerstone of monetary economics. To grasp the origins of the QTM, we must first present early ideas about money and its role in the economy. Ancient civilizations, such as Mesopotamia, Egypt, and Greece, recognized the importance of a medium of exchange. While Aristotle, among others, is argued to have highlighted the role of money as a measure of value and a medium for exchange, Bodin was probably the first who emphasized the impact of the quantity of money on prices.

The rise of mercantilism between the sixteenth and eighteenth centuries influenced monetary theories. Mercantilist thinkers focused on accumulating precious metals, particularly gold and silver, as a measure of national wealth. This perspective laid the groundwork for early quantitative theories of money, as scholars began to ponder the relationship between the money supply and economic prosperity. Next, we face a significant shift in economic thought, moving away from mercantilism toward other perspectives on money and its impact. During this period, thinkers began to question prevailing notions and develop key concepts that would influence the formulation of the QTM.

The well-known philosopher and economist David Hume made contributions which outlined how changes in the money supply could affect prices through international trade imbalances. Hume's ideas on money played a pivotal role in the QTM. He stated that changes in the money supply would ultimately influence relative prices, but not necessarily real economic variables such as output and employment. His insights provided an inspiration for further investigation by subsequent thinkers.

The economists of the Classical School, including Adam Smith and David Ricardo, in a very general sense included certain aspects of the QTM in their broader theoretical frameworks. Smith emphasized the long-run relationship between money and prices, while Ricardo highlighted the importance of relative prices. Next, Marx's and Marxists' views differ significantly from other economic perspectives. It is true that Marx himself did not extensively discuss the QTM in his works. However, Marxists have offered their interpretations and criticisms of the theory based on their broader understanding of capitalism and its dynamics. For instance, most Marxists argued that changes in the money supply act as a response to changes in money demand resulting from the total economy's movements. They view money as a 'social relation' embedded within the capitalist system. Money, in this perspective, plays a role in facilitating the exploitation and alienation of labor, reinforcing class divisions, and maintaining capitalist relations of production.

Furthermore, Marxists argue that the QTM overlooks the significance of financialization and the role of finance capital in shaping the economy. They contend that the expansion and contraction of credit, financial speculation, and the power of banks and financial institutions have substantial impacts on economic activity and are not adequately captured by a narrow focus on the money supply. Moreover, Marxists emphasize the historical specificity of money and its relationship to the economic system. They contend that the QTM, with its focus on the relationship between money and prices, does not sufficiently account for the historical development of money within capitalist societies and the distinct role it plays in the capitalist mode of production.

However, the previous centuries witnessed a revolution in economic thought with the advent of marginalist economics. This *paradigm shift* brought about new insights into the nature of value and allocation decisions. Within this framework, the QTM found its place, as neoclassical economists incorporated it into their theories. They emphasized the 'subjective' nature of value and how changes in the money supply affect individuals' marginal utility and purchasing power. The QTM continued to evolve throughout the twentieth century. The (post-)Keynesian critique highlighted the limitations of the classical QTM, as it failed to account for the complexities of aggregate demand and the potential for output gaps. However, economists like the famous neoliberal Milton Friedman and the monetarist school revitalized the QTM by emphasizing the importance of stable monetary policy. Post-Keynesian perspectives and empirical studies have also challenged the basic assumptions and implications of the QTM, focusing on the direction of causality between prices and money. In contemporary Economics, the QTM has undergone further reinterpretation and refinement, and economists have examined various factors that can influence the relationship between money and prices.

14.3 The Equation

This section analyzes the meaning and significance of the QTM equation, presenting its core concepts within economic analysis. It is often expressed as:

$$M \cdot V = P \cdot T \tag{14.1}$$

where:

- M expresses the quantity of money circulating in the economy
- V denotes the velocity of money. i.e., the average number of times a unit of currency is spent
- P represents the price level, i.e., the average level of prices in the economy
- T represents the real output, i.e., the quantity of goods and services produced

The QTM views money primarily as a medium of exchange, facilitating transactions and serving as a widely accepted means of payment. Changes in the quantity of money can influence the ability of individuals and businesses to engage in transactions and affect the overall level of economic activity. Friedman reformulated the QTM, attempting to show that it could help deal with persistent inflation and deep recessions.

According to the basic equation (14.1) of the QTM set out earlier, Friedman asserted that the velocity of money circulation stays relatively stable, similar to the volume of transactions. Given that both the velocity of circulation *V* and the volume of transactions *T* are almost constant, the primary relationship to consider is between the quantity of money *M* and the general price level *P*.

Mathematically:

$$V \equiv a$$

and

$$T \equiv b$$

with *a* and *b* being arbitrary positive constants.

By plugging these two values in Eq. (14.1), we obtain:

$$M \cdot a = P \cdot b \tag{14.2}$$

According to Friedman, changes in the quantity of money cause changes in the general price level, not the other way around. Namely, causality (→) is as follows:

$$M \rightarrow P \tag{14.3}$$

or

$$\Delta M \rightarrow \Delta P \tag{14.4}$$

where: Δ implies a change in variables *M* and *P*, respectively.

One of the crucial implications of the QTM is its connection to inflation. This theory suggests that an increase in the money supply, assuming other factors remain constant, will lead to a rise in prices, based on the direction of causality analyzed earlier. Consequently, the theory provides insights into the link between monetary policy, money supply, and inflationary pressures. Meanwhile, government fiscal policy is either ineffective or unable to impact economic activity significantly, unlike monetary policy, which can be beneficial under certain conditions.

Here's a very simple numerical example to illustrate the basic mechanism of the QTM. Let's assume the following initial conditions in a hypothetical economy: the money supply (M) is \$1000, the velocity of money (V) is 5, meaning each unit of currency is spent five times on average in a year, the price level (P) is \$10, and the real output (T) is 500 units of goods and services.

Given these values, we can use Eq. (14.1) to see how these variables relate. Substituting in the given values, we get:

$$1{,}000 \cdot 5 = 10 \cdot 500$$
$$5000 = 5000$$

Now, let's examine what happens if the money supply M increases to \$1200 while keeping the other factors constant. Let's assume that in the new conditions, the money supply M is \$1200, the velocity of money V remains 5, and the real output T remains 500. Using Eq. (14.1) again, we get:

$$1{,}200 \cdot 5 = P \cdot 500$$
$$P = \frac{6000}{500} = 12$$

So, with the increase in the money supply from \$1000 to \$1200, the price level (P) rises by 20%, from \$10 to \$12, assuming the velocity of money and the real output remain constant. This example demonstrated the basic premise of the QTM: an increase in the money supply leads to a proportional increase in the price level, assuming other factors are constant.

14.4 Consequences and Insights

As we have seen, one of the primary implications of the QTM is its relationship to inflation. The theory suggests that, assuming other factors remain constant, an increase in the quantity of money in circulation will lead to a rise in prices, with the causality direction mentioned earlier. This occurs because an excess supply of money relative to the available goods and services is supposed to put upward pressure on prices. Similarly, a decrease in the money supply will result in lower prices. Analyzing this relationship is crucial for policymakers in maintaining price stability.

The QTM has significant implications for monetary policy. Central banks and policymakers utilize the theory to guide their decisions regarding the money supply. For instance, if there is a concern about rising inflation, policymakers are supposed to implement contractionary monetary policies to reduce the growth rate of the money supply. Conversely, during periods of economic downturn or deflationary pressures, expansionary monetary policies are supposed to be needed to increase economic activity by stimulating the money supply. Milton Friedman argued that governments and central banks should establish a monetary framework to ensure the effective functioning of the private sector. He introduced the 'monetarist rule,' which advocates for a constant annual increase in the money supply to match the growth of output and population. According to this rule, the optimal approach for monetary authorities is to adjust the money supply in line with long-term real growth, while allowing the market to handle short-term fluctuations independently.

The QTM also emphasizes the role of financial intermediation and velocity in the economy. Financial intermediaries, such as banks and other financial institutions, facilitate the flow of money and credit in the economy. Changes in financial intermediation can affect the velocity of money. For example, a decrease in the velocity of money may indicate a decline in economic activity and demand, which can inform policymakers about the effectiveness of monetary policy measures.

14.5 Conclusion, Limitations, and Critiques

In summary, the QTM equation has historically offered insights into the link between the money supply and price levels in economic theory. Nonetheless, it is crucial to recognize the limitations of this theory. While the QTM provides insights, it has faced realistic challenges. For instance, changes in expectations about future inflation can influence individuals' behavior, impacting wages, prices, and the overall dynamics of the money supply. Additionally, extensions to the theory have sought to incorporate these factors and refine the understanding of how the money supply impacts economic variables. These extensions aim to provide a deeper analysis that accounts for the dynamic nature of the economy and the interactions between money and other economic factors.

For instance, the direction of causality between prices and the quantity of money is a topic of debate and different interpretations exist. While the QTM suggests a directional relationship where changes in the quantity of money cause changes in prices, there are other alternative perspectives that consider the direction of causality to be more complex and multidirectional. These alternative views emphasize that changes in prices can also influence the demand for money and the velocity of money, which in turn affects the quantity of money supplied. Famous critics, including post-Keynesianism and Marxism, argue that the quantity of money can be 'endogenous' to the economic system. They believe that the creation of credit money and demand for investment can lead to an increase in the money supply, challenging Friedman's assumption of 'exogeneity.' Marxist economists also emphasize that money is the result of the commodity production process and the expression of value and capital.

The application of the typical version of the QTM equation to economic and social spheres has faced obstacles, and empirical evidence has often *not* supported the conventional, 'exogeneity' approach. For example, during the 2006–2009 credit crunch, expansionary monetary policies did not lead to the predicted inflationary pressures and post-Keynesian and Marxist economists, with their 'endogenous' view of money, have provided a different explanation.

In light of these limitations, it is crucial to adopt a more comprehensive and holistic understanding of the relationship between prices and the quantity of money. By incorporating these diverse perspectives and embracing a broader approach to economic analysis, we can acquire a richer understanding of the complexities and dynamics of the monetary system. In conclusion, the equation of the QTM should be seen as one among many tools in the economic toolkit, rather than an 'absolute truth'. Embracing these limitations challenges us to critically examine the assumptions underlying economic theories and encourages us to examine different frameworks that consider the multidimensionality of economic phenomena. Such an inclusive approach is vital for the economy and for guiding policy decisions.

Chapter Takeaways

- The QTM states that an increase in the quantity of money, assuming other factors remain constant, will lead to higher prices.
- Changes in the money supply are said to impact economic stability and output, with an excessive increase leading to inflationary pressures and a decrease potentially resulting in economic contraction.
- The QTM provides useful insights into long-term economic trends by focusing on the relationship between changes in the money supply, economic output, and inflation.
- Financial intermediation and velocity play important roles in the theory, as changes in financial intermediation can affect the velocity of money.
- Critics argue that the QTM oversimplifies the economy and neglects factors like changes in the total economy's response and the institutional framework.
- The theory is said to have significant implications for monetary policy.
- The theory could have practical applications in guiding decisions on money supply growth targets and inflation management.
- The implications of the QTM highlight the need to consider the dynamic nature of the economy, and the interplay between different variables and the economy.
- By incorporating the insights and refinements of the theory, policymakers can strive to maintain price stability and promote sustainable economic growth.
- Different economic theories and empirical studies provide different perspectives on the nature and direction of causality between prices and the quantity of money.

Revision Questions

1. What is the relationship between the quantity of money and inflation according to the QTM?
2. How does the QTM inform monetary policy decisions?
3. Explain the implications of the QTM for economic stability.
4. What is the difference between the two directions of causality in the context of the QTM?
5. How does the QTM relate to the role of financial intermediation and velocity?
6. How does the QTM guide policymakers in managing inflation and unemployment?
7. Discuss the implications of the QTM for long-term economic trends.
8. Explain the role of inflation in the application of the QTM.
9. What are some criticisms of the typical version of the QTM?
10. How does the QTM shape our understanding of the relationship between the money supply and economic variables such as output and inflation?

CHAPTER 15

The Cost Function

Learning Objectives

- Understand the Concept of the Cost Function in Economics
- Analyze the Mathematical Foundations of the Cost Function
- Examine the Applications of the Cost Function
- Evaluate the Implications of the Cost Function
- Identify the Limitations and Critiques of the Cost Function

15.1 Introduction

In Economic Science, where choices and trade-offs constantly shape the trajectory of economies and businesses, the concept of cost stands as a fundamental cornerstone. At its heart lies the web of relationships between resources and production, encapsulated within the powerful tool known as the cost function. This mathematical construct serves as a useful tool, guiding economic agents through the landscape of decision-making, by quantifying the expenses associated with producing commodities, i.e., goods and services.

The cost function is a quantitative bridge between theory and reality, offering an approach to understanding the financial implications of resource utilization. By encapsulating the multifaceted interactions between inputs and outputs, the cost function empowers economists, entrepreneurs, and policymakers with the analytical tools needed to cope

P. G. Michaelides, *21 Equations that Shaped the World Economy*,
https://doi.org/10.1007/978-3-031-76140-9_15

with the complex economic terrain. Within the world of business, the cost function becomes a tool for managers seeking to optimize their operations. As they grapple with questions of scale, scope, and choices, the cost function unveils the trade-offs that underlie each decision. Through meticulous calculation and analysis, it reveals the most efficient pathways to minimize expenses, while taking into account factors like variable costs and fixed costs.

Beyond the boardrooms, the cost function reverberates throughout the market, influencing supply and demand equilibrium, and shaping landscapes. By analyzing the cost structures of different firms, economists can discern the origins of price differentials and market disparities. Policymakers, armed with insights from cost function analysis, can formulate regulations that promote fair competition, encourage innovation, and safeguard consumer welfare.

Additionally, the cost function contributes to a deeper understanding of resource allocation and long-term economic growth. By aggregating individual firm-level cost functions, economists can model entire industries and economies, uncovering patterns of resource distribution and efficiency on a grand scale. This knowledge informs policymakers as they design strategies to foster sustainable development, manage inflation, and stimulate investment.

15.2 The Cost Function in Economics

The development of the cost function in Economics reflects the ever-growing need for analytical tools to decipher the complexities of production, resource allocation, and market dynamics. The seeds of the cost function were sown by the Classical economists, whose theories in the eighteenth and nineteenth centuries laid the groundwork for understanding the fundamentals of Economics. Adam Smith's analysis of the division of labor, along with David Ricardo's theory of comparative advantage emphasizing cost, hinted at the inherent relationship between inputs and costs. These early insights provided a first conceptual framework that would later mature into the formalized concept of the cost function.

However, it was probably Alfred Marshall who catalyzed the emergence of the cost function as a distinct concept. Marshall introduced the concepts of variable costs and fixed costs, acknowledging that costs could be categorized based on their sensitivity to changes in production levels. This distinction recognized that certain costs, such as labor and raw materials, varied with production output, while others, like rent and capital expenditures, remained constant, regardless of output.

Marshall's contributions resonated with other generations of economists, paving the way for neoclassical economists to expand upon his framework. This period saw the articulation of the so-called Marginalists, introducing a marginal cost theory, which posited that the incremental cost of producing one more unit of output could be pivotal in determining production levels and pricing strategies. The mid-twentieth century witnessed a fusion of Economics with Mathematics, leading to a formal representation of the cost function. Figures like Paul Samuelson and Kenneth Arrow, among others, contributed to the mathematical foundations of Economics, demonstrating how mathematical models could provide insights into cost structures and their implications. This mathematical sophistication is supposed to enable economists to analyze complex scenarios.

In business management, the cost function became an indispensable tool for decision-makers. As firms dealt with the challenges of scale, scope, and choices, the cost function offered a quantitative guide to optimizing operations. The analysis of cost structures helped managers identify cost drivers, assess economies of scale, and make informed decisions. The digital age has ushered in a new era of cost analysis, facilitated by advanced computational tools and data analytics. This modern incarnation of the cost function accommodates supply chains, global market dynamics, and the integration of technology into production processes. Moreover, the cost function has extended its reach beyond traditional cost analysis, addressing contemporary concerns such as environmental sustainability, ethical considerations, and the role of innovation in shaping cost structures.

In brief, the emergence of the cost function in Economics is an example of the evolution of economic thought and the quest to understand the complex interplay of factors that shape economic outcomes. From the initial musings of Classical economists to the mathematical rigor of Neoclassical theorists, the cost function has evolved into a versatile analytical tool; however, it not without limitations.

15.3 The Equation

Let's focus on the technical aspects of the cost function, including its equation and other essential details. The total cost function, often denoted as $TC(Q)$, represents the relationship between the quantity of output Q and the corresponding total costs incurred. It allows economists, managers, and policymakers to analyze how changes in production levels impact total costs. The total cost function considers both variable costs, i.e., costs that change with the level of output, and fixed costs, i.e., costs that are constant regardless of output.

Mathematically, the total cost function TC(Q) has the following expression:

$$TC(Q) = VC(Q) + FC \tag{15.1}$$

where:

- *VC(Q)* represents the total variable costs associated with producing *Q* units of output.
- *FC* represents the total fixed costs, which is constant regardless of output.

The total cost function *TC(Q)* represents the sum of both variable and fixed costs for a given production level *Q*.

A linear cost function is a straightforward representation where costs increase proportionally with the quantity of output. The total cost function *TC(Q)* can be expressed as:

$$TC(Q) = a \cdot Q + FC \tag{15.2}$$

where:

- *TC(Q)* represents the total cost incurred by the production of *Q* units of output
- *a* is the variable cost per unit of output.
- *FC* is the total fixed cost, which is constant regardless of output.

In the linear cost function, the variable costs $a \cdot Q$ increase proportionally with the quantity of output produced *Q*. This could include costs like raw materials, labor, and other variable inputs. In the meantime, fixed costs *FC* remain practically constant, regardless of the quantity of output produced *Q*. These could encompass expenses such as rent, administrative costs, and equipment insurance and maintenance.

Cost functions and cost minimization are intertwined concepts, both offering valuable insights into resource allocation and decision-making of firms. Cost minimization is a fundamental concept that lies at the core of

Economic Science. While cost functions provide a mathematical representation of costs at different production levels, cost minimization focuses on the strategic objective of achieving a given output while using the least costly combination of resources. It revolves exactly around the idea of achieving a given level of output while using the least costly mix of inputs possible, and this is how the cost function is defined formally. Cost minimization seeks to address this challenge by computing the combination of inputs that produces the desired output, at the lowest possible cost.

In this context, let's take a look at the typical linear cost function with two (2) inputs, i.e., labor and capital. To mathematically express cost minimization for two inputs and a single output without fixed costs, firms seek to minimize the cost function C, subject to (s.t.) the production function constraint (usually a Cobb-Douglas), i.e., the idea of achieving a given level of output:

$$\begin{cases} \min : C = w \cdot L + r \cdot K \\ s.t. : Q = f(L, K) = A \cdot L^{a} \cdot K^{\beta} \end{cases} \tag{15.3}$$

where:

- w expresses the cost of labor per unit, i.e., the wage rate
- r expresses the cost of capital per unit, i.e., the rental rate
- L and K are labor and capital input quantities, respectively
- Q is the quantity of output produced
- f is the production function, usually a Cobb-Douglas, with $A > 0$, $0 < a < 1$, $0 < \beta < 1$

The goal is to estimate the optimal combination of labor L^* and capital inputs K^* that yields a given level of output Q^*, while minimizing total costs.

Similarly, the cost minimization problem for n inputs can be mathematically expressed as follows:

$$\begin{cases} \min : C = w_1 \cdot x_1 + w_2 \cdot x_2 + \ldots + w_n \cdot x_n \\ s.t. : Q = f(x_1, x_2, \ldots, x_n) = A \cdot x_1^{a_1} \cdot x_2^{a_2} \cdot \ldots \cdot x_n^{a_n} \end{cases} \tag{15.4}$$

where:

- C is the total cost
- $w_1, w_2, \ldots, w_n$ are the prices of inputs 1 through n
- $x_{1,}, x_2, \ldots, x_n$ are the quantities of inputs 1 through n
- $f(x_1, x_2, \ldots, x_n)$ is the production function, usually a Cobb-Douglas, with $A > 0$, $0 < a_i < 1$, $i = 1, 2, \ldots. n$
- Q is the desired level of output

In this formulation, for a given level of prices, the goal is to choose the quantities of inputs $x*_{1,}, x*_2, \ldots, x*_n$ to minimize the total cost (C^*), subject to the constraint that the production function $f(x_1, x_2, \ldots, x_n)$ generates the desired output Q^*.

Now, let's work through a simple numerical example. Consider a small manufacturing firm that produces widgets. The firm's total costs include both variable costs and fixed costs. Fixed Costs (FC) include the following:

- Rent for factory space: $1000 per month
- Insurance and maintenance for equipment: $500 per month
- Administrative costs: $300 per month

So, the Total Fixed Costs (FC) = 1000 + 500 + 300 = $1800 per month. And the Variable Costs (VC) include the following:

- Labor cost per widget: $10
- Raw materials cost per widget: $5
- Total Variable Cost per widget: $10 + $5 = $15

Let's use the linear cost function Eq. (15.1) to calculate the total cost for producing different quantities of widgets. Let's plug the following numbers in Eq. (15.2):

- $a = 15$, i.e., the variable cost per widget
- FC = $1800, i.e., the fixed costs

We get:

$$TC(Q) = 1800 + 15 \cdot Q$$

Now, let's calculate the total cost for producing 100 and 300 widgets.

- *Total Cost for 100 Widgets:* TC(100) = 15•100 + 1800 = \$3300
- *Total Cost for 300 Widgets:* TC(300) = 15•300 + 1800 = \$6300

This very simple numerical example demonstrates how the linear cost function can be used to determine the total cost of production at different output levels. By understanding these costs, the firm can make informed decisions about production quantities, pricing strategies, and resource allocation.

Now, let's consider a simple cost minimization problem with two inputs, labor (L) and capital K, using a Hicks-neutral Cobb-Douglas production function Q, with A = 1, $\alpha = 0.5$, and $\beta = 0.5$. This implies that the production function in Eq. (15.3) is:

$$Q = L^{0.5} \cdot K^{0.5}$$

Next, let's assume that:

- $w = 10$ is the wage rate, i.e., the cost per unit of labor
- $r = 20$ is the rental rate, i.e., the cost per unit of capital

According to Eq. (15.3), the Cost Function (C) is equal to:

$$C = 10 \cdot L + 20 \cdot K$$

The goal, according to Eq. (15.3), is to minimize the total cost *(C)*, subject to producing a given level of output Q.

So, the cost minimization problem is:

$$\begin{cases} \min : C = 10 \cdot L + 20 \cdot K \\ s.t. : Q = L^{0.5} \cdot K^{0.5} \end{cases}$$

First, let's express one input in terms of the other, using the production function constraint:

$$Q = L^{0.5} \cdot K^{0.5}$$

Solving for K:

$$K^{0.5} = \frac{Q}{L^{0.5}}$$

Or

$$\left(K^{0.5}\right)^2 = \left(\frac{Q}{L^{0.5}}\right)^2$$

and

$$K = \frac{Q^2}{L}$$

Next, we substitute K into the cost function:

$$C = 10 \cdot L + 20 \cdot \frac{Q^2}{L}$$

Now, we take the derivative of C with respect to L and set it to zero, based on the first-order conditions (FOC) (Sect. 23.3, Appendix C) to find the minimum:

$$\frac{dC}{dL} = 10 - 20 \cdot \frac{Q^2}{L^2} = 0$$

$$10 \cdot L^2 = 20 \cdot Q^2$$

$$L^2 = 2 \cdot Q^2$$

$$L = \sqrt{2} \cdot Q$$

Next, we find K using the production function:

$$K = \frac{Q^2}{L}$$

$$K = \frac{Q^2}{\sqrt{2} \cdot Q}$$

$$K = \frac{Q}{\sqrt{2}}$$

Let's say we want to produce $Q^* = 100$ units of output. To minimize costs, we shall use:

$$L^* = \sqrt{2} \cdot Q^* = \sqrt{2} \cdot 100 \approx 141.42$$

and

$$K^* = \frac{100}{\sqrt{2}} \approx 70.71$$

And the minimum total cost is:

$$C^* = 10 \cdot 141.42 + 20 \cdot 70.71 = 1414.2 + 1414.2 = 2{,}828.4$$

To check the second-order condition (SOC), we need to find the second derivative of the cost function with respect to labor and ensure that it is positive, indicating a local minimum (Sect. 23.3, Appendix C).

Taking the second derivative of $C(L)$ yields:

$$\frac{dC}{dL} = 10 - 20 \cdot \frac{Q^2}{L^2}$$

and

$$\frac{d^2C}{dL^2} = 40 \cdot \frac{Q^2}{L^3}$$

Now, we substitute $L = \sqrt{2}Q$ to get:

$$\frac{\left(d^2C\right)}{\left(dL^2\right)} = 40 \cdot \frac{Q^2}{\left(\sqrt{2}Q\right)^3} =>$$

$$\frac{d^2C}{dL^2} = 20 \cdot \frac{1}{Q\sqrt{2}}$$

Since, Q and $\sqrt{2}$ are positive, the second derivative is also positive. Therefore, the second-order condition indicates that our solution indeed minimizes the total cost.

In conclusion, to minimize costs while producing 100 units of output using a Cobb-Douglas production function with $A = 1$, $\alpha = 0.5$, and $\beta = 0.5$, the firm should use approximately 141.42 units of labor and approximately 70.71 units of capital, and the minimum total cost will be approximately \$2828.4.

15.4 Consequences and Insights

The cost function, a cornerstone of economic analysis, holds far-reaching applications that span various aspects of business operations, market dynamics, policy formulation, and investment evaluation. Its impact extends beyond mathematical equations, shedding light on fundamental economic principles and guiding crucial decision-making processes. By analyzing the cost function, firms discern the input levels that minimize costs. This process empowers them to make informed choices about expanding or contracting production, ensuring resource efficiency and viability.

Moreover, the cost function assumes a pivotal role in shaping pricing strategies. Firms, aiming for sustainability and profitability, set prices so as to ensure that variable expenses are covered, contributing to fixed costs and paving the way for success amid market fluctuations. Those endowed with lower costs inherently possess the advantage of setting potentially lower prices, gaining a foothold in market competition. Such strategic positioning enhances consumer appeal and fosters loyalty, ultimately influencing market dynamics.

Meanwhile, policymakers craft effective regulations that nurture market efficiency and safeguard consumer welfare. By evaluating the repercussions of policies for both businesses and consumers, policymakers can create an environment conducive to fair competition, innovation, and sustainable economic growth. Additionally, investors and financiers turn to cost functions as a compass in investment analysis. Cost efficiency and financial viability uncovered by these functions provide crucial insights into a firm's potential and attractiveness as an investment opportunity. Such considerations guide allocation decisions, balancing risk and reward.

Furthermore, the concept of efficiency is strongly associated with cost minimization. Through cost minimization strategies, firms optimize resource utilization, ensuring the production of desired outputs with the least resource expenditure. Lower production costs directly translate into higher profit margins, amplifying the firm's competitive advantage and financial robustness. Finally, cost minimization promotes innovation and adaptability by urging firms to put forward novel input combinations. By relentlessly seeking the most cost-effective blend of inputs, businesses not only fine-tune their operational efficiency but also foster an environment conducive to experimentation, creativity, and transformative advancements.

15.5 Conclusion, Limitations, and Critiques

As we have seen, at its core, the cost function encapsulates the multifaceted interactions between inputs and outputs, and empowers economists, entrepreneurs, and policymakers with the analytical tools needed in the economic terrain. In the context of business management, the cost function emerges as an essential asset for managers aiming to streamline their operations. Moreover, the influence of the cost function reverberates throughout the market molding competitive landscapes. By understanding the cost structures of different firms, economists can discern the origins of price differentials and market disparities. Policymakers, armed with insights from cost function analysis, can formulate regulations that promote fair competition, encourage innovation, and safeguard consumer welfare.

Of course, in the pursuit of such economic insights, it's crucial to refer to the limitations of the cost function. The assumptions and simplifications inherent in cost function analysis, such as *ceteris paribus* assumptions and linearity, might not fully capture the complexities of actual economic interactions. This could potentially lead to oversights and incomplete analyses that fail to account for dynamic factors at play. Furthermore, critiques introduce valuable perspectives that challenge the conventional application of cost functions.

For instance, behavioral economics underscores the influence of psychological biases, institutional economics highlights the role of social norms and power dynamics, and ecological economics raises concerns about the environmental impact of production decisions. Furthermore, for instance, from a Marxist perspective, the cost function analysis is fundamentally flawed as it fails to account for the exploitation and class conflict inherent in capitalist production. Marxists argue that the cost function obscures the true nature of capitalist exploitation. They contend that the costs of production, particularly the costs of labor, are not determined by the market forces of supply and demand, but rather by the power dynamics between the capitalist class and the working class. The capitalist's ability to extract surplus value from the labor of the worker is the basis of profit, not the efficient allocation of resources as suggested by the cost function. Moreover, they critique the assumption of perfect competition and the notion of equilibrium, which they view as ideological constructs that justify the existing social order. They argue that the cost function analysis fails to account for the historical and social context of production, and instead presents an ahistorical and apolitical view of economic processes.

These critiques underscore the need for a more multidisciplinary approach that accommodates diverse viewpoints and considers broader implications. Incorporating such complexity requires a willingness to adapt and evolve the application of the cost function. It calls for a dynamic framework that expresses the ever-changing economic landscape, accounting for technological advancements, shifting consumer preferences, and environmental considerations. Balancing short-term cost minimization with long-term sustainability is essential for responsible decision-making that accounts for a comprehensive range of outcomes.

In conclusion, the cost function serves as a robust tool that bridges theory and practice, offering a quantified understanding of the relationship between inputs and costs. Its applications extend across production decisions, pricing strategies, market dynamics, and policy formulation. However, its limitations and the critiques remind us of the complexity of economic theory and the need for an integrative approach. By embracing a more multidisciplinary view and incorporating diverse viewpoints, economists and decision-makers could harness the full potential of the cost function.

Chapter Takeaways

- The cost function is a vital concept in Economic Science, quantifying the relationship between inputs, outputs, and costs.
- It serves as a mathematical bridge between theory and practice, empowering economists, entrepreneurs, and policymakers with analytical tools.
- Cost minimization is a core concept linked to cost functions, focusing on achieving a given output with the least resource expenditure.
- Within business management, the cost function aids managers in optimizing operations by revealing trade-offs and cost-efficient pathways.
- The cost function's influence extends to pricing strategies, enabling firms to cover expenses, enhance competitiveness, and ensure sustainability.
- It plays a crucial role in market competition, granting firms with lower costs a competitive advantage and the ability to potentially set lower prices.
- Policymakers leverage insights from cost function analysis to design effective regulations, promote competition, and safeguard consumer welfare.
- Investors and financiers utilize cost functions for investment analysis, gauging a firm's cost efficiency and financial viability.
- The cost function's limitations include assumptions and simplifications that may not fully capture complex real-world economic interactions.
- Critiques highlight social, behavioral, institutional, and ecological perspectives, urging a multidisciplinary approach for comprehensive analysis.

Revision Questions

1. What is the fundamental role of the cost function in Economic Science?
2. How does the cost function serve as a bridge between economic theory and reality?
3. Define the cost minimization problem.
4. How does the cost function guide managers in optimizing business operations?
5. Explain how the cost function influences pricing strategies and market competition.
6. What insights can policymakers derive from analyzing the cost function?
7. How do investors and financiers benefit from understanding cost functions in investment analysis?
8. What are the limitations of cost function analysis?
9. How do alternative approaches offer critiques of the conventional cost function approach?
10. Why is a multidisciplinary approach crucial for a comprehensive understanding of the cost function's implications in economic decision-making?

CHAPTER 16

The Solow Growth Model

Learning Objectives

- Understand the Fundamentals of the Solow Growth Model
- Analyze the Equations and Dynamics of the Solow Growth Model
- Evaluate the Implications of the Solow Growth Model
- Examine the Critiques and Limitations of the Solow Growth Model
- Explore the Need for More Inclusive Growth Models

16.1 Introduction

The Solow Growth Model offers a compelling framework that can be traced back to Robert Solow's and Trevor Swan's groundbreaking work in the 1950s, where they sought to uncover the mysteries of long-term economic growth by integrating factors that were often overlooked in previous approaches. At its core, the Solow Growth Model posits that a nation's prosperity over time is not solely determined by the transient fluctuations of output but rather by the sustained accumulation of capital. It challenges conventional economic thinking by highlighting the central role played by technological progress in driving economic advancement. In doing so, the model propels us into an intellectual space where we grapple with the complex interplay of investment, innovation, and population dynamics.

P. G. Michaelides, *21 Equations that Shaped the World Economy*,
https://doi.org/10.1007/978-3-031-76140-9_16

Motivating our analysis of the Solow Growth Model is the overarching question that has captivated economists for centuries: What fuels enduring economic growth, and how can nations sustain it over time? By diving into the model, we aim to uncover the answers to this crucial question. Understanding long-term growth is not merely an academic pursuit; it is an essential endeavor with profound implications for the prosperity and well-being of economies and societies. The allure of the Solow Growth Model lies in its ability to serve as a theoretical 'laboratory' where we can simulate and experiment with different policy scenarios. As we scrutinize its equations and assumptions, we gain insights into the consequences of policies that encourage investment in capital, foster technological innovation, or manage population growth. This analytical tool became a compass for policymakers seeking strategies that balance the imperatives of short-term stability with the imperatives of sustained economic development.

16.2 The Solow Growth Model in Economics

The emergence of the Solow Growth Model marked another transformative moment in the field of Economics, providing a robust framework to analyze the dynamics of long-term economic growth. Born out of the intellectual ferment of the mid-twentieth century, the model was introduced by Robert Solow and Trevor Swan, and significantly expanded economists' understanding of the factors influencing a nation's prosperity over time.

Prior to this model, the predominant economic theories largely neglected the fundamental question of what drives sustained economic growth. The traditional framework, exemplified by the contributions of economists like Harrod and Domar, emphasized the role of savings and investment in determining economic output. However, these models lacked a comprehensive treatment of the dynamics governing the long-term growth trajectory of an economy. Robert Solow, a Massachusetts Institute of Technology economist, sought to address this gap by developing a model that incorporated the critical elements of capital accumulation, technological progress, and population growth. His model departed from the prevailing theories by introducing the concept of the so-called exogenous technological change, implying that technological progress is not (solely) a result of economic forces, but is influenced by external factors.

At the heart of the Solow Growth Model is the idea that an economy's output is determined by the interplay between its inputs and technological progress. The Solow Growth Model can be succinctly expressed through a differential equation, where the rates of change in capital stock, output, and technological progress are interlinked. This mathematical elegance allowed economists to formalize their understanding of the factors shaping long-term growth and facilitated rigorous analysis of policy implications.

The Solow Growth Model has not only stood the test of time but has also undergone refinements and extensions over the years. Economists have examined variations that incorporate human capital, endogenous technological change, and institutional factors, enriching the model's applicability to a wide array of economic scenarios. The model's impact extends beyond academia; it became an indispensable tool for policymakers grappling with the challenges of fostering sustainable economic development. By offering a systematic framework to evaluate the impact of policy decisions on capital accumulation, technological change, and overall economic growth, the Solow Growth Model is crucial in shaping economic policies across the globe.

In brief, the emergence of the Solow Growth Model represents a watershed moment in economic thought. By synthesizing insights, Solow provided the discipline with a framework to analyze the determinants of long-term economic growth. His model's enduring legacy lies not only in its theoretical elegance but also in its practical utility, offering a roadmap for understanding the complexities of economic development.

16.3 The Equation

As mentioned earlier, the Solow Growth Model is a neoclassical economic framework that seeks to explain long-term economic growth by incorporating variables such as capital accumulation, technological progress, and population growth. It is presented in a simplified form with a differential equation (d.e.) that describes the evolution of capital stock over time. The basic version of the model assumes a small, closed economy, i.e., one with no government and no trade, constant returns to scale, and a fixed savings rate. Here is the first equation of the Solow Growth Model:

$$Y(t) = F(K(t), L(t))$$

In this equation, $Y(t)$ represents the total output of the economy, $K(t)$ is the capital input, and $L(t)$ is the labor input. The function F represents the production function, which assumes constant returns to both capital and labor. For simplicity, we often write:

$$Y = F(K, L)$$

We assume that both inputs are necessary, such that:

$$F(0, L) = 0 \text{ and } F(K, 0) = 0$$

Also, the following so-called Inada conditions are met that ensure certain desirable properties of the growth process.

$$\lim_{K \to 0} \frac{\partial F}{\partial K} \to \infty$$

This condition implies that as the amount of capital (K) approaches zero, the marginal productivity of capital becomes infinitely large. In other words, when the economy has very little capital, an additional unit of capital greatly increases output. This ensures that investing in capital is highly productive when capital is scarce.

$$\lim_{K \to \infty} \frac{\partial F}{\partial K} = 0$$

This condition means that as the amount of capital (K) becomes very large, the marginal productivity of capital approaches zero. This indicates diminishing returns to capital, ensuring that endlessly accumulating capital does not lead to unbounded growth, since labor (L) is also needed.

$$\lim_{L \to 0} \frac{\partial F}{\partial L} \to \infty$$

Similarly, this condition implies that as the amount of labor (L) approaches zero, the marginal productivity of labor becomes infinitely large. When labor is very scarce, adding an additional worker significantly boosts output. This ensures that labor is highly productive when it is scarce.

$$\lim_{L\to\infty}\frac{\partial F}{\partial L}=0$$

Also, this condition means that as the amount of labor becomes very large, the marginal productivity of labor approaches zero. This reflects diminishing returns to labor, ensuring that simply increasing the labor force does not lead to unbounded growth, since capital (K) is also needed.

The production function faces constant returns to scale:

$$\lambda\cdot \mathrm{Y}=F(\lambda\cdot \mathrm{K},\lambda\cdot L),\ \lambda\geq 0$$

and for $\lambda=\frac{1}{L}$, we get:

$$\frac{Y}{L}=F\left(\frac{K}{L},1\right)$$
$$y=f(k),$$

where $y\equiv\frac{Y}{L}$, $k\equiv\frac{K}{L}$, and $f(k) = F(k,1)$

Next comes the core differential equation of the Solow Growth Model (Sect. 23.5, Appendix E). The rate of change $K'(t)$ of capital $K(t)$ with respect to time t, which is by definition equal to $K'(t)\equiv(dK(t))/dt$, is equal to the new investment $I(t)$, minus the depreciation of a share $\delta > 0$ of the already existing capital

$$K(t),\ \text{i.e., } \delta\cdot K(t).\ \text{Therefore:}$$

$$\frac{dK(t)}{dt}=I(t)-\delta\cdot K(t) \tag{16.1}$$

Now, we also assume a small, closed economy, i.e., one with no government and no international trade. Consequently, based on the income accounting equation, in a Keynesian framework, investment is equal to:

$$I(t) = S(t) = s \cdot Y(t), \tag{16.2}$$

where 0 < s < 1 is the fixed savings rate. Hence, by substituting in the capital accumulation equation, we get:

$$K'(t) = s \cdot Y(t) - \delta \cdot K(t)$$

or, dividing by $L(t)$, we get:

$$\frac{K'(t)}{L(t)} = s \cdot \frac{Y(t)}{L(t)} - \delta \cdot \frac{K(t)}{L(t)}$$

or:

$$k'(t) = s \cdot y - \delta \cdot k, \tag{16.3}$$

where:

$$y \equiv \frac{Y(t)}{L(t)}, \quad k \equiv \frac{K(t)}{L(t)}$$

and we symbolize:

$$k'(t) \equiv \frac{K'(t)}{L(t)}$$

Similarly:

$$i \equiv \frac{I(t)}{L(t)}$$

Dividing Eq. (16.2) by $L(t)$ we get:

$$\frac{I(t)}{L(t)} = \frac{S(t)}{L(t)} = \frac{s \cdot Y(t)}{L(t)}$$

or:

$$i = s \cdot y \tag{16.4}$$

Since, $y = f(k)$, Eq. (16.3) becomes:

$$k'(t) = s \cdot f(k) - \delta \cdot k \tag{16.5}$$

Technically speaking, the 'steady-state' solution k^* for any given differential equation (d.e.) of the form $k'(t) = g(k)$, where g is an arbitrary function of k, is reached when $g(k^*) = 0$ (Sect. 23.5, Appendix E). As a result, the 'steady state' here implies:

$$s \cdot f(k^*) - \delta \cdot k^* = 0 \tag{16.6}$$

Next, we assume a Hicks-neutral Cobb-Douglas production function, with constant returns to scale:

$$Y = A \cdot K^a \cdot L^{1-\alpha}, A > 0, 0 < a < 1 \tag{16.7}$$

and:

$$y = \frac{Y}{L} = \left(\frac{A \cdot K^a \cdot L^{1-\alpha}}{L} \right) = A \cdot \frac{K^a \cdot L^{1-\alpha}}{L^a \cdot L^{1-\alpha}} = A \cdot \left(\frac{K}{L} \right)^a$$

Hence:

$$y = f(k) = A \cdot k^a \tag{16.8}$$

By substituting (16.8) in (16.6), we get:

$$s \cdot A \cdot k^{*a} - \delta \cdot k^* = 0 \tag{16.9}$$

or

$$k^{*a}\left(s \cdot A - \delta \cdot k^{*1-a}\right) = 0$$

Meaning that either $k^* = 0$ or :

$$s \cdot A - \delta \cdot k^{*1-a} = 0$$

Therefore:

$$k^* = \left(\frac{s \cdot A}{\delta}\right)^{(1/1-\alpha)} \tag{16.10}$$

From a theoretical point of view, the Solow Growth Model focuses on the role of capital accumulation. The equilibrium, or 'steady state,' is reached when the investment in new capital equals the depreciation of existing capital. This leads to a so-called steady-state equilibrium where the weighted growth rates of capital and output level off.

In other words, the Solow Growth Model is a powerful framework for comprehending the dynamics of economic growth over time. Its 'equilibrium analysis' helps economists and policymakers grasp the factors that influence a nation's steady-state conditions and offers valuable insights into the forces shaping the trajectory of economies.

To illustrate a very simple numerical example of calculating the 'steady state' in the Solow Growth Model, let's consider the aforementioned version of the model with a Hicks-neutral Cobb-Douglas production function, with constant returns to scale, and the following assumptions:

- Hicks-neutral technology with A is equal to 1
- Capital share in output is equal to 0.5
- Savings rate is equal to 0.25
- Depreciation rate is equal to 0.05

We can now calculate the per-worker (i.e., divided by $L(t)$) variables of interest at the steady state. Analytically, by plugging these numbers in Eq. (16.10), we obtain the capital per worker k^* at the steady state:

$$k^* = \left(\frac{0.25 \cdot 1}{0.05}\right)^{1/(1-0.5)}$$

$$k^* = (5)^2$$

$$k^* = 25$$

And by plugging these numbers in (16.8), we get the output per worker y^* at the steady state:

$$y^* = 1 \cdot 25^{0.5}$$

$$y^* = \sqrt{25}$$

$$y^* = 5$$

Next, by plugging these numbers in Eq. (16.4), we get the investment per worker i^* at the steady state:

$$i^* = 0.25 \cdot 5$$

$$i^* = 1.25$$

Finally, by plugging these numbers in the depreciation per worker $\delta \cdot k^*$, we get:

$$\delta \cdot k^* = 0.05 \cdot 25$$

$$\delta \cdot k^* = 1.25$$

Here, investment per worker i^* indeed equals depreciation per worker $\delta \cdot k^*$. This example clearly demonstrates the 'steady-state' condition where investment per worker equals depreciation per worker, ensuring that capital per worker remains constant over time, i.e., its derivative over time is zero.

16.4 Consequences and Insights

The Solow Growth Model, a seminal contribution to economic analysis, carries significant implications for our understanding of long-term economic growth. Central to the model is the emphasis on the critical role of investment in driving economic growth. Higher savings and investment rates lead to increased capital accumulation, fostering sustained growth. Singapore serves as a practical example of this principle, with its economic transformation underscored by a commitment to high investment rates, propelling it from a developing nation to a prosperous economy.

Technological progress is another fundamental driver of long-term growth in the Solow Growth Model. While the model assumes exogenous technological change, it underscores the transformative impact of innovation on productivity and output. The information technology revolution at the end of the twentieth century serves as a practical illustration, highlighting how technological progress can reshape entire economies.

The Solow Growth Model also holds practical relevance for policymakers, offering a framework to assess the impact of various policies on economic growth. Changes in savings rates, technological policies, and population growth have direct implications for a nation's long-term trajectory. South Korea's strategic investments in education and technology during the latter half of the twentieth century exemplify how targeted policy decisions can drive technological progress and economic growth.

16.5 Conclusion, Limitations, and Critiques

The Solow Growth Model provided a foundational framework to analyze long-term economic growth. Its contributions, from the 'steady-state' solution to highlighting the role of investment and technological progress, have significantly enriched our understanding of economic development. However, the model is not without its limitations. One notable limitation lies in the model's reliance on a simplified production function, typically a Cobb-Douglas function. While this provides mathematical tractability, it may oversimplify the diverse production relationships present in actual economies. In the simplified version, the closed-economy assumption neglects the role of international trade, and the model overlooks critical factors like institutional quality, income distribution, and the impact of government policies. The mathematization, while enhancing precision, can sometimes obscure economic intuition and hinder a deeper understanding.

Furthermore, the original Solow Growth Model assumes exogenous technological change, neglecting the crucial role of endogenous forces in driving innovation. Critics argue that technological progress is not an external factor but a result of economic activities, and investment in research and development. This neglect limits the original model's ability to capture the complex feedback loops between economic growth and technological advancement. Environmental considerations are absent from the original Solow Growth Model, drawing criticism from scholars concerned with sustainability. The model's perpetual growth assumption raises questions about the environmental consequences and the finite nature of natural resources. Economists call for the integration of ecological dimensions, emphasizing the need for economic models that account for the ecological constraints and externalities associated with growth.

Some critiques challenge the Solow Growth Model's foundations and argue for a more pluralistic approach. The model's focus on market mechanisms and rational behavior is criticized for downplaying the importance of distributional issues, class dynamics, and social structures in influencing economic outcomes. Economists advocate for models that incorporate a broader range of economic behaviors, acknowledging the diversity of human decision-making and the impact of power dynamics within societies.

As we move forward, there is a call for more comprehensive models that go beyond the Solow framework. Integrating endogenous technological change, considering the impact of institutions and government policies, and accounting for environmental sustainability are essential steps that have already been put forward. A deeper understanding of economic growth requires embracing various perspectives that recognize the complexities of social and economic systems. It is important to note that several modifications and famous extensions to the Solow Growth Model exist, including models that incorporate human capital, endogenous technological change, and institutional factors, among other things. These extensions allow economists to analyze a broader range of real-world scenarios and refine their understanding of the factors influencing economic growth.

In closing, while the Solow Growth Model has been instrumental in understanding economic growth, its critiques prompt us to seek even more inclusive and multidimensional models. The evolution of Economic Science demands an integrative approach that considers diverse factors, accounting for the complexities of the real-world economic landscape.

Chapter Takeaways

- The Solow Growth Model unravels the mysteries of long-term economic growth through the integration of often-overlooked factors.
- At its core, the model emphasizes sustained capital accumulation, both physical and human, and highlighting the role of technological progress.
- The model's emergence marked a transformative moment in Economics, introducing the concept of exogenous technological change.
- The core equation of the Solow Growth Model encompasses a mathematical representation of key economic dynamics.
- The model's equilibrium state, characterized by 'steady-state' conditions, reveals insights into the factors shaping long-term growth.
- Practical implications of the Solow Growth Model include the importance of investment and the role of technological progress.
- The Solow Growth Model encourages a long-term perspective in economic planning, as illustrated by real-world examples.
- The original model's limitations involve a neglect of endogenous technological change and the absence of environmental considerations.
- Critiques challenge its foundations, emphasizing the need for pluralistic approaches that consider distributional issues and social structures.
- As Economic Science evolves, there is a call for focus on the more comprehensive models that integrate endogenous forces, institutional factors, and sustainability considerations.

Revision Questions

1. Who developed the Solow Growth Model, and what motivated its creation?
2. What are the core concepts emphasized by the Solow Growth Model in explaining long-term economic growth?
3. How does the model address the issue of technological progress, and what is the significance of exogenous technological change?
4. Describe the key equations of the Solow Growth Model and their implications for understanding economic dynamics.
5. What is the equilibrium state in the Solow Growth Model, and how does it relate to steady-state conditions?
6. Discuss the practical implications of the Solow Growth Model.
7. Provide examples illustrating the practical relevance of the Solow Growth Model for economic planning.
8. What role does technological progress play in sustaining long-term growth?
9. What are the limitations of the original Solow Growth Model, and how do critiques challenge its foundations?
10. In light of the model's limitations, what are the calls for the future development of economic models, and how does the Solow Growth Model fit into the evolving landscape of Economic Science?

CHAPTER 17

The Phillips Curve

Learning Objectives

- Understand the Basics of the Phillips Curve
- Analyze the Trade-Off Between Inflation and Unemployment
- Evaluate the Role of Inflation
- Examine the Limitations and Critiques of the Phillips Curve
- Discuss the Need for Refining Economic Models

17.1 Introduction

The study of the Phillips Curve is driven by the goal of comprehending the relationship between inflation and unemployment and its policy implications. By analyzing this relationship, economists and policymakers can acquire valuable insights into labor market dynamics, wage-setting behaviors, and the potential trade-offs between price stability and employment levels. A primary reason for studying the Phillips Curve is its significant relevance to monetary policy. Central banks are instrumental in controlling inflation and fostering economic stability. Understanding the balance between inflation and unemployment is crucial for developing effective monetary policies that aim to achieve both price stability and maximum employment.

P. G. Michaelides, *21 Equations that Shaped the World Economy*,
https://doi.org/10.1007/978-3-031-76140-9_17

For instance, if a central bank intends to lower unemployment through expansionary monetary policies, it must consider the possible effects on inflation. According to the Phillips Curve, increasing employment might lead to higher inflation, in the short term. Therefore, policymakers need to weigh the advantages of reduced unemployment against the risks of increased inflation when making their decisions. Moreover, the Phillips Curve sheds light on the different economic agents. It highlights the role of wage-setting and the bargaining power of workers in shaping inflationary pressures. Studying the Phillips Curve also provides insights into the broader economic environment. Changes in inflation and unemployment rates can reflect shifts in aggregate demand or structural changes. While the validity of the Phillips Curve has been challenged, its historical significance and influence on economic thought make it an important concept to study.

17.2 The Phillips Curve in Economics

The Phillips Curve emerged in the mid-twentieth century, and has played a significant role in macroeconomic theory and policymaking. A. W. Phillips first documented the 'inverse' relationship between wage inflation and unemployment in the 1950s. By analyzing British data, Phillips found that when unemployment was low, wages tended to rise faster, leading to higher inflation, and vice versa. This empirical observation challenged prevailing economic theories of the time and drew attention to the possibility of a trade-off between unemployment and inflation.

The emergence of the Phillips Curve coincided with the dominance of Keynesian economics. Keynesian economists embraced the idea of a trade-off between unemployment and inflation, as it aligned with their belief that government policies could manage aggregate demand to achieve desired outcomes. The Phillips Curve provided empirical support for the Keynesian view that expansionary policies could reduce unemployment, but at the cost of potentially higher inflation.

Early versions of the Phillips Curve relationship were primarily based on a 'backward-looking' approach, assuming that workers formed wage expectations based on past inflation. However, economists recognized the importance of expectations and adaptive behavior in shaping the dynamics between inflation and unemployment. The adaptive expectations hypothesis posited that workers and firms adjust their expectations about the future inflation, according to past experience, influencing their behavior in wage-setting and price-setting decisions.

The Phillips Curve's emergence has had profound policy implications. Policymakers were confronted with the question of whether they could 'fine-tune' the economy to simultaneously achieve low unemployment and low inflation. The trade-off debate revolved around the stability and durability of the Phillips Curve relationship, with some economists arguing that it represented a stable long-run trade-off and others questioning its sustainability.

Over time, challenges emerged to the Phillips Curve framework. The 1970s witnessed high inflation and high unemployment coexisting, challenging the notion of a stable trade-off. The oil crises during that period and subsequent stagflation further undermined the Phillips Curve's validity. These challenges led to the development of alternative theories, such as the well-known 'rational expectations hypothesis.' These theories suggested that the Phillips Curve was not exploitable for policy purposes and that policymakers should focus on addressing structural issues and maintaining price stability.

17.3 The Equation

This section focuses on the equation of the Phillips Curve and its importance in grasping economic dynamics. There are various formulations of the Phillips Curve equation, but the simple linear representation that captures the essence of the relationship between inflation and unemployment is as follows:

$$\pi = \pi_e - \beta \cdot \left(u - u^*\right) \tag{17.1}$$

In this equation:

- π expresses the current inflation rate
- π_e expresses the expected inflation rate
- β is a parameter that measures the sensitivity of inflation to the changes in unemployment
- u represents the current unemployment rate
- u^* expresses the natural rate of unemployment, which is the rate at which inflation remains stable in the long run

Technically speaking, the aforementioned equation expresses mathematically that there is an 'inverse relationship' between inflation and unemployment. When the unemployment rate is below the natural rate ($u < u^*$), the equation implies that inflation will be higher than expected ($\pi > \pi_e$). Conversely, when the unemployment rate is above the natural rate ($u > u^*$), inflation will be lower than expected ($\pi < \pi_e$).

More analytically, when the unemployment rate falls below the natural rate ($u < u^*$), the labor market becomes 'tight,' giving workers more leverage to negotiate higher wages. In this scenario, firms, facing a shortage of available workers, are compelled to offer higher wages to attract and retain employees. To maintain their profit margins, these firms then pass on the increased labor costs to consumers through higher prices, resulting in inflation that exceeds expectations ($\pi > \pi_e$). Conversely, when the unemployment rate rises above the natural rate ($u > u^*$), the labor market has excess capacity, and workers have diminished bargaining power. In this situation, firms can keep wages low due to the surplus of available labor and reduced demand for workers. With lower wage costs, firms face less pressure to increase prices, leading to inflation that falls below expected levels ($\pi < \pi_e$). This dynamic illustrates the trade-off between inflation and unemployment, as described by the Phillips Curve above, where changes in the labor market directly influence price stability.

The parameter β in the equation captures the degree of sensitivity of the relationship between inflation and unemployment. A higher value of β indicates a greater sensitivity of inflation to changes in unemployment, implying a 'steeper' Phillips Curve. Conversely, a lower value of β suggests a less pronounced relationship between inflation and unemployment. It should be noted that the Phillips Curve equation assumes that inflation expectations π_e are formed based on past inflation rates. However, expectations are also influenced by factors like monetary policy, fiscal policy, and external factors. In this context, such changes in inflation expectations could lead to shifts in the Phillips Curve relationship.

Let's see a very simple numerical example. Imagine an economy where economic analysts are studying the relationship between inflation and unemployment, using the Phillips Curve. For this economy, we know that the natural rate of unemployment, denoted as u^*, is estimated to be 5%. This rate represents the level of unemployment that the economy experiences when inflation is stable and not accelerating. The sensitivity of inflation to changes in unemployment, represented by β, is determined to be 0.5. The expected inflation rate, π_e, which reflects the inflation rate that workers and firms anticipate based on past experiences and current conditions, is 3%. At a particular point in time, the actual unemployment rate, u, is observed to be 4%.

By plugging these numbers in Eq. (17.1), the actual inflation rate π is calculated as follows:

$$\pi = 0.03 - 0.5 \cdot (0.04 - 0.05)$$

$$\pi = 0.035 = 3.5\%$$

In this example, the actual unemployment rate of 4% is below the natural rate of 5%. According to the Phillips Curve, this lower-than-natural unemployment rate exerts upward pressure on inflation. As a result, the actual inflation rate rises to 3.5%, exceeding the expected inflation rate of 3%. This example illustrates the trade-off between inflation and unemployment described by the Phillips Curve. Policymakers must consider this relationship when designing policies to manage economic conditions, as efforts to reduce unemployment can lead to higher inflation, while aiming for lower inflation might result in higher unemployment.

17.4 Consequences and Insights

The Phillips Curve carries important implications for understanding economic dynamics and informing policy decisions. As we have seen, according to the Phillips Curve when unemployment is low, inflation rises, and conversely, when unemployment is high, inflation tends to fall. This trade-off presents a challenge for policymakers when designing economic policies. Policies that aim to reduce unemployment through expansionary measures might trigger higher inflation, while those that focus on lowering inflation through contractionary measures could lead to increased unemployment. By understanding this trade-off, policymakers can better anticipate the outcomes of their decisions and strike a balance between acceptable levels of inflation and unemployment.

The Phillips Curve highlights the importance of inflation expectations. Expectations are crucial in wage-setting, price-setting, and decision-making processes by workers, firms, and consumers. Changes in inflation expectations can shift the Phillips Curve relationship and impact the effectiveness of various policies. Hence, policymakers must monitor and manage inflation expectations to align them with their desired inflation targets.

The concept of the natural rate of unemployment is another key implication of the Phillips Curve. The natural rate represents the equilibrium unemployment rate at which inflation remains stable and unaffected by changes in aggregate demand. Policymakers strive to reduce unemployment to levels below the natural rate but face the risk of generating higher inflation in the process. Understanding the natural rate could help policymakers set realistic employment targets and design policies that promote sustainable economic growth.

17.5 Conclusion, Limitations, and Critiques

As we have seen, the Phillips Curve illustrates an 'inverse' relationship between inflation and unemployment, in the sense that lower unemployment rates are typically associated with higher inflation, and vice versa. As a result, the Phillips Curve is highly significant in Economics because it clarifies the short-term trade-offs between inflation and unemployment.

However, when examining the limitations and critiques of the Phillips Curve, it's essential to focus on specific challenges that have emerged over time, shedding light on the complexities inherent in inflation and unemployment dynamics. One critical issue is the concept of 'stagflation,' a scenario characterized by stagnant economic growth, high inflation, and elevated unemployment levels. Stagflation challenges the traditional Phillips Curve relationship, which suggests an inverse relationship between inflation and unemployment. The coexistence of high inflation and high unemployment during 'stagflationary' periods perplexes policymakers and economists alike, as it defies the conventional wisdom of a trade-off between these two variables. This phenomenon underscores the inadequacy of simplistic models that fail to capture the interactions between supply-side dynamics, inflation expectations, and labor market conditions.

Furthermore, the Phillips Curve framework tends to oversimplify the drivers of inflation and unemployment, overlooking, among other factors, structural changes. For instance, technological advancements, globalization, and demographic shifts can profoundly influence labor market dynamics and price-setting behavior, leading to deviations from the traditional Phillips Curve trade-off. Additionally, supply-side factors, such as productivity growth, input costs, and regulatory policies, play a significant role in shaping inflationary pressures, but are often disregarded in traditional macroeconomic models.

Critics also argue that the Phillips Curve neglects the heterogeneous nature of labor markets and wage-setting mechanisms. In reality, different industries and regions exhibit varying degrees of labor market flexibility, bargaining power, and wage rigidity. Consequently, the aggregate Phillips Curve may mask divergent inflationary trends within specific sectors or geographic areas, leading to misinterpretations of overall price dynamics and suboptimal policy responses.

Moreover, the Phillips Curve framework relies on the assumption of adaptive expectations, wherein agents form their inflation forecasts based on past experiences and observed trends. However, empirical evidence suggests that inflation expectations are often influenced by a wide range of factors, including monetary policy announcements, central bank credibility, and global economic conditions. Failure to account for the complexities of inflation expectations can undermine the accuracy of Phillips Curve predictions and distort policymakers' assessment of inflationary risks.

In response to these challenges, economists advocate for alternative approaches that embrace a more holistic view of inflation and unemployment dynamics. Some economists, for example, emphasize the role of institutional arrangements, power relations, and income distribution in shaping economic outcomes. By incorporating a broader range of factors into economic analysis, these approaches offer alternative insights into the drivers of inflation and unemployment, paving the way for more effective policy interventions.

In summary, while the Phillips Curve remains a useful concept for understanding the relationship between inflation and unemployment, its limitations highlight the need for a more comprehensive and flexible approach to economic analysis. By acknowledging critiques and embracing alternative perspectives, policymakers can develop more robust models and policies that address the complexities of modern economies and promote sustainable growth and stability. In conclusion, the Phillips Curve remains a valuable tool for policymakers in achieving macroeconomic stability. However, its implications must be considered alongside alternative theories to account for the evolving nature of the economy.

Chapter Takeaways

- The Phillips Curve expresses the trade-off relationship between inflation and unemployment, guiding experts in finding a balance between the two variables.
- Inflation expectations play a pivotal role in influencing economic outcomes and must be managed to align with desired inflation targets.
- Inflation expectations significantly influence wage-setting, price-setting, and decision-making processes by workers, firms, and consumers.
- The Phillips Curve assists policymakers in making informed decisions about macroeconomic stabilization and policy formulation.
- The trade-off between inflation and unemployment requires policymakers to diligently consider the potential consequences of their policy choices.
- The concept of the natural rate of unemployment provides insights for setting realistic employment targets and promoting sustainable economic growth.
- Understanding the natural rate of unemployment helps policymakers establish realistic employment goals and design effective policies.
- Policymakers must continuously refine economic models and conduct research to enhance their understanding of inflation and unemployment dynamics.
- Challenges arise when the Phillips Curve relationship breaks down during periods of 'stagflation', necessitating the consideration of supply-side factors and external changes.
- The evolving nature of the economy and alternative theories must be considered alongside the Phillips Curve to address its limitations and enhance policy effectiveness.

Revision Questions

1. What is the key trade-off described by the Phillips Curve?
2. How do inflation expectations shape economic outcomes?
3. What insights does the natural rate of unemployment provide for policymakers?
4. What challenges arise when the Phillips Curve relationship breaks down?
5. Why is continued research and refinement of economic models necessary?
6. What role do inflation expectations play in wage-setting, price-setting, and decision-making processes?
7. How does understanding the natural rate of unemployment help policymakers set employment targets?
8. How does the Phillips Curve guide policymakers in macroeconomic decision-making?
9. What considerations must policymakers keep in mind when balancing inflation and unemployment?
10. Why is it important to incorporate alternative theories alongside the Phillips Curve?

CHAPTER 18

The Gravity Equation

Learning Objectives

- Analyze the Theoretical Foundations of the Gravity Equation
- Understand the Fundamentals of the Gravity Equation
- Examine the Extended Form of the Gravity Equation
- Evaluate the Empirical Applications of the Gravity Equation
- Identify the Limitations and Critiques of the Gravity Equation

18.1 Introduction

In the vast landscape of international trade and economic interactions, the Gravity Equation stands as an enduring framework that seeks to unravel the flow of goods, services, and investments internationally. Borrowing its name from Physics' law of universal gravitation, this economic model is an indispensable tool in the economist's toolkit. The Gravity Equation not only provides a powerful lens through which to examine the patterns of global trade but also sheds light on the factors influencing economic relationships.

The Gravity Equation has evolved into a fundamental concept in International Economics, transcending its initial application in the analysis of trade flows. Its versatility has allowed researchers to analyze diverse economic phenomena, ranging from the determinants of foreign direct investment to the spatial distribution of economic activity within

P. G. Michaelides, *21 Equations that Shaped the World Economy*,
https://doi.org/10.1007/978-3-031-76140-9_18

countries. This chapter will analyze the Gravity Equation, focusing on its roots, theoretical foundations, and empirical applications across various dimensions.

We will discuss how this 'gravitational force' operates at both macro and micro levels, influencing the choices made by nations, firms, and individuals. Theoretical underpinnings will be leveraged to provide an understanding of the factors that contribute to the gravitational pull between economic entities. Additionally, we will argue that advancements in the availability of rich datasets have enabled researchers to refine and expand the applications of the Gravity Equation over time.

From the trade patterns among nations to the localized clustering of industries within regions, the Gravity Equation serves as a unifying force that brings coherence to the complex web of economic relationships. By examining the dynamics encapsulated in this equation, we aim to provide our readers with an analysis of the forces shaping the world of international trade.

18.2 Gravity Equation in Economics

The emergence of the Gravity Equation in Economics marks a pivotal moment in the field's evolution, representing a departure from traditional approaches and the introduction of a metaphorical bridge between the laws of Physics and Economics. The roots of this emergence can be traced to the post-World War II era, a period characterized by reconstruction, globalization, and an increasing interest in understanding the dynamics of international trade. As we know, in the aftermath of World War II, economists faced the demanding task of comprehending the complex web of global economic interactions. Nations sought to rebuild, establish cooperative frameworks, and facilitate international trade. Against this backdrop, some economists sought inspiration from Physics, particularly Newtonian Physics, to develop a model that could capture the underlying forces governing economic interactions between nations.

Among them, Tinbergen's vision was revolutionary. Drawing parallels between economic entities and physical objects subjected to gravitational forces, he formulated the Gravity Equation. This equation proposed that the volume of trade is proportional to the product of the countries' economic masses and inversely proportional to the square of the actual geographic distance between them. This innovative application of Physics to

Economics laid the groundwork for a novel approach to understanding international economic relations.

The early applications of the Gravity Equation were primarily focused on unraveling the mysteries of international trade patterns. The model's simplicity and empirical success in explaining the relationship between economic size and geographic proximity to trade flows captured the attention of economists. As the equation gained traction, researchers began to analyze its theoretical insights and applicability to a broader range of economic phenomena. What started as a model primarily reliant on economic size and distance soon evolved into a more sophisticated framework. Economists began to recognize the need for additional factors to refine the Gravity Equation. Cultural affinities, language similarities, and institutional compatibilities were introduced, expanding the model's theoretical underpinnings. This evolution enabled the Gravity Equation to transcend its original application, becoming a helpful tool for analyzing various dimensions of economic interactions.

The 1970s and 1980s witnessed significant advances, providing economists with tools to refine the Gravity Equation. Some methodological refinements broadened the model's scope, enabling economists to focus on new economic relationships. The late twentieth century brought about a data revolution that further propelled the Gravity Equation. The availability of large-scale datasets and advancements in computational capabilities enabled economists to test the model. The Gravity Equation, once limited by data constraints, transformed into a powerful tool capable of dissecting economic interactions at levels previously unattainable.

18.3 The Equation

In this section, we set out the technical aspects of the Gravity Equation. At the heart of the Gravity Equation is a simple formula:

$$T_{ij} = \frac{M_i \cdot M_j}{D_{ij}}, \tag{18.1}$$

where:

- T_{ij} expresses the volume of trade or economic interaction between countries i and j

- M_i and M_j express the economic masses (e.g., GDP) of countries i and j, respectively
- D_{ij} expresses the distance between countries i and j

The Gravity Equation draws an analogy from Newton's law of gravity in Physics, where the gravitational force between two objects is directly proportional to their masses and inversely proportional to the square of the distance between them. In trade theory, the equation suggests that trade volume is directly proportional to the economic sizes of the trading countries and inversely proportional to the distance between them. This means larger economies tend to trade more with each other, while greater distances reduce trade.

However, the simplicity of the formula is deceptive, as the real power of the Gravity Equation lies in its capacity for refinement. While the core equation highlights the significance of economic size and geographic proximity, the Gravity Equation has evolved to incorporate additional factors that contribute to economic interactions. The theoretical insights extend to include cultural similarities, language affinity, and institutional compatibility. This extended model acknowledges the multidimensional nature of economic relationships, recognizing that factors beyond mere size and distance influence trade patterns.

When extending these theoretical insights of the Gravity Equation to include cultural similarities, language affinity, and institutional compatibility, the model becomes more extended. Let's incorporate these factors into an extended Gravity Equation:

$$T_{ij} = \frac{M^{\alpha}{}_{i} \cdot M^{\beta}{}_{j} \cdot C^{\gamma} \cdot L^{\delta} \cdot \mathrm{I}^{\varepsilon}}{D^{\varphi}{}_{ij}}, \tag{18.2}$$

where:

- T_{ij} still expresses the volume of trade or economic interaction between countries i and j, respectively
- M_i and M_j express the economic masses (e.g., GDP) of countries i and j
- C represents a measure of cultural similarity
- L represents a measure of language affinity
- I represents a measure of institutional compatibility

- D_{ij} expresses the distance between countries i and j

The exponents ($\alpha, \beta, \gamma, \delta, \varepsilon, \phi$) reflect the respective impact of each factor on economic interactions. Here's a compact explanation of each term:

- M^{α}_{i}, M^{β}_{j}: Economic masses of the two countries raised to exponents (α and β) capture the basic idea that larger economies exert more gravitational pull.
- C^{γ}, L^{δ}, I^{ε}: These terms account for cultural similarities C, language affinity L, and institutional compatibility I. The exponents γ, δ, and ε signify the influence of these factors on trade patterns. For instance, a higher value for γ suggests that countries with greater cultural similarities engage in more trade.
- D^{φ}_{ij}: The inverse relationship with distance D_{ij} is maintained, but the exponent ϕ allows for the dampening effect of distance to be adjusted based on its significance in the context of the specific model.

The exponents do not necessarily have to be positive, but deviations from positivity should be supported by theoretical or empirical justification. Without such justification, the standard assumption is that all exponents are positive. This extended Gravity Equation acknowledges that economic interactions are shaped by a variety of factors, recognizing the multidimensional nature of international relationships. The inclusion of cultural, linguistic, and institutional elements enhances the model's ability to take into consideration the complexities of economic dynamics, beyond the simplistic size and distance considerations in the initial formulation.

The Gravity Equation's multifaceted character is showcased through its empirical applications. Researchers employ econometric techniques to estimate the parameters of the Gravity Equation and apply it to contexts involving foreign direct investment, migration flows, and the spatial distribution of economic activities. The model's ability to adapt to various contexts highlights its empirical robustness.

To address potential econometric challenges, researchers often resort to advanced techniques when estimating the parameters of the Gravity Equation. The success of the Gravity Equation is closely tied to the quality and availability of data. As we know, recent decades have witnessed a data revolution, providing researchers with access to large-scale datasets and computational tools. This evolution has enabled economists to analyze economic relationships, unlocking new possibilities for understanding the complexities of global economic dynamics.

Let's see a simple numerical example to illustrate the Gravity Equation in the context of trade between two countries. Assume that country i has a GDP M_i of $1000 billion, country j has a GDP M_j of $500 billion, and the distance D_{ij} between country i and country j is 2000 km. By plugging these numbers in the basic Gravity Equation (18.1), we get:

$$T_{ij} = \frac{1000 \cdot 500}{2000}$$

or:

$$T_{ij} = 250$$

So, the trade volume T_{ij} between country i and country j would be 250 units of trade volume.

Now, let's extend the equation to include cultural similarity C, language affinity L, and institutional compatibility I. Assume the following values:

- Economic masses and distance as before.
- Cultural similarity is equal to 0.8 in a scale from 0 to 1
- Language affinity is equal to 0.9 in a scale from 0 to 1
- Institutional compatibility is equal to 0.85 in a scale from 0 to 1
- Exponents are equal to $\alpha = 1, \beta = 1, \gamma = 1, \delta = 1, \varepsilon = 1, \phi = 1$

By plugging these values in the extended Gravity Equation (18.2), we get:

$$T_{ij} = \frac{1000^1 \cdot 500^1 \cdot 0.8^1 \cdot 0.9^1 \cdot 0.85^1}{2000^1}$$

or

$$T_{ij} = 152.5$$

Therefore, the trade volume T_{ij} between country i and country j, considering the extended factors, would be 152.5 units of trade volume.

18.4 Consequences and Insights

As we have seen, the Gravity Equation is a relevant tool for modeling trade patterns between countries. It implies that larger economies will be involved in more substantial trade volumes, whereas distance serves as a natural dampener. The trade relationship between the United States and China aligns with the Gravity Equation's insights. Despite the considerable distance, the sheer economic masses of these two nations contribute to substantial trade flows.

The model suggests that countries with geographical proximity are more likely to engage in significant economic interactions. This has implications for regional integration efforts. The European Union exemplifies the impact of regional integration. Proximity, along with shared cultural and historical ties, has led to a deep economic integration among EU member states. Beyond physical distance, the Gravity Equation implies that factors such as cultural similarities, language affinity, and institutional compatibility significantly influence economic relationships. For instance, the United States and the United Kingdom, sharing a common language and having historically strong cultural ties, showcase the importance of non-geographical factors in shaping economic interactions.

Policymakers can use the insights from the Gravity Equation to formulate effective trade policies. By understanding the factors influencing economic interactions, governments can develop strategies that align with these dynamics. Japan's trade policy, which has historically focused on strengthening economic ties with neighboring Asian countries, reflects a strategic alignment with the insights of the Gravity Equation. The Gravity Equation suggests that countries are more likely to participate in global value chains with nations that possess complementary economic characteristics. China's integration into global value chains, particularly in manufacturing, aligns with the Gravity Equation. Its economic mass and industrial capabilities attract collaboration from countries seeking to benefit from China.

The model extends beyond trade to explain foreign direct investment (FDI) patterns, suggesting that countries with economic synergies are more likely to attract investments from each other. The US–Canada economic relationship, characterized by significant FDI flows, demonstrates how proximity, shared language, and institutional compatibility contribute to cross-border investments. The Gravity Equation is also, broadly speaking, applicable to migration, implying that countries with closer economic ties, cultural similarities, and linguistic affinities are likely to experience higher migration flows. The migration patterns within the European Union, where citizens can freely move across member states, align with the Gravity Equation's implications, based on economic, cultural, and language ties.

The Gravity Equation's insights are vast and encompass various aspects of economic interactions. Whether modeling trade flows, understanding regional integration, or informing policy decisions, the model equips readers with a useful framework for understanding the complex dynamics of the global economy. Practical examples across different economic scenarios underscore the real-world applicability of the Gravity Equation in shaping our understanding of international economic relationships.

18.5 Conclusion, Limitations, and Critiques

In conclusion, the Gravity Equation stands as another vital tool in Economics, offering valuable insights into the dynamics of international economic relationships. Originating from the metaphorical connection to Newtonian Physics, the model has evolved to incorporate not only economic size and distance but also cultural, linguistic, and institutional factors.

However, like any model, the Gravity Equation has its limitations. These limitations highlight the necessity of a deeper understanding and the acknowledgment that while the model provides valuable insights, it does not capture the full complexity of global economic interactions. The Gravity Equation, even in its extended form, may not account for all relevant factors influencing economic relationships. Omitted variables, such as geopolitical considerations, or technological advancements can impact trade patterns but are not explicitly captured. Furthermore, the model assumes homogeneity in economic entities, overlooking heterogeneity within countries. This oversimplification may lead to misinterpretations, especially in contexts where internal economic disparities play a significant role. The traditional versions of the Gravity Equation are inherently static and may not fully capture the dynamic nature of economic relationships.

Critiques of the Gravity Equation also challenge some of its underlying assumptions. For instance, critics argue that the Gravity Equation tends to overlook power relations and structural inequalities in the global economic system. Countries with historical advantages or greater economic power may disproportionately influence trade patterns, potentially leading to skewed interpretations. Others criticize the inclusion of cultural factors, asserting that cultural affinity does not necessarily dictate economic interactions. They argue that cultural determinism oversimplifies the complexities of trade. Other economists challenge the assumption that institutional compatibility translates into increased interactions. They argue that institutional frameworks are shaped by power dynamics and may not reflect mutual interests.

In the current globalized landscape, the Gravity Equation remains relevant. Beyond its focus on trade, it informs our understanding of global value chains, investment decisions, and regional clustering. Researchers continue to extend the model, incorporating new variables and dimensions to adapt to the evolving nature of economic interactions. The Gravity Equation, with its simplicity and capacity for refinement, is an example of interdisciplinary thinking in Economics. Its theoretical foundations, coupled with empirical applications and methodological advancements, make it a vital tool for economists. Complementing its insights with other models, considering broader contextual factors, and embracing diverse perspectives will contribute to a deeper understanding of the landscape of international economics.

Chapter Takeaways

- The Gravity Equation emerged post-World War II, drawing inspiration from Newtonian Physics to model economic interactions.
- Application of gravity principles to Economics laid the foundation for the model, in the early 1960s.
- The model posits that trade volume between two countries is proportional to the two countries' economic masses and inversely proportional to their distance.
- Beyond trade, the Gravity Equation has been applied to foreign direct investment, migration, and the spatial distribution of economic activities.
- Cultural, linguistic, and institutional factors are incorporated into the extended Gravity Equation, acknowledging multidimensional influences.
- The model's success in explaining diverse economic phenomena highlights its empirical robustness.

(*continued*)

(continued)

- Advanced methods address challenges in estimating Gravity Equation parameters.
- Recent decades have seen a data revolution, enabling economists to analyze economic relationships with unprecedented granularity.
- The Gravity Equation remains relevant in a globalized landscape, informing global value chains, investment decisions, and regional economic clustering.
- Despite its power, the model has limitations, including omitted variables and a static nature.

Revision Questions

1. How does the Gravity Equation draw parallels with Newtonian Physics?
2. Explain the core equation of the Gravity Model and its implications for modeling trade patterns.
3. How has the Gravity Equation evolved from its original focus on trade to encompass various economic phenomena?
4. What are the cultural, linguistic, and institutional factors incorporated into the extended Gravity Equation?
5. Why are such crucial factors often neglected?
6. Describe the empirical applications of the Gravity Equation beyond trade, providing examples.
7. What role has the data science revolution played in transforming the Gravity Equation into a dynamic and powerful analytical tool?
8. Discuss the global relevance of the Gravity Equation.
9. What are the limitations of the Gravity Equation, and how do they impact its applicability to real-world economic scenarios?
10. How do critiques challenge the assumptions of the Gravity Equation, and what alternative perspectives do they offer in understanding international economics?

CHAPTER 19

The Granger Causality Equation

Learning Objectives

- Understand the Basics of Granger Causality in Economics
- Analyze the Methodology of Granger Causality
- Evaluate the Implications of Granger Causality
- Examine the Applications of Granger Causality
- Identify the Limitations of Granger Causality

19.1 Introduction

Deciphering the temporal sequences and causal links in economic phenomena is a pursuit that has preoccupied economists for decades. At the forefront of this investigative journey stands Granger causality, a key concept that has proven instrumental in shedding light on the time-ordered relationships between economic variables. In its essence, causality necessitates more than the identification of statistical correlations or regressions. Granger causality, named after Clive Granger, introduces a temporal dimension, offering a framework to discern whether the past values of one variable can be considered a useful predictor of future values in another.

The historical roots of Granger causality trace back to the 1960s when Clive Granger and Robert Engle developed time series models to analyze economic relationships. As we walk through the evolution of Granger

P. G. Michaelides, *21 Equations that Shaped the World Economy*,
https://doi.org/10.1007/978-3-031-76140-9_19

causality, we encounter its pioneering applications and its subsequent integration into the toolkit of modern economists seeking to unravel cause-and-effect relationships in a temporal context. In essence, Granger causality serves as a bridge between theory and empirical analysis, offering a statistical lens through which causation in economic systems can be measured.

19.2 Granger Causality in Economics

Traditional economic analyses predominantly focused on cross-sectional regressions and simple correlations, often falling short in capturing the evolving nature of economic processes over time. The need for a deeper understanding of causation, especially one that acknowledged the temporal dimension of economic variables, spurred the development of Granger causality. In this context, Clive Granger and Robert Engle, in the early 1960s, recognized that to truly comprehend the cause-and-effect relationships in Economics, researchers needed to examine the predictive power of variables. The fundamental question was whether past values of a particular economic variable could be useful in predicting the future values of another variable. This marked a significant departure from a traditional view, which tended to treat variables as synchronous and static.

The methodology introduced by Granger causality represented an important leap forward. Vector autoregression (VAR) models, a key component in Granger causality analysis, allowed economists to capture the dynamic interplay between economic variables. By incorporating lagged values of variables into the models, researchers could discern not only contemporaneous associations, but also the temporal sequences of events. This temporal dimension became a critical tool for analyzing the structures inherent in economic systems.

Some of the earliest applications of Granger causality were in the field of macroeconomics. Economists began using Granger causality to analyze the temporal relationships between variables like GDP, inflation, and interest rates. This provided insights into the propagation of shocks and the efficacy of policy interventions over time. For instance, Granger causality analysis became particularly influential in understanding the dynamics of monetary and fiscal policies.

As the empirical applications of Granger causality expanded, its influence extended into diverse subfields of Economic Science. For instance, in financial economics, researchers used Granger causality to examine the relationships between asset prices, interest rates, and other financial variables. In international trade, it helped unravel the temporal dynamics of trade relationships and the transmission of economic shocks across borders. Of course, the evolution of Granger causality did not occur in isolation. It unfolded alongside broader shifts in economic methodology, emphasizing the importance of dynamic modeling and recognizing the temporal dimension as being central to economic analysis. The concept's adaptability and versatility contributed to its enduring relevance in economic research.

19.3 The Equation in Economics

More technically speaking, Granger causality is a statistical hypothesis test employed in Economics to assess whether one time series can be considered a predictor of another, providing a means to infer a causal relationship between the two variables. The basic idea behind the Granger causality test involves running regression models with lagged values of the variables in question. If past values of a variable statistically significantly improve the prediction of future values of another variable, Granger causality is said to exist.

The equation for a bivariate Granger causality test involves regressing variable Y_t on its own past values as well as the past values of the variable X_t :

$$Y_t = a + \beta_1 \cdot Y_{t-1} + \beta_2 \cdot Y_{t-2} + \ldots + \beta_p \cdot Y_{t-p} + \gamma_1 \cdot X_{t-1} + \gamma_2 \cdot X_{t-2} + \ldots + \gamma_p \cdot X_{t-p} + \varepsilon_t \quad (19.1)$$

In this equation:

- Y_t expresses the dependent variable
- a is the intercept
- $\beta_1, \beta_2, \ldots, \beta_p$ express the coefficients on the lags of Y_t
- $\gamma_1, \gamma_2, \ldots, \gamma_p$ express the coefficients on the lags of X_t
- $X_{t-1}, X_{t-2}, \ldots, X_{t-p}$ express the past values of X_t
- $Y_{t-1}, Y_{t-2}, \ldots, Y_{t-p}$ express the past values of Y_t

- ε_t expresses the error term, which is assumed to be *i.i.d.*

The null hypothesis H_0 for Granger causality is that the lagged values $X_{t-1}, X_{t-2},\ldots, X_{t-p}$ of X_t do *not* help in predicting Y_t beyond what is already contained in the lagged values $Y_{t-1}, Y_{t-2},\ldots, Y_{t-p}$ of Y_t.

Mathematically, this means:

$$H_0 : \gamma_1 = \gamma_2 = \ldots = \gamma_p = 0$$

The test involves comparing the significance of the coefficients $\gamma_1, \gamma_2,\ldots, \gamma_p$ associated with the lagged values $X_{t-1}, X_{t-2},\ldots, X_{t-p}$ of X_t. If these coefficients are jointly significant, then there is evidence *not* to accept the null hypothesis, suggesting that X_t indeed 'Granger causes' Y_t. Note that the inclusion of lagged values in the model is crucial. The idea is that the past values of the variables may contain information about the future values. The choice of the number of lags is typically determined based on statistical criteria or on an assumption by the researcher derived from economic theory.

Therefore, the *F*-test, in the context of Granger causality, involves testing the joint significance of all the lagged variables $X_{t-1}, X_{t-2},\ldots, X_{t-p}$ of the independent variable X_t, in predicting the dependent variable Y_t. It assesses whether the inclusion of these lagged variables improves the overall model's explanatory power. A statistically significant *F*-statistic indicates that at least one of the lagged variables $X_{t-1}, X_{t-2},\ldots, X_{t-p}$ provides meaningful information for predicting the dependent variable Y_t, beyond what is already explained by its own lagged values $Y_{t-1}, Y_{t-2},\ldots, Y_{t-p}$.

The test statistics are then compared to relevant critical values from the *F*-distribution, to determine statistical significance. The critical values depend on the chosen significance level, e.g., 10%, 5%, or 1%. As far as the interpretation of the results is concerned, If the lagged values of X_t are found to be statistically significant in predicting Y_t, it suggests that X_t Granger causes Y_t.

Let's see a very simple example. Suppose we have yearly data on investment I_t and industrial production IP_t, over a period of time. We want to test whether past changes in investment Granger cause changes in industrial production. In this context, the dependent variable Y_t is now the industrial production IP_t, and the independent X_t is the investment I_t. Therefore, based on Eq. (19.1), we will construct a relevant bivariate model, to test for Granger causality, assuming a time lag of one (1) year. A lag of one (1) year is chosen because the researcher knows that the economic effects of investment on industrial production usually manifest within a short time frame.

Hence, by plugging these variables in Eq. (19.1) with one (1) time lag, we get:

$$IP_t = a + \beta_1 \cdot IP_{t-1} + \gamma_1 \cdot I_{t-1} + \varepsilon_t$$

Now, assume the estimated coefficients from the model are $\beta_1 = 0.8$ and $\gamma_1 = 0.6$. Next, we need to perform an *F*-test on the lagged value of investment I_{t-1}, to determine if it significantly improves the prediction of industrial production IP_t, beyond what is already captured by the past value of industrial production IP_{t-1}. More precisely, typically the *F*-test in this context assesses whether the inclusion of I_{t-1} improves the overall model's explanatory power.

Mathematically, this means:

$$H_0 : \gamma_1 = 0$$

Assume that the relevant *F*-statistic of the *F*-test for γ_1 is significant. The statistical significance confirms that this relationship is unlikely to be due to random chance, suggesting a meaningful causal influence of investment on industrial production over time. Based on the results of the Granger causality test:

- We *reject* the null hypothesis H_0, above, that past values of investment do *not* help predict industrial production beyond past industrial production values alone.
- Therefore, we conclude that investment Granger causes changes in industrial production in our case. Note that in this specific scenario, where a single coefficient is being tested, the F-test simplifies to the t-test, providing an equivalent conclusion about significance.

19.4 Consequences and Insights

The Granger causality test, with its emphasis on temporal precedence and the predictive power of one variable over another, holds implications across various domains within Economic Sciences. In policy evaluation, economists leverage Granger causality to assess the effectiveness of economic policies over time. For instance, by scrutinizing whether changes in interest rates Granger cause changes in inflation rates, policymakers gain insights into the transmission channels of monetary policy and its impact on overall economic conditions.

Within financial economics, Granger causality proves instrumental in understanding market dynamics and lead–lag relationships between different financial instruments. For instance, researchers might investigate whether past fluctuations in stock prices Granger cause changes in bond yields, offering valuable information for shaping investment strategies. Examining international trade, Granger causality helps unveil the transmission mechanisms through which economic variables influence each other. Researchers might examine whether changes in exchange rates Granger cause variations in export volumes, shedding light on the channels through which currency fluctuations impact global trade patterns. Granger causality could also be employed in identifying the sources of economic fluctuations. In this context, economists might investigate whether sudden increases in oil prices Granger cause changes in inflation rates, aiding policymakers in understanding the origins of inflationary pressures and formulating appropriate responses.

Furthermore, investors utilize Granger causality to inform their decision-making processes. For example, if past values of corporate earnings Granger cause changes in stock prices, investors may factor this information into their investment strategies, anticipating potential movements in the stock market. Moreover, Granger causality can contribute to early crisis prediction. By investigating whether certain macroeconomic variables Granger cause changes in economic and/or financial stability indicators, economists can even develop early warning mechanisms for potential economic downturns, allowing for proactive crisis management.

19.5 Conclusion, Limitations, and Critiques

In conclusion, the Granger causality test stands as another powerful tool in the economist's toolkit, offering a dynamic lens through which temporal relationships between economic variables can be investigated. However, the Granger causality test, despite its widespread use and contributions to Economics, is not without limitations and has faced critiques from various perspectives.

One significant limitation lies in its susceptibility to spurious regression, especially when variables share common trends or structural breaks in the data. In brief, spurious regression refers to a statistical phenomenon where two or more time series variables appear to be related through regression analysis, producing misleadingly high coefficients and significant results, despite lacking a true causal relationship. Omitted variable bias is another concern, as the test assumes the inclusion of all relevant variables; omitting important factors can lead to biased results. The linearity assumption may also be a limitation, as the test assumes a linear relationship between variables, potentially providing inaccurate results if the true relationship is nonlinear.

Additionally, the accuracy of the Granger causality test relies on precise variable measurement, and any measurement errors or the use of proxies may introduce 'noise' into the analysis. The assumption of stationarity is crucial, and violations of this assumption can result in spurious causality. Furthermore, the test establishes only temporal precedence, requiring additional evidence or theoretical reasoning to discern causation accurately. In small sample sizes, the test may lack the power to detect true causality, increasing the risk of errors. Endogeneity issues, where variables simultaneously influence each other, are also raised as concerns not fully addressed by the Granger causality test.

Critiques also focus on the philosophical limitations of the test. While Granger causality identifies predictive relationships, it falls short of establishing philosophical causation, which involves a deeper understanding of the mechanisms driving the relationship. Critics argue that the test may oversimplify the dynamic complexity of economic systems, neglecting feedback loops and nonlinear dynamics. Economists emphasize the importance of context and qualitative understanding in interpreting causality, suggesting that Granger causality may overlook qualitative aspects and specific contextual factors shaping economic relationships. Some perspectives advocate for alternative approaches, such as agent-based modeling or systems dynamics, which better capture the complexities of economic interactions and offer a more holistic view of causation.

In closing, while the Granger causality test remains a valuable quantitative tool, its application requires caution and should be complemented by a broader understanding of economic theory, history, context, and alternative methodologies to ensure a more robust analysis of economic causation. Consequently, the application of Granger causality demands careful consideration.

Chapter Takeaways

- Granger causality traces its roots back to the 1960s, evolving from the need to analyze the predictive power of economic variables over time.
- The Granger causality test utilizes autoregressive models, particularly vector autoregression (VAR), to capture dynamic interplays between economic variables.
- Some of the earliest applications were in macroeconomics, examining temporal relationships between variables.
- Granger causality expanded its influence into financial economics, international trade, and various subfields.
- The Granger causality equation regresses the dependent variable on its own past values and the past values of the independent variable. The null hypothesis tests whether lagged values of the independent variable improve predictions.
- Granger causality aids in evaluating the effectiveness of economic policies, offering insights into the transmission channels of monetary and fiscal interventions.
- Investors utilize Granger causality to inform decision-making, incorporating the predictive power of past values of variables like corporate earnings.
- Granger causality demands caution in interpretation, considering potential spurious correlations, omitted variables, and economic reasoning.
- Critics highlight the test's limitations in establishing true causation in the philosophical sense, emphasizing the need for a deeper understanding of mechanisms driving relationships.
- The chapter highlights the importance of a holistic understanding of economic relationships, recognizing Granger causality as a valuable tool.

Revision Questions

1. What are the historical origins of Granger causality, and how did it contribute to a shift in Economic Science?
2. Explain the methodology of Granger causality, focusing on the role of autoregressive models.
3. How did Granger causality influence empirical applications in Economics?
4. Provide an overview of the Granger causality equation and the hypothesis it tests.
5. How do investors leverage Granger causality in decision-making, and what considerations should be kept in mind when interpreting its results?
6. Analyze the applications of Granger causality in various fields of Economic Science, highlighting its role in uncovering lead–lag relationships and economic shocks.
7. In what ways does Granger causality aid in policy evaluation?
8. What are the cautionary considerations in interpreting Granger causality results?
9. Discuss the philosophical limitations of Granger causality.
10. How did Granger causality contribute to the evolution of economic methodology, emphasizing dynamic modeling and temporal dimension?

CHAPTER 20

Black-Scholes Formula

Learning Objectives

- Analyze the Emergence of the Black-Scholes Equation
- Understand the Basics of the Black-Scholes Formula
- Evaluate the Assumptions of the Black-Scholes Model
- Examine the Limitations of the Black-Scholes Formula
- Recognize the Importance of Continuous Refinement

20.1 Introduction

In financial markets, where risk and opportunity go hand-in-hand, the valuation of derivates guides investors and risk managers. The Black-Scholes Equation, a ***magnum opus*** in Finance, transcends its mathematical origins to become a powerful tool shaping the decisions that steer portfolios and corporate strategies. As we embark on this chapter's journey, our motivation lies not just in presenting the mathematical model, but also in recognizing the impact it has had on the making of modern Finance.

The inception of the Black-Scholes Equation was a response to the pressing need for a standardized approach to options pricing. The early 1970s witnessed a financial landscape undergoing seismic shifts, with the demand for a reliable model to value options becoming increasingly urgent. Fischer Black, Myron Scholes, and Robert Merton responded to

P. G. Michaelides, *21 Equations that Shaped the World Economy*,
https://doi.org/10.1007/978-3-031-76140-9_20

this call, delivering a model that not only addressed the immediate challenges but also laid the foundation for a new era in quantitative finance.

The chapter begins with a presentation of the context, motivated by the desire to comprehend the driving forces that led to the creation of the Black-Scholes Equation. The backdrop reveals the economic and financial dynamics of the time as well as the intellectual fervor and practical necessity that catalyzed the birth of this groundbreaking model. Next, moving beyond historical motivations, we analyze the heart of the Black-Scholes Equation, deciphering the Mathematics that underpins its elegance. Each term in the equation carries significance, and our aim is to demystify these components, fostering an understanding that transcends the confines of Mathematics.

Yet, the power of the Black-Scholes Equation is not confined to academia. Its applications influence financial institutions, shaping investment strategies and risk management practices. By uncovering these applications, we aim to inspire a deeper appreciation for the practical implications and limitations of the model. From traders making split-second decisions to corporate finance professionals evaluating strategic moves, the Black-Scholes Equation is regarded as a key tool in financial decision-making.

Motivated by a quest for continuous improvement, we also confront the assumptions and limitations that underlie the Black-Scholes model. By understanding the model's sensitivity to deviations from assumptions, we empower decision-makers to handle the Black-Scholes Equation with caution in various market conditions. Finally, as we examine the extensions and criticisms of the Black-Scholes model, our motivation is to foster a spirit of inquiry. As we know, no model is infallible, and the ongoing dialogue surrounding the Black-Scholes Equation is an example of the dynamism of financial markets. By examining criticisms, we encourage a mindset that supports continuous refinement.

20.2 Black-Scholes Equation in Economics

The emergence of the Black-Scholes Equation is by itself a fascinating chapter in the evolution of financial theory and quantitative modeling. Born out of the changing market dynamics, the equation represented a quantum leap in the understanding and valuation of financial derivatives, particularly options. In the early 1970s, financial markets were struggling with the complexities of options trading. The lack of a standardized model for pricing options posed a considerable challenge. Traders, investors, and financial institutions were in dire need of a method that could provide a mathematically rigorous approach to assess the value of options. It was against this backdrop of practical necessity that Fischer Black, Myron Scholes, and Robert Merton collaborated to create a path-breaking solution.

Black, Scholes, and Merton brought together diverse expertise, i.e., Economics, Finance, and Mathematics, respectively, to tackle the multifaceted problem of options pricing. Fischer Black, drawing on his background in Economics, contributed insights into risk and financial markets. Myron Scholes, with his expertise in Finance, provided a deep understanding of option pricing dynamics. Robert Merton, with a strong foundation in Mathematics, brought a mathematical rigor to the model. Their collaborative efforts culminated in the publication of the Black-Scholes Formula, a work that not only provided a solution to the problem at hand but also laid the groundwork for a new paradigm in Finance. The Black-Scholes Equation itself is an elegant expression of the so-called fair market value of a European-style option.

The equation introduced the idea of a 'risk-neutral' environment, where investors show no preference for risk regarding expected returns. This notion, along with assumptions like consistent volatility and efficient markets, offered a versatile framework applicable to various financial instruments. The Black-Scholes Equation, celebrated for its simplicity and mathematical beauty, emerged as a fundamental pillar in contemporary financial theory. The impact of the Black-Scholes Equation was transformative. Financial markets, armed with a standardized method for pricing options, experienced a surge in activity. Traders and investors could now quantify the value of options, enabling more informed decision-making. Financial institutions adopted the model for risk management, and academic institutions incorporated it into their curricula. The equation became a foundational pillar in the education of future generations of financial professionals. Hence, the emergence of the Black-Scholes Equation was based on the power of interdisciplinary collaboration and intellectual synergy.

20.3 The Equation

The Black-Scholes Equation or Black-Scholes-Merton formula is a partial differential equation (PDE) that describes how the derivative price changes over time and in response to changes in the underlying asset price (Sect.

23.6, Appendix F). It takes into consideration factors such as volatility, interest rates, and the option's value. Solving this equation allows analysts to derive the theoretical price of an option under certain assumptions, providing insights into its fair value and helping investors make educated decisions.

We consider a stock that pays no dividends and we construct a derivative that has a fixed maturation, and its payoff depends on the values of the stock at that moment, such as a European call or put option. Then, the Black-Scholes Equation for this derivative and the non-dividend-paying stock is given by:

$$\frac{1}{2}\cdot(\sigma\cdot S)^2\cdot\frac{\partial^2 V(S,t)}{\partial S^2}+r\cdot S\cdot\frac{\partial V(S,t)}{\partial S}+\frac{\partial V(S,t)}{\partial t}-r\cdot V(S,t)=0$$

Or, simply:

$$\frac{1}{2}\cdot(\sigma\cdot S)^2\cdot\frac{\partial^2 V}{\partial S^2}+r\cdot S\cdot\frac{\partial V}{\partial S}+\frac{\partial V}{\partial t}-r\cdot V=0, \tag{20.1}$$

where:

- $V(S, t)$ is the price of the option as a function of the underlying stock price S at time t. In the context of the Black-Scholes model, as mentioned above, the option is usually assumed to be a European option, meaning it can only be exercised at maturity, i.e., at the end of the period.
- $\frac{\partial V}{\partial t}$ is the partial derivative of V with respect to time. This term represents the rate of change of the option price with respect to time. It indicates how the option price evolves over time.
- $\frac{\partial V}{\partial S}$ is the partial derivative of V with respect to the stock price. This term represents the sensitivity of the option price to changes in the underlying asset price S. It indicates how much the option price changes for a small change in the asset price.
- $\frac{\partial^2 V}{\partial S^2}$ is the second partial derivative of V with respect to the stock price. This term represents the curvature of the option price with

respect to the underlying asset price S. It measures the convexity or concavity of the option price curve relative to changes in the underlying asset price.

- σ is the volatility of the underlying asset, where volatility measures the degree of variation of a financial asset's price over time. In the Black-Scholes Equation, volatility is assumed to be constant and represents the standard deviation (s.d.) of the asset's returns.
- r is the risk-free interest rate. This is the theoretical return on an investment with no risk of financial loss. In the Black-Scholes model, it is assumed that investors can borrow and lend money at this fixed, risk-free rate.
- $\frac{\partial V}{\partial S}$ is the partial derivative of V with respect to the stock price. This term represents the sensitivity of the option price to changes in the underlying asset price S. It indicates how much the option price changes for a small change in the asset price.

In another formulation, the Black-Scholes Eq. (20.1) provides an expression of the rate of change of the price of the option with respect to time $\frac{\partial V}{\partial t}$, as a simple linear combination of: (i) the price of the option itself V, (ii) the rate of change of the option with respect to the stock price $\frac{\partial V}{\partial S}$, (iii) and the acceleration of that change $\frac{\partial^2 V}{\partial S^2}$. All the other variables, namely r, S, and σ, appear in the form of coefficients of those terms. Consequently, rearranging the terms of Eq. (20.1), we get:

$$\frac{\partial V}{\partial t} = r \cdot V + (-r \cdot S) \cdot \frac{\partial V}{\partial S} + \left(-\frac{1}{2} \cdot (\sigma \cdot S)^2 \right) \cdot \frac{\partial^2 V}{\partial S^2} \tag{20.2}$$

Note that in the absence of the terms representing the price of the option V, and its rate of change with respect to the stock price $\frac{\partial V}{\partial S}$, the equation takes the form of the so-called heat equation in one dimension used in Engineering and Physics, which has the general form:

$$\frac{\partial u(x,t)}{\partial t} = a^2 \cdot \frac{\partial^2 u(x,t)}{\partial x^2}, \tag{20.3}$$

with $u(x, t)$ being the temperature at the point x and time t, and a^2 is a positive constant that expresses the thermal diffusivity of the medium.

Here, it is important to stress that the aforementioned Black-Scholes Equation doesn't have a simple closed-form solution for all cases, i.e., a straightforward, analytical solution for every situation. If we have boundary and terminal conditions, the PDE can be solved using Numerical Analysis and other advanced methods leveraged in Engineering, such as a type of 'finite difference method.' However, even analytically, its solution has led to the development of some formulas which provide a theoretical pricing framework for European call and put options. Although such formulas provide a theoretical price for European options, they are based on several assumptions about the market, such as constant volatility, constant interest rates, and no transaction costs. Of course, the actual option prices may differ significantly when markets deviate from these assumptions.

Let's see a very simple numerical example to illustrate the components of the Black-Scholes Equation. Suppose we want to find the value of a European call option. Here are the given parameters:

- Stock Price is equal to \$50
- Time to Maturity is equal to 1 year
- Volatility is equal to 20% per annum
- Risk-Free Interest Rate is equal to 5% per annum

We focus on setting up the equation with these values, recognizing the different terms involved. Let's plug the numbers in each term of Eq. (20.1).

Plugging numbers in the first term of Eq. (20.1), we get:

$$\frac{1}{2} \cdot (0.2 \cdot 50)^2 \cdot \frac{\partial^2 V}{\partial S^2} = 50 \cdot \frac{\partial^2 V}{\partial S^2}$$

Plugging numbers in the second term of Eq. (20.1), we get:

$$0.05 \cdot 50 \cdot \frac{\partial V}{\partial S} = 2.5 \cdot \frac{\partial V}{\partial S}$$

The third term of Eq. (20.1) has no numbers to plug in and remains unchanged:

$$\frac{\partial V}{\partial t}$$

Plugging numbers in the fourth term of Eq. (20.1), we get:

$$-0.05 \cdot V$$

Substituting all these values into the Black-Scholes Eq. (20.1), we get:

$$50 \cdot \frac{\partial^2 V}{\partial S^2} + 2.5 \cdot \frac{\partial V}{\partial S} + \frac{\partial V}{\partial t} - 0.05 \cdot V = 0$$

Or, dividing by 5, we get:

$$10 \cdot \frac{\partial^2 V}{\partial S^2} + 0.5 \cdot \frac{\partial V}{\partial S} + \frac{\partial V}{\partial t} - 0.01 \cdot V = 0$$

This is the simplified form of the Black-Scholes partial differential equation (PDE) with the given parameters. This example helps illustrate how the parameters are incorporated into the Black-Scholes Equation. The actual solution would involve advanced numerical methods or other techniques, which are beyond our scope.

20.4 Consequences and Insights

The advent of the Black-Scholes Equation in Finance ushered in a shift, not just in theoretical frameworks but in how financial decisions are made and risk is managed. One of the profound implications of this groundbreaking model lies in the democratization of options trading. Prior to the Black-Scholes model, options trading was a complex task, often limited to institutional players. The standardized approach provided by the Black-Scholes Equation made options pricing more transparent and accessible to a relatively wide range of investors. This democratization contributed to the exponential growth of options markets, enabling individual investors to participate in strategies that were once considered exclusive to financial institutions and sophisticated market participants.

Beyond accessibility, the Black-Scholes Equation has had a transformative impact on risk management practices within financial institutions. By providing a quantifiable and standardized measure of option values, the model became an indispensable tool for assessing and mitigating risk. Financial institutions could now employ the Black-Scholes framework to understand their exposure to tailor their risk management plans accordingly. For example, banks and investment firms utilize the Black-Scholes model to hedge their portfolios against adverse market movements, ensuring a more resilient financial stance in the face of uncertainties. In corporate finance, the Black-Scholes model is a key tool in mergers and acquisitions (M&A) activities. The valuation of options, often embedded in various financial instruments, becomes a crucial factor in assessing the potential risks related to M&A transactions. The supposed precision offered by the Black-Scholes Equation enhances the accuracy of financial evaluations, enabling more informed decision-making in the corporate landscape.

20.5 Conclusion, Limitations, and Critiques

As we have seen, the Black-Scholes Equation, a landmark in Finance, has undeniably shaped the contours of options pricing and risk management. Its elegant mathematical framework provided a standardized method for evaluating derivatives, and especially European-style options, making it an indispensable tool for investors and financial institutions. By democratizing access to options trading, the model expanded market participation and empowered a broader spectrum of investors.

However, despite being widely accepted, the model is not immune to criticism, and this acknowledgment has spurred further developments in Financial Engineering. Its assumptions of efficient markets and a risk-neutral world have been subject to scrutiny. Also, the model assumes that there are no transaction costs, that there are no limits to short-selling, and, additionally, that it is possible to lend and borrow money at a fixed and risk-free rate. Furthermore, it assumes that the market prices move in a random way, or as we say, follow a Brownian motion, and that the movement of the mean and market volatility are constant, i.e., stay the same over time.

Critiques revolve around broader issues surrounding the Black-Scholes model, raising concerns about its influence on market dynamics. One critique posits that the widespread use of the model may contribute to 'herding behavior' and market trends divorced from underlying economic fundamentals. More analytically, this means that many traders might follow the same strategies or make similar decisions based on the model, rather than on actual economic fundamentals. Because so many people rely on the same model for pricing options, it can create market trends that don't reflect the true economic situation. Instead, prices may move based on collective behavior rather than underlying economic realities. The reliance on options pricing models, including Black-Scholes, might exacerbate market volatility and contribute to the formation of financial bubbles.

In this context, the Black-Scholes model's role in exacerbating market risk during periods of financial stress is a subject of scrutiny. The model assumes a continuous and smooth market process, neglecting the potential for sudden shocks or discontinuities. During the credit crunch of 2006–2009, this became evident as the model struggled to account for extreme events, leading to underestimations of risks associated with complex financial instruments. Financial institutions, relying heavily on the model for risk management, found themselves ill prepared for the systemic challenges that unfolded during the crisis. In other words, the credit crunch exemplified the model's limitations in a painful real-world crisis scenario. The assumptions embedded in the Black-Scholes Equation did not adequately capture the extremely complex and discontinuous nature of the market disruptions during the financial crisis. Financial institutions using the model for risk assessment faced severe difficulties in hedging their exposures. The underestimation of risks related to mortgage-backed securities and complex derivatives, influenced by the model, apparently played a role in the severity of the crisis.

The limitations and critiques of the model highlight the need for continuous refinement and a cautious approach to financial modeling. While the model remains a popular tool, financial practitioners and academics recognize the importance of considering alternative models and adapting to changing market conditions. Stochastic volatility models and other extensions have emerged as attempts to address the shortcomings of the Black-Scholes framework. In essence, the Black-Scholes Equation's journey is one of undeniable impact and continuous evolution. It serves as a historical benchmark in Finance, prompting ongoing discussions on the interplay between mathematical models and the unpredictable dynamics of financial markets. As the financial landscape advances, the legacy of the model underscores the importance of dynamic, adaptable models that could better capture the complexities inherent in Finance.

Chapter Takeaways

- The Black-Scholes Equation is a powerful model in Finance, providing a standardized approach to valuing options.
- Fischer Black, Myron Scholes, and Robert Merton collaboratively crafted the model in response to the pressing need for a reliable options pricing framework.
- The equation's historical context reveals the intellectual fervor and practical necessity that led to its creation.
- The Black-Scholes Equation is not confined to academia; its applications extend to shaping investment strategies, risk management practices, and corporate finance decisions.
- The model's assumptions, including constant volatility and efficient markets, have been subject to scrutiny.
- The model's impact on options trading democratized access, allowing a broader range of investors to participate in strategies once exclusive to financial institutions.
- In corporate finance, the Black-Scholes model plays a pivotal role in mergers and acquisitions (M&A).
- Ongoing critiques and developments highlight the dynamic nature of financial markets and the need for continuous refinement in quantitative models.
- The Black-Scholes Equation's legacy underscores its enduring impact on financial economics and the imperative of adapting models to evolving market conditions.
- The credit crunch of 2006–2009 exposed the real-world limitations of the Black-Scholes model, particularly in handling extreme market conditions and unforeseen events.

Revision Questions

1. What motivated the development of the Black-Scholes Equation?
2. Describe the collaborative efforts of Fischer Black, Myron Scholes, and Robert Merton in creating the model.
3. What are the key assumptions underlying the Black-Scholes Equation, and how have they been criticized?
4. How did the Black-Scholes Equation democratize options trading in financial markets?
5. How has the model influenced risk management practices within financial institutions?
6. Explain the real-world applications of the Black-Scholes Equation and its enduring legacy in modern Finance.
7. Analyze the implications of the model in Corporate Finance, specifically in the valuation of employee stock options.
8. What role did the Black-Scholes Equation play during the credit crunch of 2006–2009, and what limitations were exposed?
9. Discuss the ongoing dialogue surrounding the model and its implications for financial markets.
10. What alternatives and extensions address its limitations?

CHAPTER 21

Chaos Theory

Learning Objectives

- Understand the Fundamentals of Chaos Theory
- Analyze Chaotic Behavior in Economic Systems
- Evaluate the Applications of Chaos Theory in Economic Science
- Examine the Limitations of Chaos Theory Models
- Recognize the Importance of Initial Conditions in Chaos Theory

21.1 Introduction

The field of Economics has long been fascinated with understanding the behavior of complex systems. Traditional economic models, based on stable and predictable assumptions, have faced challenges in capturing the dynamics of real-world economies. In response to these limitations, the emergence of Chaos Theory has provided a fresh perspective that attempts to embrace the inherent complexity and unpredictability of economic systems. Chaos Theory is a branch of Science that emerged in the 1960s and 1970s as a result of the work of Engineers, Physicists, and Mathematicians. Chaos Theory, rooted in the study of complex systems and nonlinear dynamics, has found significant applications in Economic Science, offering

P. G. Michaelides, *21 Equations that Shaped the World Economy*,
https://doi.org/10.1007/978-3-031-76140-9_21

new insights into financial markets, economic growth, and various areas of economic analysis.

This chapter examines the fascinating world of Chaos Theory and its implications for Economics. We briefly set out the historical background of Chaos Theory, tracing its origins into the study of nonlinear systems. Notably, the influential contributions of pioneers like Edward Lorenz and Benoit Mandelbrot have shaped the development of Chaos Theory and its application in understanding complex systems. The chapter then turns to the specific application of Chaos Theory in Economic Science. We examine how Chaos Theory has challenged traditional economic models by acknowledging the inherent complexity and unpredictability of economic systems. By embracing nonlinearity and acknowledging the limitations of rational behavior assumptions, Chaos Theory offers a new lens through which economists can analyze the behavior of economic agents and the dynamics of various economic phenomena.

One of the significant contributions of Chaos Theory in Economics lies in its applications. In this chapter, we highlight the importance of recognizing the inherent instability and unpredictability of economic systems, urging policymakers to adopt flexible policies that can adapt to changing economic conditions. By understanding the potential for feedback loops and nonlinear effects, policymakers can better cope with economic complexities and mitigate unexpected outcomes. Of course, while Chaos Theory offers useful insights, we will also acknowledge its limitations.

21.2 Chaos Theory in Economics

Well before Chaos Theory emerged in Economics, there was a growing interest in the study of nonlinear dynamics. Broadly speaking, nonlinear dynamics refers to the study of systems whose output is not linearly related to their input(s). There is no doubt that nonlinear systems are quite complex and very difficult to predict. One of the key pioneers in the field of nonlinear dynamics was Edward Lorenz, a Meteorologist who was studying the behavior of the atmosphere. In the early 1960s, Lorenz was running simulations of weather patterns. He noticed that small changes in the initial conditions of the simulations led to large differences in the final outcomes. Such phenomena gave birth to the concept of the famous 'butterfly effect' because, loosely speaking, the theory suggested that the flap of a butterfly's wings, e.g., in Greece could set off a tornado, e.g., in

Arizona. Lorenz's work on the 'butterfly effect' led to a growing interest in the study of nonlinear systems.

In the late 1960s and early 1970s, Engineers, Physicists, and Mathematicians started to develop new quantitative techniques for studying nonlinear systems, including Chaos Theory. For instance, one of the first applications of Chaos Theory came from the behavior of population dynamics. A very simple model was developed for the growth of a population, which was called the 'logistic' map. The 'logistic' map is a nonlinear system, and it can exhibit chaotic behavior under certain conditions. The work on the logistic map was one of the first examples of Chaos Theory in action, and it helped to popularize the field.

A famous pioneer in the field of Chaos Theory was Benoit Mandelbrot, who was studying fractals. Fractals are inherent geometrical formations characterized by self-replication across multiple levels of magnification. They possess a unique property wherein their immanent patterns repeat themselves, albeit with variations, when observed at different scales. Mandelbrot developed the concept of the fractal dimension, which provides a way of measuring the complexity of a fractal. Mandelbrot's work on fractals provided a new framework for analyzing the behavior of complex systems, and it helped to inspire a new generation of scientists, studying chaotic systems.

21.3 The Equation

The emergence of Chaos Theory in Economics took place when economists started to question the validity of traditional economic models. Traditional economic models were, and still are, based on the assumption that the economy is a rather stable and essentially predictable system, which in turn is based on the belief that economic agents behave rationally. However, after numerous recessionary phases it became increasingly clear that these underlying assumptions did not always hold in practice. The economy is a complex system that is subject to many different influences, and economic agents do not always behave rationally. In this context, some economists started to develop new models and approaches that took into account the complexity and unpredictability of the economy. Chaos Theory was one of the most influential of these new approaches, which provided a new framework for understanding complex systems' behavior, and it gained popularity among economists.

Chaos Theory has found numerous applications in Economic Sciences. One of the most practical applications of Chaos Theory in Finance is in the study of financial markets. Chaos Theory provides a relevant context for analyzing the behavior of financial markets, and it has been used to develop new models for capturing the behavior of stocks and other financial variables. Another important application of Chaos Theory in Economics is in the study of economic growth. Economic growth is a complex process that is subject to many different influences, and it can exhibit chaotic behavior. Chaos Theory has been used to develop new models for understanding the dynamics of economic growth, and it has helped to shed new light on the factors that drive economic growth. Chaos Theory has also been applied to certain areas of Economics, including Macroeconomics, International Trade, and Game Theory. In each of these areas, it provides a relatively fresh quantitative framework for understanding the behavior of the systems considered.

The mathematical expressions of Chaos Theory can be complex and difficult to understand. However, there are some key concepts and equations that are relatively easily understandable and central to the study of Chaos Theory. Very loosely speaking, a system exhibiting chaotic behavior is one in which its time series appears to adhere to a stochastic model, despite being entirely deterministic and lacking any random factors! This surprising characteristic denotes 'unpredictability.' In other words, a system demonstrating chaotic behavior behaves unpredictably over time, despite being entirely deterministic and lacking random factors!

As we shall see later on, in Chaos Theory, such systems are extremely sensitive to initial conditions, meaning extremely small changes in the starting state can lead to very different outcomes. However, surprisingly, unlike stochastic systems which incorporate randomness into their behavior, chaotic systems are entirely predictable if initial conditions and governing equations are known. To put it another way, in chaotic systems, irregular behavior does not result from irregular causes. The apparent randomness in their behavior is a consequence of their extreme sensitivity to initial conditions, making long-term predictions challenging or impossible beyond a certain point.

Let us consider a first-order difference equation (d.e.) (Sect. 23.7, Appendix G) of the general form:

$$X_{t+1} = f(X_t, \mu) \equiv f_\mu(X_t), t = 0,1,2\ldots \tag{21.1}$$

where: $X_t \in \mathbb{R}, f: \mathbb{R}^2 \longrightarrow \mathbb{R}$ or $f_\mu : \mathbb{R} \rightarrow \mathbb{R}$.

When f is nonlinear, the ensuing dynamics can be extremely complex, which leads to chaos. To introduce some chaotic dynamics, we consider $f_\mu(X_t)$: $[0,1] \longrightarrow [0,1]$, i.e., $f_\mu(X_t)$ maps a closed interval $[0,1]$ to itself. A very simple example is the logistic growth function:

$$f_\mu(X_t) = \mu \cdot X_t \cdot (1 - X_t)$$

such that:

$$X_{t+1} = \mu \cdot X_t \cdot (1 - X_t), 1 \leq \mu \leq 4 \tag{21.2}$$

Values of the parameter μ close to 4 lead to chaos.

In another formulation, the aforementioned equation can be expressed as:

$$X_{t+1} = 4 \cdot a \cdot X_t \cdot (1 - X_t) a \in [0, 1], \tag{21.3}$$

Here, values of the parameter a close to 1 lead to chaos.

In Eq. (21.2), for a given value of μ at time $t = 0$ we start with an initial value X_0, and with $t = 0$ and the value of X_0, we calculate X_1. Next, with the aid of the value of X_1, we set $t = 1$ to compute X_2, and so on. The process is deterministic and depends on the initial value of X_0. The initial value is determined by a good guess or previous knowledge of the system studied.

But is there any sort of 'equilibrium' in the model? Theoretically, yes, there is. To compute the so-called steady state or 'fixed point' in Eq. (21.2) we set $X_{t+1} = X_t$ and the steady state X^* (Sect. 23.7, Appendix G) is equal to:

$$X^* = f(X^*)$$

Therefore:

$$X^* = \mu \cdot X^* \cdot (1 - X^*)$$

Or

$$X^* = \mu \cdot X^* - \mu \cdot X^{*2}$$

Rearranging:

$$\mu \cdot X^{*2} + X^* - \mu \cdot X^* = 0$$

and

$$X^* \left(\mu \cdot X^* + 1 - \mu \right) = 0$$

Implying that, either:

$$X^* = 0$$

or

$$\mu \cdot X^* + 1 - \mu = 0$$

And solving for X^*, we obtain:

$$\mu \cdot X^* = \mu - 1$$

and, assuming $\mu \neq 0$, we obtain the non-trivial 'steady state' or 'fixed point':

$$X^* = \frac{\mu - 1}{\mu} \tag{21.4}$$

However, this 'steady state' for values of μ larger than 3 is unstable and in practice it is not observed. Even the slightest disturbance causes it to diverge. It is like trying to balance a plate on the tip of your finger. Any small movement will cause it to fall.

One of the most crucial characteristics of chaos is that if two identical systems start at two very close initial points, these systems can diverge widely after some time, expressing their sensitivity to the initial conditions. For example, for $\mu = 3.99$ and for the three different initial conditions

$X_0 = 0.98, 0.99, 0.995$, the trajectories after say $t = 40$ periods diverge widely. In other words, while the system is theoretically deterministic, in practice it becomes totally unpredictable, since even the slightest uncertainty inherent in the initial value grows extremely fast. Precisely, this short-lived initial 'predictability' distinguishes 'deterministic' chaos from pure 'randomness.'

The logistic growth function is one of the most famous equations in Chaos Theory. In Economics, the logistic map may be used, for instance, to model the adoption of new technologies. In this context, according to Eq. (21.1), the population size X_t represents the proportion of individuals who have adopted the new technology at a certain time. Using the logistic map, one can determine the population size X_{t+1} representing the proportion of individuals who have adopted the new technology at time *t+1*, by assuming that this proportion is related to the share of people who have already adopted the technology, as well as to those who have not done so yet. Mathematically:

$$X_{t+1} = r \cdot X_t \cdot (1 - X_t),\ 1 \le r \le 4 \tag{21.5}$$

The adoption rate is represented by the parameter r, and values of r close to 4 lead to chaos. For a low r value, indicating a slow rate of adoption, the proportion of individuals who adopt the technology increases gradually over time. Nonetheless, as the value of r increases, the rate of adoption increases, and the proportion of individuals who adopt the technology can manifest complex and unpredictable behaviors, including chaos. In addition to analyzing the conditions under which the adoption of new technologies may exhibit chaotic behavior, the logistic map may also be used to determine factors that may influence the adoption rate. Important factors that influence parameter r, for example, may be the availability of information, the cost of adoption, as well as social and cultural factors. It is important for policymakers to understand the factors that affect the adoption rate of new technologies in order to develop strategies to promote their adoption.

Speculative bubbles in financial markets are another example of the logistic map equation in Finance. The concept of a speculative bubble is used to describe an asset's price rising rapidly due to the expectation of future price increases, instead of its value. It is possible that the price of an asset can collapse rapidly if investors start to sell their holdings, resulting in significant losses for investors. The logistic map can be used to model the dynamics of speculation bubbles. In this context, the parameter r represents the rate at which investors enter or exit the market. A low level of speculation results in a slow and steady increase in the price of an asset. Nevertheless, as speculation increases, the price of the asset can exhibit complex and unpredictable behavior, such as the occurrence of bubbles and their collapse. A logistic map enables economists to analyze the conditions under which speculative bubbles form and collapse, along with the factors that influence speculation rates. There are numerous factors that can influence the level of speculation, for example, market sentiment, investor expectations, and the availability of credit. In order to reduce the likelihood and severity of financial crises, policymakers should be aware of the factors that contribute to the formation of speculative bubbles.

Let's see a very simple numerical example. In the bustling tech hub of Silicon Valley, two innovative companies, TechWave and FutureGizmo, are racing to release their groundbreaking new technologies. Both companies have near-identical starting points in terms of market readiness and consumer interest. Their marketing strategies, pricing models, and even the core features of their products are strikingly similar. As they launch their products, the adoption rates of their technologies follow a logistic growth function. This model, influenced by numerous factors such as consumer behavior, market conditions, and promotional strategies, will illustrate the impact of minute differences in initial adoption rates. The intrinsic growth rate of adoption, represented by the parameter r, is set at 3.99, indicating a highly competitive and rapidly changing market. This setting will reveal how slight variations could lead to dramatically different paths for TechWave and FutureGizmo.

We use the logistic map Eq. (21.5) to model the adoption of technology, where $r = 3.99$. By plugging this value in Eq. (21.5), we get:

$$X_{t+1} = 3.99 \cdot X_t \cdot (1 - X_t)$$

We start with initial values $X_0 = 0.7000$ for TechWave and $X_0 = 0.7001$ for FutureGizmo. We notice that the difference in the initial values is in the fourth decimal place, i.e., practically non-existent! Now, let's calculate the adoption rates for both TechWave and FutureGizmo over 40 iterations.

- TechWave ($X_0 = 0.7000$)

$$X_1 = 3.99 \cdot 0.7000 \cdot (1 - 0.7000) = 0.8379$$

$$X_2 = 3.99 \cdot 0.8379 \cdot (1 - 0.8379) = 0.5419$$

....

$$X_{31} = 3.99 \cdot 0.9260 \cdot (1 - 0.9260) = 0.2734$$

$$X_{32} = 3.99 \cdot 0.2734 \cdot (1 - 0.2734) = 0.7925$$

$$X_{33} = 3.99 \cdot 0.7925 \cdot (1 - 0.7925) = 0.6560$$

$$X_{34} = 3.99 \cdot 0.6560 \cdot (1 - 0.6560) = 0.9004$$

$$X_{35} = 3.99 \cdot 0.9004 \cdot (1 - 0.9004) = 0.3579$$

$$X_{36} = 3.99 \cdot 0.3579 \cdot (1 - 0.3579) = 0.9170$$

$$X_{37} = 3.99 \cdot 0.9170 \cdot (1 - 0.9170) = 0.3038$$

$$X_{38} = 3.99 \cdot 0.3038 \cdot (1 - 0.3038) = 0.8439$$

$$X_{39} = 3.99 \cdot 0.8439 \cdot (1 - 0.8439) = 0.5256$$

$$X_{40} = 3.99 \cdot 0.5256 \cdot (1 - 0.5256) = 0.9949$$

- Future Gizmo (X_0 = 0.7000)

$$X_1 = 3.99 \cdot 0.7001 \cdot (1 - 0.7001) = 0.8377$$

$$X_2 = 3.99 \cdot 0.8377 \cdot (1 - 0.8377) = 0.5424$$

....

$$X_{31} = 3.99 \cdot 0.9597 \cdot (1 - 0.9597) = 0.1544$$

$$X_{32} = 3.99 \cdot 0.1544 \cdot (1 - 0.1544) = 0.5209$$

$$X_{33} = 3.99 \cdot 0.5209 \cdot (1 - 0.5209) = 0.9958$$

$$X_{34} = 3.99 \cdot 0.9958 \cdot (1 - 0.9958) = 0.0169$$

$$X_{35} = 3.99 \cdot 0.0169 \cdot (1 - 0.0169) = 0.0662$$

$$X_{36} = 3.99 \cdot 0.0662 \cdot (1 - 0.0662) = 0.2467$$

$$X_{37} = 3.99 \cdot 0.2467 \cdot (1 - 0.2467) = 0.741$$

$$X_{38} = 3.99 \cdot 0.7416 \cdot (1 - 0.7416) = 0.7646$$

$$X_{39} = 3.99 \cdot 0.7646 \cdot (1 - 0.7646) = 0.7181$$

$$X_{40} = 3.99 \cdot 0.7181 \cdot (1 - 0.7181) = 0.8077$$

In a highly competitive and rapidly changing market, represented by $r = 3.99$, the logistic map equation reveals how extremely small differences in initial conditions, practically non-existent, can lead to vastly different outcomes. The initial difference in adoption rates is in the fourth decimal place, seemingly negligible. TechWave and FutureGizmo, starting from $X_0 = 0.7000$ and $X_0 = 0.7001$ respectively, both follow a path described by the exact same equation. However, this extremely small difference in the fourth decimal place (!), which is practically non-existent, results in chaotic behavior in their final values. For instance, over 40 iterations, TechWave reaches X_{40}=0.9949 and FutureGizmo reaches X_{40} = 0.8077. Similarly, over 39 iterations, TechWave reaches X_{39}= 0.5256 and FutureGizmo reaches X_{39}=0.7181, etc.

These results highlight how extremely small differences in the initial conditions, which are practically non-existent in the fourth decimal place, can lead to significantly divergent adoption paths in a highly sensitive and dynamic market, characterized by uncertainty. For both companies, the adoption rates exhibit fluctuations and complex patterns typical of chaotic systems. Even though their starting points were nearly identical, the subsequent iterations show divergent trajectories, making it difficult to predict long-term adoption patterns, since we can never know the initial conditions with, for instance, higher than fourth-decimal-place accuracy! This underscores the sensitivity of the logistic map to initial conditions and highlights the chaotic nature of certain economic and financial phenomena, illustrating the concept of chaos.

21.4 Consequences and Insights

It is essential to note that, while the logistic growth function is useful in providing insights, e.g., into the adoption of new technologies in Economics, it is a highly simplified model that does not accurately reflect the complexity of real-world economic systems. Therefore, policymakers should exercise caution when using economic models to inform policy decisions since real-world markets are influenced by a range of factors that are very difficult to model and predict. Although the logistic map does not offer a complete picture of the nonlinear and unpredictable behavior of markets, it provides a suitable framework for understanding the nonlinear and unpredictable behavior of these markets, and thus could assist policymakers in developing strategies for managing risks.

One of the key implications of Chaos Theory is that economic systems are inherently unstable, unpredictable, and subject to sudden changes. This means that policymakers need to be prepared for unexpected events, and they need to have flexible policies that can adapt to changing economic conditions.

Furthermore, Chaos Theory also suggests that policymakers need to take a holistic approach to economic policy. Economic systems are complex and interconnected, and changes in one area can have unexpected effects in other areas. Therefore, policymakers need to consider the system as a whole, rather than focusing only on individual parts in isolation.

21.5 Conclusion, Limitations, and Critiques

In conclusion, Chaos Theory has emerged as an important perspective for understanding complex systems in Economics. It has been used to develop new models for understanding the behavior of financial markets, economic growth, and other important economic phenomena. It has also provided important insights into the unpredictability and nonlinearity of economic systems, and it can have important policy implications for economists and policymakers.

Despite its many applications and insights, it is important to acknowledge that Chaos Theory is not a panacea. One limitation is that the predictions and insights generated by Chaos Theory models may not always be accurate or applicable in real-world situations. Another serious limitation of Chaos Theory in Economics is that it can be difficult to interpret and understand the results of Chaos Theory models. Chaos Theory models can generate complex patterns of behavior, and it can be very challenging to determine what these patterns mean or how they should be interpreted. Finally, these models are *by definition* extremely sensitive to initial conditions and parameter values, and even extremely small changes in these values can lead to significantly different outcomes, as we have seen.

Chaos Theory encourages economists to acknowledge the interconnectedness and interdependence of various economic factors and agents.

It prompts a shift from 'reductionist' and 'equilibrium-based' thinking to a more 'holistic' and 'dynamic approach.' This shift allows for a more realistic assessment of the uncertainties and risks present in economic and financial systems, enabling policymakers to better anticipate and respond to potential disruptions. Furthermore, Chaos Theory opens up new avenues for policy considerations. Policymakers must recognize the inherent limitations in predicting and controlling complex systems and embrace a more adaptive and flexible approach. They should be cautious of unintended consequences and be prepared to adjust policies in response to changing conditions. However, while Chaos Theory has certain limitations, it remains an important tool for understanding and analyzing complex economic systems. As the field of Economics continues to evolve, it is highly likely that Chaos Theory will continue to play an important role in shaping our understanding of the economic and financial systems.

Chapter Takeaways

- Chaos Theory studies complex systems, including their behavior in the fields of Economics and Finance.
- The emergence of Chaos Theory in Economics came about as traditional economic models struggled to capture the complexity of economic systems.
- Edward Lorenz and Benoit Mandelbrot were key pioneers in the field, making significant contributions to the study of nonlinear dynamics and fractals.
- Chaos Theory has found applications in various areas of Economics Science, such as Economic Growth, Technological Change, and Financial Markets.
- The logistic map equation, a key concept in Chaos Theory, can be used to model the adoption of new technologies and the dynamics of speculative bubbles.
- Chaos Theory highlights the inherent instability and unpredictability of economic systems, requiring policymakers to adopt flexible policies.

(*continued*)

(continued)

- Feedback loops play a crucial role in economic systems, as small changes can be amplified and lead to large and unexpected outcomes.
- Policymakers should consider the interconnectedness of economic systems, recognizing that changes in one area can have unforeseen effects in other areas.
- Policymakers should exercise caution and supplement Chaos Theory with economic theory and empirical evidence when making policy decisions.
- While Chaos Theory provides valuable insights, it is often based on models that may not capture the full complexity of real-world economic systems.

Revision Questions

1. What is Chaos Theory and how does it relate to Economics and Finance?
2. Who were some key pioneers in the development of Chaos Theory?
3. How did the emergence of Chaos Theory challenge traditional economic models?
4. What are some important applications of Chaos Theory in Economics?
5. How does the logistic map equation relate to the adoption of new technologies in Economics?
6. How can Chaos Theory be applied to the study of speculative bubbles in financial markets?
7. What are some implications of Chaos Theory for economists and policymakers?
8. What is the significance of feedback loops in economic and financial systems and how can they impact outcomes?
9. Why is it important for policymakers to consider the interconnectedness of economic systems?
10. What are some limitations of Chaos Theory?

CHAPTER 22

Epilogue

In this fascinating intellectual journey, we encountered a variety of theories, concepts, frameworks, and methodologies that offered useful insights into the complexities of the global economy. Each chapter served as a 'building block' in our evolving understanding of economic and financial phenomena. These building blocks, when viewed collectively, hopefully reveal the dynamic interplay of economic and financial forces that shape the functioning of societies, the lives of individuals, and, therefore, the trajectory of economies.

The exploration of these diverse economic and financial principles deepens our appreciation for the complexity and interconnectedness of economic and financial systems. For instance, understanding the foundational role of interest rates allows us to grasp how financial decisions, investment strategies, and macroeconomic policies are interwoven with the behavior of borrowers and savers. The study of statistical distributions and regression analysis provide information on how to interpret vast amounts of economic and financial data. Our journey also highlights the significance of production functions and profit rates, which offer insights into how resources are allocated, industries grow, and wealth is generated within economies. By examining these concepts, we gain a clearer understanding of the mechanisms driving economic productivity and the challenges of achieving sustainable and equitable growth. The exploration of equilibrium concepts, the input-output framework, and risk management

P. G. Michaelides, *21 Equations that Shaped the World Economy*,
https://doi.org/10.1007/978-3-031-76140-9_22

strategies underscores the importance of balance and interdependencies within markets. These frameworks illustrate how supply and demand dynamics, sectoral interconnections, and financial stability are critical to the smooth functioning of economies. They also emphasize the need for robust policies and adaptive strategies to mitigate risks and enhance economic resilience.

Moreover, our investigations into growth models, trade theories, and financial equations reveal the fundamental principles guiding long-term economic development, international trade patterns, and financial market behavior. These models and theories provide a comprehensive view of how economies expand, adapt, and interact on a global scale, highlighting the role of innovation, investment, and policy in shaping economic outcomes. As we dive into more abstract theories such as profit rate, game theory, causality analysis, and chaos theory, we are reminded of the limitations of traditional economic models and the necessity for alternative approaches. These advanced theories challenge us to think critically about the unpredictable and often unstable nature of economic and financial systems, urging us to consider new perspectives.

In reflecting on this extensive exploration, it becomes evident that Economics and Finance are not static but ever-evolving. The continuous dialogue, refinement, and adaptation of alternative economic theories and methods are imperative for addressing the dynamic and unpredictable challenges faced by modern economies. Our analysis has reinforced the importance of embracing diverse perspectives, fostering interdisciplinary collaboration, and remaining open to innovative ideas.

As we close this exploration into the economic equations that have shaped our world, it's important to note that the complex web of mathematical models we've examined is not just a collection of abstract concepts, but the very foundation upon which our global political economy stands. These equations—whether they govern international trade, or monetary policy—are more than just symbols and numbers; they are the keys to uncovering the forces that have driven societies, individuals, and civilizations to rise and fall, fortunes to be made and lost. This book was born out of a desire to demystify the complexities of Economic Science and make them accessible to a wider audience. The academic world often shrouds these concepts in jargon and complexity, but our goal has been to bridge that gap, presenting these ideas in clear, jargon-free, and straightforward language. We wanted to ensure that anyone—whether a student, a professional, an academic, or just a curious reader—could grasp the profound impact these equations have on our lives.

In other words, in writing this book, we sought to open doors to a broader, more inclusive conversation about Economics and Finance, one that is not confined to the halls of academia but is accessible to all who wish to understand the world we live in. The equations we've explored are not just historical milestones but living scientific tools that continue to shape our future. If this book has made the complex world of Economic Science a bit more understandable, if it has sparked curiosity or deepened your understanding, then it has fulfilled its purpose. As you move forward, I hope this book has given you a clearer understanding of these concepts. Thank you for joining me on this fascinating journey!

CHAPTER 23

Mathematical Appendix

23.1 Appendix A

First-Order Partial Derivative

The partial derivative of a function $f(x,y,\ldots)$ with respect to one of its variables, say x, is the derivative of f with respect to x, while holding the other variables constant. It measures how f changes as x changes, with all other variables fixed. Formally, the partial derivative of f with respect to x is defined as:

$$\frac{\partial f}{\partial x} = \lim_{\Delta x \to 0} \frac{f(x+\Delta x, y, \ldots) - f(x, y, \ldots)}{\Delta x}$$

It is denoted as $\frac{\partial f}{\partial x}$ or f_x. For the partial derivative to exist at a point, the function f must be defined in an open neighborhood around that point, and of course the aforementioned limit should exist.

First-Order Condition (FOC)

Given a function $f(x,y)$ that is twice differentiable in a neighborhood containing the point (x^*, y^*), where x and y are independent variables, we aim to find the critical points (x^*, y^*). To find the critical points, we need to set

P. G. Michaelides, *21 Equations that Shaped the World Economy*,
https://doi.org/10.1007/978-3-031-76140-9_23

the first-order partial derivatives of $f(x,y)$, with respect to x and y equal to zero, respectively:

$$\frac{\partial f(x,y)}{\partial x} = 0 \text{ and } \frac{\partial f(x,y)}{\partial y} = 0$$

Solving these two equations yields the critical points (x^*, y^*). These points are candidates for local minima, local maxima, or saddle points.

These first-order conditions (FOC) are necessary but not sufficient by themselves to determine the nature of these points. Further analysis, such as examining the second-order conditions (SOC), would be required to classify them. Employing these FOC conditions is instrumental in deriving the intercept in the simple OLS regression.

23.2 Appendix B

The relevant theory behind the total derivative, when considering the total differential $d(lnY)$ of lnY, is grounded in multivariable calculus, specifically in the properties of differentiable functions and their differentials. Additionally, we also apply the so-called chain rule for functions of multiple variables, when taking the derivative $\frac{d(lnY)}{dt}$.

Total Differential

The total differential of a function f with several independent variables x_1, x_2, ..., x_n is a foundational concept in multivariable calculus. For the total differential to be defined, the function $f(x_1, x_2, \ldots, x_n)$ must be differentiable. When function $f(x_1, x_2, \ldots, x_n)$ is differentiable, the total differential df is given by:

$$df = \sum_{i=1}^{n} \frac{\partial f}{\partial x_i} \cdot dx_i = \frac{\partial f}{\partial x_1} \cdot dx_1 + \frac{\partial f}{\partial x_2} \cdot dx_2 + \ldots + \frac{\partial f}{\partial x_n} \cdot dx_n$$

Here, $\frac{\partial f}{\partial x_i}$ denotes the partial derivative of f with respect to x_i, and dx_i represents an infinitesimal change in x_i. This formula expresses how the function f changes in response to infinitesimal changes dx_1, dx_2, ..., dx_n in its respective variables x_1, x_2, ..., x_n.

Chain Rule

The chain rule provides a method for computing the derivative of a composite function. When a function g depends on an intermediate variable h, which in turn depends on another variable t, the chain rule allows us to find the rate of change of g with respect to t. To apply the chain rule, both g and h must be differentiable functions.

Formally, if $g = g(h(t))$, then the chain rule states that:

$$\frac{dg}{dt} = \frac{dg}{dh} \cdot \frac{dh}{dt}$$

This can be generalized to functions of multiple variables. If g is a function of several variables, $u_1, u_2, \ldots, u_m$ each of which is a function of t, then the chain rule generalizes to:

$$\frac{dg}{dt} = \sum_{i=1}^{m} \frac{\partial g}{\partial u_i} \cdot \frac{du_i}{dt} = \frac{\partial g}{\partial u_1} \cdot \frac{du_1}{dt} + \frac{\partial g}{\partial u_2} \cdot \frac{du_2}{dt} + \ldots + \frac{\partial g}{\partial u_m} \cdot \frac{du_m}{dt}$$

This requires g to be differentiable with respect to the variables $u_1, u_2, \ldots, u_m$ and each variable $u_1, u_2, \ldots, u_m$ to be differentiable with respect to t.

The concepts of total differential and chain rule are essential for understanding how the growth rates of different factors contribute to the overall growth rate of an economic output. These concepts together provide a relevant framework for analyzing the dynamics of the Cobb-Douglas production function.

23.3 Appendix C

Let's see the first-order condition (FOC) and second-order condition (SOC) in the context of single-variable optimization problems, which are relevant for Cost Minimization and Utility Maximization. We will discuss both minimization and maximization.

First-Order Condition (FOC)

For a function $f(x)$ that is twice differentiable on a real interval I containing the point c, a critical point $x = c$ is a point where the first derivative of f is zero, namely:

$$\left.\frac{df(x)}{dx}\right|_{x=c} = 0$$

Second-Order Condition (SOC)

For the same function, the second-order condition involves the second derivative evaluated at this critical point $x = c$.

(a) If $\left.\frac{d^2f(x)}{dx^2}\right|_{x=c} > 0$, then at the critical point c, f has a local minimum.

(b) If $\left.\frac{d^2f(x)}{dx^2}\right|_{x=c} < 0$, then at the critical point c, f has a local maximum.

(c) If $\left.\frac{d^2f(x)}{dx^2}\right|_{x=c} = 0$, then the SOC is inconclusive, and other methods must be used to determine the nature of the critical point.

The FOC helps identify potential points of interest (critical points), while the SOC helps determine whether these points are local minima or maxima. For a function that is twice differentiable, the first-order condition (FOC) and second-order condition (SOC) are crucial tools in single-variable optimization, leveraged among other concepts, in Cost Minimization and Utility Maximization.

23.4 Appendix D

In Input-Output (IO) Analysis and General Equilibrium (GE), vectors and matrices are used.

Vector

A vector X in an n-dimensional space is an ordered list of n numbers, defined either vertically (nx1) or horizontally (1xn), as follows:

$$X = \begin{pmatrix} x_1 \\ x_2 \\ . \\ . \\ . \\ x_n \end{pmatrix}$$

or

$$X = (x_1, x_2, \ldots, x_n)$$

By definition, transposition (T) of vector X is, respectively, equal to:

$$X^T = \begin{pmatrix} x_1 \\ x_2 \\ . \\ . \\ . \\ x_n \end{pmatrix}^T = (x_1, x_2, \ldots, x_n)$$

or

$$X^T = (x_1,\ x_2, \ldots, x_n)^T = \begin{pmatrix} x_1 \\ x_2 \\ . \\ . \\ . \\ x_n \end{pmatrix}$$

Matrix

A $n \times n$ matrix A is a rectangular array of numbers with n rows and n columns:

$$A = \begin{pmatrix} a_{11} & \cdots & a_{1n} \\ \vdots & \ddots & \vdots \\ a_{n1} & \cdots & a_{nn} \end{pmatrix}$$

Transposition of matrix A is, by definition, equal to:

$$A^T = \begin{pmatrix} a_{11} & \cdots & a_{n1} \\ \vdots & \ddots & \vdots \\ a_{1n} & \cdots & a_{nn} \end{pmatrix}$$

In general, the number of rows and columns in a matrix may vary. However, when they are equal, the $n \times n$ matrix is called a 'square matrix.'

Matrix Multiplication

Now, let's go through the mathematical theory for multiplying two 2×2 matrices.

Assume:

$$A = \begin{pmatrix} a_{11} & a_{12} \\ a_{21} & a_{22} \end{pmatrix} \text{and } B = \begin{pmatrix} b_{11} & b_{12} \\ b_{21} & b_{22} \end{pmatrix}$$

The product of the two matrices A and B is equal to a new matrix C:

$$C = \begin{pmatrix} c_{11} & c_{12} \\ c_{21} & c_{22} \end{pmatrix}$$

such that:

$$C = A \cdot B$$

or

$$C = \begin{pmatrix} a_{11} & a_{12} \\ a_{21} & a_{22} \end{pmatrix} \cdot \begin{pmatrix} b_{11} & b_{12} \\ b_{21} & b_{22} \end{pmatrix}$$

Specifically, by definition, the elements of matrix C are equal to:

$$C = \begin{pmatrix} a_{11} \cdot b_{11} + a_{12} \cdot b_{21} & a_{11} \cdot b_{12} + a_{12} \cdot b_{22} \\ a_{21} \cdot b_{11} + a_{22} \cdot b_{21} & a_{21} \cdot b_{12} + a_{22} \cdot b_{22} \end{pmatrix}$$

Note that for any two arbitrary matrices A and B, $A \cdot B \neq B \cdot A$.

Determinant and (Non)-Singularity

The determinant of an $n \times n$ matrix A, usually denoted as $\det(A)$, is a scalar value, i.e., a number that provides important information about the matrix, such as whether it is invertible. Therefore:

(a) If $\det(A) = 0$, then matrix A is called 'singular' and does not have an inverse matrix.

(b) If $\det(A) \neq 0$, then matrix A is called 'non-singular' and has an inverse, usually denoted as A^{-1}, such that $A \cdot A^{-1} = I = A \cdot A^{-1}$, where:

$$I = \begin{pmatrix} 1 & \cdots & 0 \\ 0 & \ddots & 0 \\ \vdots & & \vdots \\ 0 & \cdots & 1 \end{pmatrix}$$

and I is the so-called unity matrix, which has unity (1) in its main diagonal, and zero (0) elsewhere, as above.

Note that for any nxn matrix A, it holds that: $A \cdot I = I \cdot A = A$. However, as we have seen, for arbitrary nxn square matrices A and B it holds that: $A \cdot B \neq B \cdot A$.

Inverse of a 2 × 2 Matrix

Assuming that $\det(A) \neq 0$, then the inverse of a 2×2 matrix A:

$$A = \begin{pmatrix} a & b \\ c & d \end{pmatrix}$$

is given by:

$$A^{-1} = \frac{1}{\det(A)} \cdot \begin{pmatrix} d & -b \\ -c & a \end{pmatrix}$$

where:

$$\det(A) = a \cdot d - b \cdot c$$

In the context of Input-Output (IO) analysis, matrices and inverse matrices are used to represent technical coefficients (A) and the so-called Leontief inverse matrix $(I - A)^{-1}$, respectively, Also, vectors are used to represent quantities such as final demand (Υ), outputs produced (X), and other economic variables. In addition, in the context of General Equilibrium (GE), vectors are used to represent prices (p), quantities (z), etc.

23.5 Appendix E

A differential equation (DE) is an equation that involves functions and their derivatives. It describes how a particular quantity changes with respect to another, often time. Differential equations are widely used in various scientific disciplines, including Economics, and in the Solow Growth Model.

First-Order Differential Equation

An ordinary differential equation (ODE) involves functions of a single variable and their derivatives. A first-order differential equation involves the first derivative of the function. The general form of a first-order ODE is:

$$\frac{dy}{\partial t} = f(y,t)$$

where:

- y is the variable of interest
- t is another variable, usually time
- $\frac{dy}{\partial t}$ is the first derivative of y with respect to t

f is a given function

Definition of 'Equilibrium' or 'Steady State'

In the context of a first-order differential equation, the 'equilibrium' or 'steady state' refers to a situation where some variable of interest no longer changes over time.

Hence, for a general first-order differential equation of the form:

$$\left.\frac{dx}{\partial t}\right| = g(x)$$

the steady state x^* is defined as the value of x at which the rate of change is zero:

$$\left.\frac{dx}{dt}\right|_{x=x^*} = g\left(x^*\right) = 0$$

At this point, the system is said to be in 'equilibrium' or in 'steady state.'

The first-order differential equation is crucial for understanding long-term economic growth, as it helps determine the evolution of capital in the economy, according to the Solow Growth Model. Furthermore, the steady state of the capital per worker provides a tool for evaluating the effects of changes in savings rates, technology, and depreciation rates on the overall economy.

23.6 Appendix F

A partial differential equation (PDE) is an equation that involves the function and the partial derivatives of an unknown multivariable function. PDEs are used to formulate problems involving functions of several variables, and are either solved analytically or numerically. The Black-Scholes Equation is a famous PDE in Economics and Finance.

Partial Differential Equation

Formally, a PDE for a function $u(x_1, x_2, \ldots, x_n)$ is an equation of the form:

$$F\left(x_1, x_2, \ldots, x_n, u, \frac{\partial u}{\partial x_1}, \frac{\partial u}{\partial x_2}, \ldots, \frac{\partial^2 u}{\partial x_1^{\,2}}, \frac{\partial^2 u}{\partial x_1 \partial x_2}, \ldots\right) = 0$$

where F is some given function.

The order of a PDE refers to the highest derivative present in the equation. For example, if the highest derivative in the equation is a second derivative, the PDE is of second order.

The first-order partial derivative of a function $f(x, y, \ldots)$ with respect to one of its variables was presented earlier (Sect. 23.1, Appendix A).

Second-Order Partial Derivative

Now, a second-order partial derivative is the partial derivative of a partial derivative. For a function $f(x, y)$, the second-order partial derivative with respect to x is denoted as $\frac{\partial^2 f}{\partial x^2}$ or f_{xx} and is defined as:

$$f_{xx} = \frac{\partial^2 f}{\partial x^2} = \frac{\partial}{\partial x}\left(\frac{\partial f}{\partial x}\right)$$

Similarly, the mixed second-order partial derivative with respect to x and y is denoted as f_{xy} and is defined as:

$$f_{xy} = \frac{\partial^2 f}{\partial x \partial y} = \frac{\partial}{\partial y}\left(\frac{\partial f}{\partial x}\right) = \frac{\partial}{\partial x}\left(\frac{\partial f}{\partial y}\right) = f_{yx}$$

This mixed derivative measures how the partial derivative of f with respect to x changes as y changes. The equality $f_{xy} = f_{yx}$ holds true under certain conditions.

23.7 Appendix G

First-Order Difference Equation

A difference equation (DE) is a mathematical relation that expresses the value of a sequence or a discrete-time process as a function of its previous values. Difference equations are fundamental in the study of discrete dynamical systems and are used to model a wide variety of phenomena in Economics and other fields. The general form of a first-order difference equation is given by:

$$X_{t+1} = f(X_t, \mu) \equiv f_\mu(X_t), t = 0, 1, 2, \ldots$$

where:

$X_t \in R$ is the state variable at time t

μ is a parameter that may influence the dynamics

$f_\mu : R \rightarrow R$ is a function that maps the state variable from one time step to the next

The function f determines how the state evolves over time. Depending on the nature of f, the behavior of the sequence $\{X_t\}$ can range from simple and predictable to highly complex and chaotic.

The Logistic Map: A Nonlinear First-Order Difference Equation

Consider a simple nonlinear difference equation known as the logistic map. This equation is typically used to model population growth, where X_t represents the proportion of the maximum population at time t. The logistic map equation is given by:

$$X_{t+1} = \mu \cdot X_t \cdot (1 - X_t)$$

where:

$$0 \le X_t \le 1 \text{ and } 0 \le \mu \le 4.$$

This is a classic example of a simple nonlinear dynamical system that can exhibit chaotic behavior. This equation is a first-order difference equation, meaning that the value of the variable at the next time step $(t + 1)$ depends only on its value at the current step (t).

While there is no general closed-form solution for the logistic map due to its nonlinear nature, the equation's dynamics can be understood through various methods, such as numerical simulations.

Steady State

Now, consider a general first-order difference equation of the previous form:

$$X_{t+1} = f(X_t)$$

where X_t is the current state, X_{t+1} is the next state, and $f: R \to R$ is a continuous function. A 'steady state,' or 'fixed point,' is a value X^* of X, such that:

$$X^* = f(X^*)$$

To find the 'steady states' or 'fixed points,' we solve this equation in order to find all values of X that satisfy this equation. The solutions X^* are the 'steady states' or 'fixed points' of the system.

The logistic map serves as a paradigmatic example in the study of Chaos Theory in Economics and Finance, demonstrating how very simple nonlinear systems can produce complex behavior.

Summary

In this book, each chapter served as a critical piece in understanding the multifaceted landscape of modern economies. Chapter 1 provided a dive into the far-reaching influence of simple and compound Interest Rates within Economics and Finance, tracing their origins, evolution, and significance in shaping financial decisions, investment strategies, and macroeconomic policies. The chapter examined the implications of interest rates at both micro and macro levels, highlighting their role in guiding borrowing, spending behaviors, saving patterns, and economic growth, while also acknowledging their limitations and the need for a balanced approach.

Chapter 2 presented the Normal Distribution in Economics. The normal distribution, also known as the Gaussian distribution, is a vital tool in Economics, capturing central tendencies and variability across diverse economic domains. This chapter studied its symmetrical, 'bell-shaped' curve, parameters, and their applications. While recognizing its elegance and prevalence, the chapter also addressed its limitations and critiques, advocating for approaches that accommodate non-normality and heterogeneity.

Chapter 3 examined the role of Ordinary Least Squares (OLS) regression in Economics, unraveling its principles, applications, and implications in economic analysis. OLS is a fundamental tool for estimating parameters in regression models, offering simplicity, interpretability, and versatility. The chapter presented its emergence, mathematical foundation, and

P. G. Michaelides, *21 Equations that Shaped the World Economy*,
https://doi.org/10.1007/978-3-031-76140-9

applications across various fields, while also addressing its limitations and critiques.

Chapter 4 examined the production function in Economics. The production function, a cornerstone of modern economic analysis, expresses the relationships governing the transformation of inputs into commodities. This chapter studied its origins, refinement through neoclassical principles, and applications in economic growth, industry dynamics, and resource allocation. While acknowledging its power, the chapter also critiqued assumptions and advocated for a holistic understanding that embraces historical specificity, social dynamics, and environmental impacts.

Chapter 5 examined the Profit Rate in Economics. Rooted in Classical and Marxist traditions, the profit rate's analysis illustrated the complexities of modern economies. The chapter examined its impact on policy domains, technological innovation, investment, and economic growth, while recognizing key limitations and critiques. Despite challenges, understanding the profit rate aids policy decisions in stability, income equality, and more.

Next, in Chap. 6, the concept of General Equilibrium (GE) represented as a cornerstone in neoclassical Economics, offering insights into the delicate dance between supply, demand, and prices that underpins market dynamics. This chapter examined GE theory, its basic principles, and applications in economic analysis, policy decisions, and market efficiency. It discussed challenges and limitations, showcasing its enduring relevance and impact on economic theory and practice.

In Chap. 7, Wassily Leontief's Input-Output (IO) framework redefined economic analysis by uncovering the interdependencies in modern economies. This chapter shed light on its applications, while acknowledging limitations and critiques. Its capacity to unravel interdependencies and guide policy decisions underscores its value for economists, policymakers, and researchers.

In Chap. 8, the Break-Even Point (BEP) was defined as a pivotal concept in Finance, representing the minimum level of activity required for a business to cover its costs and then 'break even'. This chapter examined its multifaceted nature, role in risk management, and implications, while acknowledging limitations and addressing critiques.

Next, in Chap. 9, the Fisher equation was set out as a foundational pillar in economic theory, expressing the connections between nominal interest rates, real interest rates, and expected inflation. The chapter examined its emergence, mathematical formulation, and implications for financial decisions, investment strategies, and monetary policies, while also acknowledging its limitations and critiques.

Chapter 10 focused on Net Present Value (NPV) in Economic Sciences, tracing its evolution and implications. It examined its theoretical foundations, practical applications, and limitations, highlighting its impact on corporate finance, public finance, and environmental economics.

Chapter 11 analyzed the Income Accounting Identity, tracing its roots and practical applications in economic analysis and policy formulation. It provided insights into aggregate economic performance, equilibrium income, and implications for policymaking and business strategy.

Chapter 12, examined the notion of Nash Equilibrium, a pivotal pillar in Game Theory, and elucidated its implications for economic outcomes and decision-making dynamics within competitive contexts. It discussed its assumptions, applications, and critiques, providing insights into strategic interactions and collective outcomes.

In Chap. 13, the Capital Asset Pricing Model (CAPM) was examined for its role in reshaping how risk and return are understood, assessed, and navigated in financial markets. The chapter discussed its assumptions, applications, limitations, and critiques, offering insights into portfolio management and asset valuation.

In Chap. 14, the historical emergence and evolution of the Quantity Theory of Money (QTM) reflected the intellectual journey of economists seeking to understand the inherent dynamics of monetary systems. This chapter shed light on its implications for policy decisions and analyses of inflation and financial stability, while recognizing critiques and alternative approaches.

In Chap. 15, the Cost Function serves as a fundamental concept in Economic Science, offering insights into resource allocation, market dynamics, and decision-making processes. The chapter examined its emergence, applications, and implications across various economic spheres, while acknowledging limitations and critiques.

Chapter 16 set out the Solow Growth Model, crafted by Robert Solow and Trevor Swan, which remains a pivotal framework in Economic Science, unraveling the complexities of long-term economic growth. Our investigation went through its genesis, equations, implications, and critiques, providing insights into investment dynamics and technological progress.

Chapter 17 looked at the Phillips Curve, a fundamental concept in Macroeconomics, which examines the relationship between inflation and unemployment. The chapter provided an overview of its insights, implications, and critiques, emphasizing the importance of refining economic models to enhance understanding of inflation and unemployment dynamics.

In Chap. 18, the Gravity Equation in international trade was presented. The Gravity Equation, rooted in Newtonian Physics, offers insights into international trade and economic relationships. This chapter shed light on its historical evolution, theoretical foundations, empirical applications, and limitations, providing a framework to predict trade patterns and guide policy formulation.

Chapter 19 dived into the Granger causality equation. This study traversed Granger causality's roots, methodological aspects, practical applications, and critical assessments in economic analysis. The chapter examined its implications for policy evaluation, forecasting, and market dynamics, while acknowledging limitations and philosophical considerations.

In Chap. 20, we examined the famous Black-Scholes Equation. The Black-Scholes Formula, a seminal contribution to Finance, revolutionized the field by equipping researchers with a quantitative framework for valuing options. The chapter focused on its historical context, emergence, implications, and ongoing dialogue surrounding its assumptions and applications.

Finally, Chap. 21, the final chapter, examined Chaos Theory. Economics and Finance have become more complex than ever, and Chaos Theory is increasingly important in understanding this complexity. The chapter shed light on its implications for economic modeling, and policymaking, while recognizing challenges and limitations.

Bibliography

Abramovitz, M. (1956). Resource and Output Trends in the United States Since 1980. *American Economic Review, 46*(2), 5–23.

Agarwal, R. P., & Sen, S. K. (2006). *Probability and Statistics, World Scientific* (1st ed.).

Aghion, P., & Howitt, P. (1988). *Endogenous Growth Theory*. MIT Press.

Ahuja, H. L. (2019). *Modern Microeconomics: Theory and Applications* (19th ed.). S. Chand Publishing.

Arnold, V. I. (1992). *Ordinary Differential Equations* (1st ed.). Springer.

Arrow, K. J., & Debreu, G. (1954). Existence of an Equilibrium for a Competitive Economy. *Econometrica, 223*, 265–290.

Asano, A. (2013). *An Introduction to Mathematics for Economics* (1st ed.). Cambridge University Press.

Axler, S. (2015). *Linear Algebra Done Right* (3rd ed.). Springer.

Babichenko, Y., & Rubinstein, A. (2020). Communication Complexity of Approximate Nash Equilibria. *Games and Economic Behavior, Vol., 134*(July), 376–398.

Balasko, Y. (1988). *Foundations of the Theory of General Equilibrium*. Academic Press.

Ballandonne, M., & Rubin, G. (2020). Robert Solow's Non-Walrasian Conception of Economics. *History of Political Economy, 52*, 827–861.

Barro, R. J., & Sala-i-Martin, X. (1995). *Economic Growth*. McGraw-Hill.

Berk, J., & DeMarzo, P. (2019). *Corporate Finance* (5th ed.). Pearson.

Bernholz, P. (2016). *Monetary Regimes and Inflation: History, Economic and Political Relationships* (2nd ed.). Edward Elgar Publishing.

P. G. Michaelides, *21 Equations that Shaped the World Economy*,
https://doi.org/10.1007/978-3-031-76140-9

Besanko, D., & Braeutigam, R. (2019). *Microeconomics: Theory and Applications* (5th ed.). Wiley.

Beyer, W. H. (2010). *Differential Equations: An Introduction to Theory and Applications* (1st ed.). Springer.

Blaug, M. (1995). *Why Is the Quantity Theory of Money the Oldest Surviving Theory in Economics, The Quantity Theory of Money, from Locke to Keynes and Friedman.* Edward Elgar Publ Comp.

Blaug, M. (1992). *The Methodology of Economics: Or, How Economists Explain* (2nd ed.). Cambridge University Press.

Blaug, M. (2009). *The Evolution of Economic Thought* (5th ed.). Wiley-Blackwell.

Bodin, J. (1578). *Discours sur le rehaussement et diminution des monnoyes.* Chez Iacques Du Puys.

Boianovsky, M., & Hoover, K. (2014). In the Kingdom of Solovia: The Rise of Growth Economics at MIT: 1956–70. *History of Political Economy, 46,* 198–228.

Borel, E. (1921). La théorie du jeu et les equation intégrales à noyau symétrique gauche. *ComptesRendus de l'Académie des Sciences, 1304–1308,* 173.

Bowles, S., & Edwards, R. (2005). *Understanding Capitalism: Competition, Command, and Change* (3rd ed.). Oxford University Press.

Box, G. E. P., Jenkins, G. M., & Reinsel, G. C. (2015). *Time Series Analysis* (5th ed.). Wiley.

Boyce, W. E., & DiPrima, R. C. (2012). *Elementary Differential Equations and Boundary Value Problems* (10th ed.). Wiley.

Boyd, S., & Vandenberghe, L. (2004). *Convex Optimization* (1st ed.). Cambridge University Press.

Braun, M. (2013). *Differential Equations and Their Applications: An Introduction to Applied Mathematics* (4th ed.). Springer.

Brealey, R. A., Myers, S. C., & Allen, F. (2019). *Principles of Corporate Finance* (13th ed.). McGraw-Hill Education.

Brealey, R., Myers, S., & Marcus, A. (2014). *Fundamentals of Corporate Finance* (9th ed.). McGraw-Hill Education.

Brock, W. A., & Hommes, C. H. (1998). Heterogeneous Beliefs and Routes to Chaos in a Simple Asset Pricing Model. *Journal of Economic Dynamics and Control, 22,* 1235–1274.

Brockwell, P. J., & Davis, R. A. (2002). *Introduction to Time Series and Forecasting* (2nd ed.). Springer.

Cameron, A. C., & Trivedi, P. K. (2005). *Microeconometrics* (2nd ed.). Cambridge University Press.

Chatfield, C. (2004). *The Analysis of Time Series: An Introduction* (6th ed.). Chapman and Hall/CRC.

Chiang, A. C., & Wainwright, K. (2005). *Fundamental Methods of Mathematical Economics* (4th ed.). McGraw-Hill Education.

Chiang, E. (2018). *Core Microeconomics* (1st ed.). Worth Publishers.

Chong, E. K. P., & Zak, S. H. (2013). *Introduction to Optimization* (4th ed.). Wiley.
Chung, K. L. (2001). *Probability and Statistics* (4th ed.). Springer.
Cochrane, J. H. (2005). *Asset Pricing* (Rev. ed.). Princeton University Press.
Cochrane, R. (2016). *The Secret Life of Equations: The 50 Greatest Equations and How They Work*. Firefly.
Cottle, C. C. (2004). *Options Trading: The Hidden Reality* (1st ed.). Wiley.
Cournot, A. (1838). *Recherches sur les Principes Mathématiques de la Théorie des Richesses*. Hachette.
Crease, R. (2010). *The Great Equations: Breakthroughs in Science from Pythagoras to Heisenberg*. W. W. Norton.
Damodaran, A. (2014). *Applied Corporate Finance* (4th ed.). Wiley.
Damodaran, A. (2014). *Corporate Finance: Theory and Practice* (4th ed.). Wiley.
Daskalakis, C., Goldberg, P. W., & Papadimitriou, C. H. (2009). The Complexity of Computing a Nash Equilibrium. *SIAM Journal on Computing, 39*(3), 195–259.
Davis, M. D. (1983). *Game Theory: A Nontechnical Introduction* (1st ed.). Dover Publications.
De la Fuente, A. (2000). *Mathematical Methods and Models for Economists* (1st ed.). Cambridge University Press.
DeGroot, M. H., & Schervish, M. J. (2011). *Probability and Statistics* (4th ed.). Pearson.
Denison, E. (1967). *Why Growth Rates Differ*. The Brookings Institution.
Diebold, F. X. (2018). *Elements of Forecasting* (4th ed.). Cengage Learning.
Dinov, I. (2018). *Probability and Statistics* (1st ed.). Springer.
Dixit, A. K. (1990). *Optimization in Economic Theory* (1st ed.). Oxford University Press.
Dixit, A. K., & Skeath, S. (2009). *Games of Strategy* (3rd ed.). W.W. Norton & Company.
Dorfman, R., Samuelson, P., & Solow, R. (1958). *Linear Programming and Economic Analysis* (1st ed.). McGraw-Hill.
Dornbusch, R., Fischer, S., & Startz, R. (2014). *Macroeconomics* (12th ed.). McGraw-Hill Education.
Douglas, E. J. (2019). *Managerial Economics: Theory, Applications, and Cases* (2nd ed.). Wiley.
Drakopoulos, S., & Karagiannis, A. (2003). *History of Economic Thought: An Overview*. Kritiki Publications.
Drazen, A. (2000). *The Political Economy of Public Policy* (1st ed.). Cambridge University Press.
Duffie, D. (2001). *Dynamic Asset Pricing Theory* (3rd ed.). Princeton University Press.

Edwards, C. H., Jr. (1995). *Advanced Calculus of Several Variables* (1st ed.). Academic Press.

Ehrhardt, M. (2019). *Eugene Brigham, Corporate Finance: A Focused Approach* (7th ed.). Cengage Learning.

Ekelund, R. B., & Hebert, R. F. (2007). *A History of Economic Theory and Method* (3rd ed.). Waveland Press.

Evans, A. J. (2020). *Economics: A Complete Guide for Business.* London Publishing Partnership.

Evans, L. C. (2010). *Partial Differential Equations* (2nd ed.). American Mathematical Society.

Evans, M. J., & Rosenthal, J. S. (2009). *Probability and Statistics* (4th ed.). Springer.

Ferguson, N. (2008). *The Ascent of Money: A Financial History of the World* (1st ed.). Penguin Books.

Fitzpatrick, P. M. (2010). *Advanced Calculus* (2nd ed.). Springer.

Folland, G. B. (2009). *Advanced Calculus* (1st ed.). Princeton University Press.

Friedman, M., & Jovanovich, H. B. (1992). *Money Mischief: Episodes in Monetary History* (1st ed.).

Friedman, M., & Schwartz, A. J. (1971). *A Monetary History of the United States, 1867–1960* (1st ed.). Princeton University Press.

Fumio, H. (2000). *Econometrics* (1st ed.). Princeton University Press.

Gentle, J. E. (2007). *Matrix Algebra: Theory, Computations, and Applications in Statistics* (2nd ed.). Springer.

Gleick, J. (1987). *Chaos: Making a New Science* (1st ed.). Penguin Books.

Godley, W., & Lavoie, M. (2012). *Monetary Economics: An Integrated Approach to Credit, Money, Income, Production and Wealth* (2nd ed.). Palgrave Macmillan.

Goodhart, C. (1991). *The Evolution of Central Banks.* The MIT Press.

Greene, W. H. (2018). *Econometric Analysis* (8th ed.). Pearson.

Greenwald, B., & Stiglitz, J. E. (1987). Keynesian, New Keynesian, and New Classical Economics. *Oxford Economic Papers, 39*, 119–133.

Gulick, D. (1992). *Chaos Theory Simplified* (1st ed.). McGraw-Hill Education.

Gupta, D. S. (1997). *The Political Economy of Globalization.* Springer.

Gupta, R. C. (2017). *Business Economics: Theory and Applications* (1st ed.). McGraw-Hill Education.

Hamilton, J. D. (1994). *Time Series Analysis* (2nd ed.). Princeton University Press.

Hayek, F. A. (1953), The Counter-Revolution of Science., Collier-Macmillan.

Heilbroner, R. L. (2011). *The Worldly Philosophers: The Lives, Times and Ideas of the Great Economic Thinkers.* Simon and Schuster.

Helpman, E. (2004). *The Mystery of Economic Growth* (1st ed.). Belknap Press.

Hensher, D. A., & Button, K. J. (2000). *Business Economics* (1st ed.). Cambridge University Press.

Hirschey, M. (2019). *Essentials of Managerial Economics* (1st ed.). Cengage Learning.

Horn, R. A., & Johnson, C. R. (2012). *Matrix Analysis* (2nd ed.). Cambridge University Press.

Huang, C.-f., & Litzenberger, J. M. (1988). *Foundations for Financial Economics* (1st ed.). North Holland.

Hull, J. C. (2017). *Options, Futures, and Other Derivatives* (10th ed.). Pearson.

Hunt, E. K. (2002). *History of Economic Thought* (3rd ed.). M.E. Sharpe.

Itoh, M., & Lapavitsas, C. (1999). *Political Economy of Money and Finance*. Macmillan.

Jacques, I. (2013). *Mathematics for Economics and Business* (8th ed.). Pearson.

Jaffe, W. (Ed.) (1965). *Correspondence of Leon Walras and Related Papers* (3 vols.). North-Holland.

Jarrow, R., & Turnbull, S. (2000). *Financial Derivatives: Pricing and Risk Management* (1st ed.). South-Western College Publishing.

Johnson, H. G. (1971). The Keynesian Revolution and the Monetarist Counter-Revolution. *American Economic Review, 61*(2), 1–14.

Johnston, J., & DiNardo, J. (1997). *Econometric Methods* (4th ed.). McGraw-Hill Education.

Joshi, M. S. (2008). *The Concepts and Practice of Mathematical Finance* (2nd ed.). Cambridge University Press.

Karagiannis, A. (2001). *Economic Methodology*. Kritiki Publications.

Keat, P. G., & Yale, P. K. (2016). *Economics for Managers* (8th ed.). Pearson.

Kennedy, P. (2008). *A Guide to Econometrics* (6th ed.). MIT Press.

Keynes, J. M. (1936). *The General Theory of Employment, Interest, and Money* (1st ed.). Harcourt Brace Jovanovich.

Klein, M. (2013). *Mathematics for Economists with Applications* (1st ed.). Routledge.

Kreps, D., & Wilson, R. (1982). Sequential equilibria. *Econometrica, 50*, 863–894.

Krugman, P. (1979). A Model of Balance of Payments Crises. *Journal of Money, Credit, and Banking, 11*, 311–325.

Krugman, P. (1981). Trade, Accumulation and Uneven Development. *Journal of Development Economics, 8*(2), 149–161.

Krugman, P. (1990). *Rethinking International Trade*. MIT Press.

Krugman, P. (1995). *Development, Geography and Economic Theory*. MIT Press.

Krugman, P., Obstfeld, M., & Melitz, M. (2018). *International Trade: Theory and Policy* (11th ed.). Pearson.

Krugman, P., & Wells, R. (2018). *Microeconomics, Worth Publishers* (5th ed.).

Kurz, H., & Salvadori, N. (2000). The Dynamic Leontief Model and the Theory of Endogenous Growth. *Economic Systems Research, 12*(2), 255–265.

Kurz, H. D., & Salvadori, N. (2010). *Economic Thought: A Brief History* (1st ed.). Routledge.

Lancaster, K. (2014). *Mathematical Economics* (1st ed.). Dover Publications.

Lange, O. (1936). On the Economic Theory of Socialism: Part One. *The Review of Economic Studies, 4*(1), 53–71.
Lavoie, M. (1984). The Endogenous Flow of Credit and the Post Keynesian Theory of Money. *Journal of Economic Issues, 771-797*, 18.
Lawson, T. (1997). *Realism and Economic Methodology* (1st ed.). Routledge.
Lay, D. C. (2015). *Linear Algebra and Its Applications* (5th ed.). Pearson.
Leigh, D., & Gilbert, H. (2007). *Economies of Representation, 1790–2000: Colonialism and Commerce* (pp. 200–201). Ashgate Publishing, Ltd.
Leontief, W. (1986). *Input-Output Economics* (2nd ed.). Oxford University Press.
Levy, D. M. (1999). *The History of Economic Thought: A Critical Perspective* (1st ed.). Routledge.
Lewis, M. (2010). *The Big Short: Inside the Doomsday Machine* (1st ed.). W.W. Norton & Company.
Lipsey, R. G. (1999). *The Development of Economic Thought* (1st ed.). Oxford University Press.
Ljungqvist, L., & Sargent, T. J. (2018). *Recursive Macroeconomic Theory* (3rd ed.). MIT Press.
Lovric, M. (2011). *Probability and Statistics* (1st ed.). Springer.
Lucas, R., Jr. (1988). On the Mechanisms of Economic Development. *Journal of Monetary Economics, 22*(1), 3–42.
Machaj, M. (2023). *Monetary Policy and Inflation: Quantity Theory of Money* (1st ed.). Routledge.
Makridakis, S., Wheelwright, S. C., & Hyndman, R. J. (1998). *Forecasting: Methods and Applications* (3rd ed.). Wiley.
Mankiw, N. *Gregory, Principles of Macroeconomics*. Cengage Learning.
Mariolis, T. (2010). *Essays in the Logical History of Political Economy*. Matura.
Marx, K. (1990). *Capital* (Vol. 1). Penguin Classics.
Marx, K. (1991). *Capital* (Vol. 3). Penguin Classics.
Marx, K. (1993). *Grundrisse. Foundations of the Critique of Political Economy*. Penguin Classics.
Marx, K., & Engels, F. (1985). *The Communist Manifesto*. Penguin Classics.
Marx, K. (1867). *Capital: A Critique of Political Economy* (Vol. 1, 1st ed.). Penguin Classics.
Mas-Colell, A. (2009). *The Equilibrium Manifold: Postmodern Developments of the Theory of General Economic Equilibrium*. MIT Press.
Mas-Colell, A. (2011). *The General Equilibrium Theory of Value*. Princeton University Press.
Mas-Colell, M. W., & Green, J. (1995). *Microeconomic Theory*. Oxford University Press.
Mason, J. W. (2017). *The History of Economic Thought: A Short Guide* (1st ed.). Routledge.

McAleer, M. J. (2016). *Economic Growth and Development: Theories, Criticisms, and an Alternative Growth Model* (1st ed.). Peter Lang.

McCloskey, D. N. (1998). *The Rhetoric of Economics* (2nd ed.). University of Wisconsin Press.

McConnell, C. (2018). *Macroeconomics* (20th ed.). McGraw-Hill Education.

McDonald, R. A. (2016). *Business Economics: A Practical Guide* (1st ed.). Wiley.

Medema, S. G., & Samuels, W. J. (2003). *The History of Economic Thought: A Reader* (2nd ed.). Routledge.

Mendenhall, W., Beaver, R. J., & Beaver, B. M. (2012). *Introduction to Probability and Statistics* (14th ed.). Cengage Learning.

Michaelides, P. G. and Papadakis, T.-E. (2023), History of Economic Ideas., Palgrave-Macmillan.

Milios, J., Dimoulis, D., & Economakis, G. (2018 [2002]). *Karl Marx and the Classics, An Essay on Value, Crises and the Capitalist Mode of Production.* Routledge.

Milios, J., & Sotiropoulos, D. P. (2009). *Rethinking Imperialism: A Study of Capitalist Rule.* Palgrave Macmillan.

Mills, T. C. (2016). *Time Series Econometrics: A Concise Introduction* (1st ed.). Cambridge University Press.

Milonakis, D., & Fine, B. (2013). *From Political Economy to Economics: Method, the Social and the Historical in the Evolution of Economic Theory.* Routledge.

Mollo, M. L. R. (1999). The Endogeneity of Money: Post-Keynesian and Marxian Concepts Compared. In P. Zarembka (Ed.), *Economic Theory of Capitalism and Its Crises, Research in Political Economy, 17* (pp. 3–26). Jai Press.

Moore, B. J. (1988). *Horizontalists and Verticalists: The Macroeconomics of Credit Money.* Cambridge University Press.

Mornati, F. (2018). *Vilfredo Pareto: An Intellectual Biography Volume I.* Palgrave Studies in the History of Economic Thought.

Moss, D. A. (2007). *A Concise Guide to Macroeconomics* (1st ed.). Harvard Business Review Press.

Myerson, R. B. (1999). Nash Equilibrium and the History of Economic Theory. *Journal of Economic Literature, 37*(3), 1067–1082.

Nash, J. (1950a). The Bargaining Problem. *Econometrica, 18*, 155–162.

Nash, J. (1950b). Equilibrium Points in n-person Games. *Proceedings of the National Academy of Sciences U.S.A., 36*, 48–49.

Nash, J. (1951). Noncooperative Games. *Annals of Mathematics, 54*, 289–295.

Nash, J. (1996). *Essays on Game Theory.* Edward Elgar.

Nicholson, W. (2017). *Microeconomic Theory: Basic Principles and Extensions* (12th ed.). Cengage Learning.

O.E.C.D. (1996), Research and Development Expenditures in Industry, .

Ohlin, B. (1933). *Interregional and International Trade.* Harvard University Press.

Olver, P. J., & Shakiban, C. (2006). *Applied Linear Algebra* (1st ed.). Prentice Hall.

Orrell, D. (2010). *Economyths: Ten Ways Economics Gets It Wrong*. Wiley.
Osborne, M. J. (2004). *An Introduction to Game Theory* (2nd ed.). Oxford University Press.
Pask, C. (2015). *Great Calculations: A Surprising Look Behind 50 Scientific Inquiries*. Prometheus.
Peitgen, H.-O., Jürgens, H., & Saupe, D. (2004). *Chaos and Fractals: New Frontiers of Science* (2nd ed.). Springer.
Pemberton, M., & Rau, N. (2015). *Mathematics for Economists: An Introductory Textbook* (4th ed.). Manchester University Press.
Peters, E. E. (1996). *Chaos Theory in the Financial Markets* (2nd ed.). Wiley.
Pindyck, R., & Rubinfeld, D. (2018). *Microeconomics* (9th ed.). Pearson.
Rodrik, D. (2011). *The Globalization Paradox: Democracy and the Future of the World Economy* (1st ed.). W.W. Norton & Company.
Rohatgi, V. K., & Saleh, A. K. M. E. (2015). *Probability and Statistics* (2nd ed.). Wiley.
Romer, D. (2019). *Advanced Macroeconomics* (5th ed.). McGraw-Hill Education.
Romer, P. (1986). Increasing Returns and Long-Run Growth. *Journal of Political Economy, 94*, 1002–1037.
Romer, P. (1990). Endogenous Technological Change. *Journal of Political Economy, 98*, 71–102.
Rosenberg, A. (1988). *The Methodology of Economics and Other Social Sciences* (1st ed.). Academic Press.
Ross, S., & Westerfield, R. (2018). *Jeffrey Jaffe Corporate Finance* (12th ed.). McGraw-Hill Education.
Rousseas, S. (1986). *Post Keynesian Monetary Economics*. M. E. Sharpe.
Rubin, I. I. (1979). *A History of Economic Thought*. Ink Links.
Rumsey, D. J. (2011). *Probability and Statistics* (2nd ed.). For Dummies.
Samuelson, P. (1947). *Foundations of Economic Analysis*. Harvard University Press.
Samuelson, W. F., & Marks, S. G. (2015). *Managerial Economics* (8th ed.). Wiley.
Sargent, T. J. (1993). *Bounded Rationality in Macroeconomics*. Clarendon Press.
Sarno, L., & Taylor, M. P. (2002). *The Economics of Exchange Rates* (pp. 245–264). Cambridge University Press.
Schelling, T. C. (1980). *The Strategy of Conflict* (1st ed.). Harvard University Press.
Schumpeter, J. A. (1912). *The Theory of Economic Development*. Harvard University Press [1934].
Schumpeter, J. A. (1939). *Business Cycles*. McGraw-Hill.
Schumpeter, J. A. (1954). *History of Economic Analysis*. Routledge.
Schumpeter, J. A. (2010). *Capitalism, Socialism and Democracy*. Routledge.
Schumpeter, J. A. (1994). *The History of Economic Ideas* (1st ed.). Transaction Publishers.
Screpanti, E., & Zamagni, S. (2005). *An Outline of the History of Economic Thought*. OUP Oxford.

Sen, A. K. (1960). *Choice of Techniques*. Basil Blackwell.
Sen, A. K. (1970a). *Collective Choice and Social Welfare*. Holden Day.
Sen, A. K. (1981b). *Poverty and Famines: An Essay on Entitlement and Depression*. Oxford University Press.
Sen, A. K. (1984). *Resources, Values and Development*. Blackwell and Harvard University Press).
Sen, A. K. (1997). Maximization and the Act of Choice. *Econometrica, 65*(4), 745–779.
Sen, A. K. (1999). *Development as Freedom*. Oxford University Press.
Sen, A. (1999). *Development as Freedom* (1st ed.). Knopf.
Sheldon, N. (2015). *Option Volatility and Pricing: Advanced Trading Strategies and Techniques* (2nd ed.). McGraw-Hill Education.
Simon, C. P., & Blume, L. (1994). *Mathematics for Economists* (1st ed.). W.W. Norton & Company.
Skidelsky, R. (1995). *J.M. Keynes and the Quantity Theory of Money, The Quantity Theory of Money, from Locke to Keynes and Friedman*. Edward Elgar Publ Comp.
Smith, A. (1981). *An Inquiry into the Nature and Causes of the Wealth of Nations*. Liberty Classics.
Solow, R. (1956). A Contribution to the Theory of Economic Growth. *Quarterly Journal of Economics, LXX*, 65–94.
Solow, R. (1957). Technical Change and the Aggregate Production Function. *Review of Economics and Statistics, 39*(3), 312–320.
Solow, R. A. (2014). *The Classical Theory of Economic Growth* (1st ed.). Princeton University Press.
Sotiropoulos, D. P., Milios, J., & Lapatsioras, S. (2013). *A Political Economy of Contemporary Capitalism and Its Crisis: Demystifying Finance*. Routledge.
Spaniel, W. (2011). *Game Theory 101: The Complete Textbook* (1st ed.). CreateSpace Independent Publishing Platform.
Spivak, M. (1965). *Calculus on Manifolds: A Modern Approach to Advanced Calculus* (1st ed.). Addison-Wesley.
Stachurski, J. (2009). *Economic Dynamics: Theory and Computation* (2nd ed.). MIT Press.
Starr, R. M. (2011). *General Equilibrium Theory: An Introduction*. Cambridge University Press.
Stewart, I. (2012). *Seventeen Equations That Changed the World*. Profile Books.
Stiglitz, J. E. (2002). *Globalization and Its Discontents* (1st ed.). W.W. Norton & Company.
Strang, G. (2016). *Introduction to Linear Algebra* (5th ed.). Wellesley-Cambridge Press.
Sumpter, D. (2020). *The Ten Equations That Rule the World: And How You Can Use Them*. Penguin.

Sydsaeter, K., & Hammond, P. J. (2016). *Further Mathematics for Economic Analysis* (2nd ed.). Pearson.

Sydsaeter, K., Hammond, P. J., & Strom, A. (2016). *Essential Mathematics for Economic Analysis* (5th ed.). Pearson.

Tadelis, S. (2013). *Game Theory: An Introduction* (1st ed.). Princeton University Press.

Ten Raa, T. (2006). *The Economics of Input-Output Analysis* (1st ed.). Cambridge University Press.

Thirlwall, A. (2001). *Growth and Development.* Papazisis Publications.

Thomas, P. (2007). *The Economic Thought of Karl Marx* (1st ed.). Routledge.

Thornton, P. (2014). *The Great Economists: Ten Economists Whose Thinking Changed the Way We Live.* Pearson UK.

Tirole, J. (2006). *The Theory of Corporate Finance* (1st ed.). Princeton University Press.

Tobin, J. (1972). Friedman's Theoretical Framework. *Journal of Political Economy, 80,* 852–863.

Todaro, M. P., & Smith, S. C. (2015). *Economic Development* (12th ed.). Pearson.

Tse, T. (2015). *Corporate Finance: The Basics* (1st ed.). Routledge.

Tsoulfidis, L. (2010). *Competing Schools of Economic Thought.* Springer Science & Business Media.

van Staveren, I. (2021). *Alternative Ideas from 10 (Almost) Forgotten Economists.* Springer Nature Press.

Varian, H. R. (1992). *Microeconomic Analysis.* W. W. Norton Company.

Varoufakis, G. (2007b). *Game Theory.* Gutenberg Publications.

von Neumann, J. (1928). On the Theories of Parlor Games. *Mathematische Annalen, 100,* 295–320.

von Neumann, J., & Morgenstern, O. (2004). *Theory of Games and Economic Behavior* (60th Anniversary Commemorative ed.). Princeton University Press.

Walker, D. A. (1987). In J. Eatwell, M. Milgate, & P. Newman (Eds.), *Walras, Leon, The New Palgrave: A Dictionary of Economics, Vol. 4 (Q to Z).* Macmillan Press.

Walpole, R. E., Myers, R. H., Myers, S. L., & Ye, K. (2011). *Probability and Statistics for Engineers and Scientists* (9th ed.). Pearson.

Walras, L. (1954). *Elements of Pure Economics* (W. Jaffe, Trans.). Allen and Unwin.

Widder, D. V. (1989). *Advanced Calculus* (1st ed.). Dover Publications.

Wilensky, H. L. (2002). *The Political Economy of the Welfare State* (1st ed.). Routledge.

Woods, N. (2000). *The Political Economy of Globalization* (1st ed.). Palgrave Macmillan.

Woodward, W. A., Gray, H. L., & Elliott, A. T. (2017). *Applied Time Series Analysis* (2nd ed.). Wiley.

Wooldridge, J. M. (2018). *Introductory Econometrics: A Modern Approach* (7th ed.). Cengage Learning.
Wray, L. R. (2015). *Modern Money Theory: A Primer on Macroeconomics for Sovereign Monetary Systems* (1st ed.). Palgrave Macmillan.
Yueh, L. (2018). *What Would the Great Economists Do?* Picador.

The manufacturer's authorised representative in the EU is Springer Nature Customer Service Centre GmbH, Europaplatz 3, 69115 Heidelberg, Germany. If you have any concerns regarding our products, please contact ProductSafety@springernature.com

Printed and bound by CPI Group (UK) Ltd, Croydon, CR0 4YY
01/10/2026
02225933-0001